Approaches to Academic Reading and Writing

MARTIN L. ARNAUDET

MARY ELLEN BARRETT

English Language Institute
The American University
Washington, D.C.

Prentice Hall Regents, Englewood Cliffs, NJ 07632

Library of Congress Cataloging in Publication Data

ARNAUDET, MARTIN L.
   Approaches to academic reading and writing.

   Includes bibliographical references and index.
      1. English language—Text-books for foreign speakers.
   2. English language—Rhetoric.   3. Report writing.
   I. Barrett, ·Mary Ellen.   II. Title.
   PE1128.A66 1984   428.2'4   83–10968
   ISBN   0-13-043679-8

Editorial/production supervision and
   interior design: F. Hubert
Cover design: 20/20 Services, Inc.,
   Mark W. Berghash
Manufacturing buyer: Harry P. Baisley

for Kate, Ned, and Frank, who cooperated

© 1984 by Prentice-Hall, Inc., Englewood Cliffs, New Jersey 07632

All rights reserved. No part of this book may be
reproduced, in any form or by any means,
without permission in writing from the publisher.

Printed in the United States of America

10   9   8   7   6   5

ISBN   0-13-043679-8

Prentice-Hall International (UK) Limited, *London*
Prentice-Hall of Australia Pty. Limited, *Sydney*
Prentice-Hall Canada Inc., *Toronto*
Prentice-Hall Hispanoamericana, S.A., *Mexico*
Prentice-Hall of India Private Limited, *New Delhi*
Prentice-Hall of Japan, Inc., *Tokyo*
Simon & Schuster Asia Pte. Ltd., *Signapore*
Editora Prentice-Hall do Brasil, Ltda., *Rio de Janeiro*

Contents

Preface

APPROACHES TO ACADEMIC READING AND WRITING IS INTENDED FOR USE as a guide for advanced learners of English as a foreign language whose goal is mastery of written English as it is used in an academic environment. This would include students currently enrolled in regular academic courses at colleges or universities in an English-speaking country who need a support level course in English as well as those students and scholars abroad who must read and write English in order to pursue their professional interests. The text assumes a high level of proficiency in English usage and a basic academic vocabulary on the part of the students who will be using it. Generally speaking, a student should have a TOEFL score of 550 or above to successfully handle the material in this book.

The purpose of the text is twofold: to guide students toward intensive analytical reading of academic prose, and to provide them with the writing skills necessary to academic writing assignments, from short essay exam answers to complex research papers. The reading sections of this book are designed to help students recognize the elements of organization, basic thought relationships, and textual coherence devices common to academic writing. Many of the texts which are used in the reading analysis and recognition sections of the text are later "recycled" to be used as the basis for writing assignments. The text is therefore *not* a "reader" in the traditional sense, but rather, as the title suggests, provides practical approaches to the special intensive reading that is required of students and scholars.

The chapters dealing with writing use the notional-functional approach. Each one focuses on a particular type of writing task which students and scholars are commonly asked to perform, and each provides the students with the tools necessary to accomplish these tasks. The topics traditionally dealt with in a composition text—rhetorical patterns, stylistics, specificity of examples, usage, and so on—are incorporated into the various chapters so that the writing task is not subservient to the elements being taught. The writing tasks which we have selected for inclusion here are ones which we have found to be of most *practical* help to the students. Once again, as the title suggests, we offer the students guidance in approaching these tasks. We are aware that there are many ways to write, for example, a critical review or a research paper, but our strong feeling is that if a learner of English as a second language becomes proficient in *one approach* to the task— one which is acceptable in any circumstance—then that student will be able to write successfully in other course work or in professional activities.

In an effort to provide realistic reading and writing assignments, we have included three resource chapters with this text. Our guidelines in compiling these chapters were that they be representative of academic prose and also general enough in content for students to be able to relate to the information, no matter what their major fields of interest. These resource chapters form the basis for the reading analysis and provide data for the writing assignments. Thus the text is largely self-contained.

Because most academic writing assignments are usually preceded by reading assignments, we have placed the reading analysis and recognition chapters first. For this reason, and because the lessons are carefully sequenced, incorporating concepts taught in earlier chapters into the later ones, we suggest that this book be used in sequence. A Teacher's Guide, which incorporates suggestions for use of the text and supplemental exercises, is available.

Acknowledgments

We gratefully acknowledge the help and encouragement we have received from our students and our colleagues at the English Language Institute. Their willingness to experiment with our efforts and their subsequent insightful and frequently detailed comments were of immeasurable assistance. Our particular thanks are extended to Dr. Gilbert D. Couts and Dr. Robert P. Fox. We also wish to thank Charles G. Morris, Stephen P. Robbins, Joseph L. Massie, and Leon P. Baradet for graciously allowing us to use large portions of their work as resource material for ours.

1 Identifying Controlling Ideas

KEY TERMS
  Controlling Idea
  Supporting Idea

UNDERSTANDING GENERAL ORGANIZATIONAL PATTERNS
  Deduction
  Textual Coherence
  Induction (Final Placement)
  Deduction / Restatement
  Implied Controlling Idea

A SPECIAL CASE: INTRODUCTIONS
  Deductive Introductions
  Nondeductive Introductions

EXPOSITORY WRITING ATTEMPTS TO CLARIFY AND EXPLAIN IDEAS IN TERMS OF OTHER IDEAS. In well-written academic expository prose, such as that found in a class textbook, the ideas are unified and presented according to certain general organizational patterns. This chapter will discuss (1) key elements involved in these organizational patterns, (2) kinds of patterns which you might expect to find in a text, and (3) kinds of linguistic devices by which authors insure that their texts come across clearly to readers.

KEY TERMS

A good understanding of the organization of an introductory textbook—a paragraph, a chapter section, a chapter, or even an entire book—depends to a large extent on the student's understanding of two key terms: **controlling idea** and **supporting idea.**

Controlling Idea

The controlling idea is the author's most general statement. It is called a controlling idea because it controls or limits which ideas and information the author will include in the text, as well as the selection of rhetorical devices.

A well-written controlling idea should alert the reader to the nature of these choices by means of *key words or phrases* relating to the subject under discussion. For example, when the author of a psychology textbook states that behavioral psychology is not the same as cognitive psychology, it is quite likely that, if the difference is not just being mentioned in passing, then what follows will be related to this contrast—that is, the text which follows will show *how* behavioral and cognitive psychology differ. Or an author who is writing about the general subject of communication might offer the following summary:

> There are three types of barriers which inhibit good communication: physical, human, and semantic.

Such a controlling idea suggests that the text which follows it will be developed by providing factual information; the three terms will be defined, and the reasons why they inhibit good communication will be discussed. The text is also limited specifically to the discussion of these *three* barriers; you do not expect to find information about other possible barriers.

The controlling idea of a paragraph has traditionally been referred to as the topic sentence. This terminology, however, can sometimes be misleading. Frequently, more than one sentence is used to clarify the controlling idea. Moreover, this controlling idea does not always control just one paragraph; it sometimes determines the content of a long series of paragraphs, of a chapter, or of an entire book. For these reasons, we will avoid using the term *topic sentence*.

Supporting Idea

Once you have located the controlling idea of a text, you can be sure that the remainder of the ideas—we shall call them supporting ideas—relate somehow to the controlling idea and are organized in reference to it. Supporting ideas are more specific than their controlling idea. They represent smaller parts of the entire subject and therefore relate to it in some way. For example, in a textbook whose stated purpose is to describe human nonverbal communication, the author might write about any of the following:

• types of nonverbal communication
• subtypes of each type
• differences or similarities between two types or subtypes
• effects of nonverbal communication on the communication process
• examples of nonverbal communication

Each of the above ideas is less general than the bigger idea of nonverbal communication; thus, they might all be included in a complete description of it.

In this book we will symbolize these "levels of generality" by what are called *branching diagrams*[1]: abstract visual representations of the ways in which writers arrange their ideas. As you read these diagrams from left to right (that is, from the first to the second, third, and further levels), the ideas will become less general—or, if you prefer, more specific. Study the following branching diagram. Most of the other diagrams in this book, though not identical to it, will nonetheless be constructed in much the same fashion.

---

[1] Later on in the book, we will suggest that you use a more conventional representation—the formal outline.

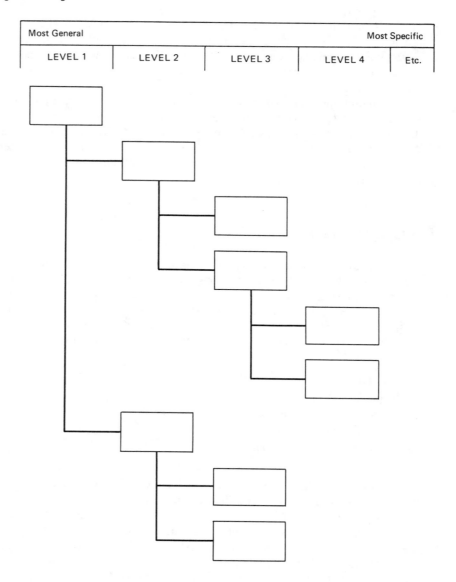

Most General				Most Specific
LEVEL 1	LEVEL 2	LEVEL 3	LEVEL 4	Etc.

UNDERSTANDING GENERAL ORGANIZATIONAL PATTERNS

One of the keys to accurate reading and writing is the ability to single out, from among all the ideas in a text, the controlling idea. In other words, where is an author most likely to place a controlling idea in relation to his or her supporting ideas? Where should *you* place a controlling idea when you write?

There are two main methods of arrangement, as well as several variations which are really combinations of the two main methods. As we examine each of these methods, we will also list a certain number of techniques which help to link ideas once they have been arranged.

Deduction

In academic prose, the most common place for a controlling idea is *near the beginning* of a text—the first or second sentence of a paragraph, or the first few sentences combined; or the first paragraph(s) of a longer text, such as an essay or a book chapter. A writer who uses this method announces the controlling idea with clear key words or phrases almost immediately; the supporting ideas that follow then refer the reader back to an already-known point of reference. This particular method of organizing ideas is called **deduction**. The diagram below symbolizes the deductive arrangement of ideas in writing:

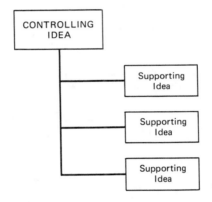

The text that follows is an example of this type of organization. The writer starts out by announcing a general idea, namely that there are certain kinds of nonverbal clues in any conversation. He then proceeds to give more specific ideas—*kinds* of clues—which all refer back to the general idea and are included in it.

    In addition to the words which a speaker uses to convey meanings in a conversation, the hearer has to deal with certain kinds of nonverbal clues. The first kind is body movements. A body position or movement does not by itself have a precise or universal meaning, but when it is linked with spoken language, it gives fuller meaning to a sender's
5   words. Intonations, too, influence the hearer's perception of what is being said. An intonation can change the meaning of a verbal message, adding information not actually contained in the words themselves. The facial expression of the speaker conveys still another kind of nonverbal message. Facial expressions can show many of the speaker's characteristics that would not be obvious in a written transcript of the conversation. The
10   final kind of unspoken signal which the speaker sends has to do with the way he spaces himself, in terms of physical distance, from the listener. What is considered proper

spacing in various kinds of situations is dependent largely on the norms of the culture involved. How the speaker respects or disregards those cultural norms always has significance for the hearer. (Adapted from *Organizational Behavior*, p. 230.)

1–1
VISUALIZE

Directions: Visualize the organization of the preceding text by labeling the diagram.

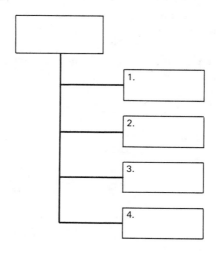

Textual Coherence

No matter where the controlling idea is located, writers use various techniques to remind readers how one part of a text is related or linked to another and how a text moves naturally from one idea to another. These techniques can be used to link (1) parts of a sentence, (2) different sentences, or (3) larger sections of a text. This linking—we will call it **coherence**—is particularly useful in longer texts, where a reader often needs to be reminded of the author's train of thought. However, coherence devices are quite common even in shorter texts like the sample paragraph you have just read.

Coherence Device: SYNONYMS

When authors want to insure that an important idea or word is carried from one section of a text to another, they can substitute a synonymous word, phrase, or grammatical structure. Note the use of synonyms in the preceding sample text:

   In addition to the words which a ⎡speaker⎤ uses to convey meanings in a conversation, the hearer has to deal with certain kinds of nonverbal clues. The first kind is body movements. A body position or movement does not by itself have a precise or universal meaning, but when it is linked with spoken language, it gives fuller meaning to a
5 ⎡sender⎤'s words. Intonations, too, influence the hearer's perception of what is being

said. An intonation can change the meaning of a verbal message, adding information not actually contained in the words themselves. The facial expression of the speaker conveys still another kind of nonverbal message. Facial expressions can show many of the speaker's characteristics that would not be obvious in a written transcript of the
10   conversation. The final kind of unspoken signal which the speaker sends has to do with the way he spaces himself, in terms of physical distance, from the listener. What is considered proper spacing in various kinds of situations is dependent largely on the norms of the culture involved. How the speaker respects or disregards those cultural norms always has significance for the hearer.

1–2
EXEMPLIFY / VISUALIZE / DISCUSS

Directions: Find other examples of synonymous expressions in the preceding text. Circle or box them, and connect them with lines.

1–3
WRITE

Directions: Use the information in the chart below (adapted from *Essentials of Management*, pp. 101–102) as the basis for a short (2-paragraph) composition. Each paragraph should be developed *deductively*, with a clear controlling idea expressed in the first sentence.

- Paragraph 1: Relate the information in the chart. This chart has no title; this means that you will have to analyze the information and develop a controlling idea which will be an effective beginning sentence for the paragraph. You may use the preceding sample paragraph ("Types of Nonverbal Signals") as your model.
- Paragraph 2: Make a judgment as to which type in the chart seems to you to be the most *effective*. Explain why. Do not use any personal pronouns in your paragraph. (*I, my, our,* etc.). Be sure that the controlling idea is expressed in the first sentence of the paragraph.

Type	*Characteristics*	*Mode of Operation*
the dictatorial leader	dominant; critical, negative attitude toward subordinates	punishment or replacement of subordinates who do not perform
the benevolent-autocratic leader	strong personality; respected by and has personal allegiance of subordinates	subordinates forced to rely on leader for job satisfaction
the democratic leader	cooperative, communicative	participation in all stages of management encouraged
the laissez-faire leader	complete dependence on subordinates; "just another member of the group"	group members allowed to act individually, sometimes in conflicting directions

Induction (Final Placement)

The other main method of organizing ideas is the exact opposite of deduction: **induction**. Inductive writing starts out by giving a certain number of major and/or minor supporting ideas. It then proceeds to a statement of the more general controlling idea, which is located somewhere near the end of the text. Induction is most often used when the subject matter is controversial or when the writer is trying to convince the reader to accept his or her conclusions.

The inductive method can be symbolized as follows:

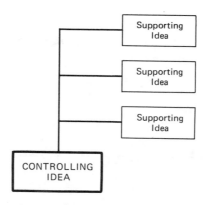

The text which follows is an example of this type of organization. You will notice that it contains basically the same ideas as the text which was used to exemplify deduction. However, these ideas have been rearranged to illustrate the *opposite* process: the first idea stated is not the controlling idea; after giving all his more specific ideas, the writer concludes by stating his more general controlling idea to which all the previous ideas refer.

The way a speaker moves his body during a conversation adds to, and often complicates, verbal communication. Although a body position or movement does not by itself have a precise or universal meaning, when it is linked with spoken language, it gives fuller meaning to the sender's words. Intonation, too, influences the hearer's perception of
5   what is being said. Intonations can actually change the meaning of a verbal message, adding information not contained in the words themselves. Facial expressions are just as important as intonation patterns. The facial expression of the speaker can show many of his characteristics that would not be obvious in a written transcript of the conversation. The hearer also has to interpret the way the speaker spaces himself, in terms of physical
10 distance, from the hearer. What is considered proper spacing in various kinds of situations is largely dependent on cultural norms. How the speaker respects or disregards those norms always has meaning for the hearer. Thus, in addition to the verbal content of a spoken message, the hearer must take into account these four types of *nonverbal* communication.

   This basic difference in organization is one which you must be well aware of if you hope to become an effective reader and writer. Deduction is somewhat clearer than induction, for it makes the organization of ideas more immediately apparent. However, you must also understand the inductive method of arranging ideas, since certain texts you will have to study will be organized inductively.

1–4
VISUALIZE

Directions: Visualize the organization of the preceding text by constructing and labeling a diagram of your own, based on the abstract model just given.

Coherence Device: REPETITION

   If a writer does not want to find a synonym for an important word or idea, he can simply *repeat* it, either exactly or by using a related word form. Consider the writer's use of repetition in the same text that was used to demonstrate induction:

   The way a speaker moves his body during a conversation adds to, and often complicates, verbal communication. Although a body position or movement does not by itself have a precise or universal meaning, when it is linked with spoken language, it gives fuller meaning to the sender's words. Intonation, too, influences the hearer's
5   perception of what is being said. Intonations can actually change the meaning of a verbal message, adding information not contained in the words themselves. Facial expressions are just as important as intonation patterns. The facial expressions of the speaker can show many of his characteristics that would not be obvious in a written transcript of the conversation. The hearer also has to interpret the way in which the
10   speaker spaces himself, in terms of physical distance, from the hearer. What is considered proper spacing in various kinds of situations is largely dependent on cultural norms. How the speaker respects or disregards those norms always means something to the hearer. Thus, in addition to the verbal content of a spoken message, the hearer must take into account these four types of nonverbal communication.

1–5
EXEMPLIFY / VISUALIZE / DISCUSS

   A. How many other examples of repetition can you find in the above text? Underline them.
      1. Which of the examples represent repetition of the *exact* word or phrase?
      2. In which examples do you notice a change in the form of the word(s)?
   B. In which sentence of the text does the reader discover precisely what the four kinds of things refer to?
   C. In which paragraph—this one (induction) or the preceding one (deduction)—is the reader able to grasp the overall organization more quickly? Why?

1–6
WRITE

Directions: Rewrite the first paragraph assigned in Exercise 1–3, using inductive development. Remember that in this type of organization, the controlling idea is saved until the end. You might want to consider using the word *these* in your final sentence to add coherence to your paragraph.

Deduction / Restatement

A word of caution is in order concerning the two preceding sample texts. Many texts do not use either the purely deductive or the purely inductive arrangement, and even in shorter texts, some variations are possible. One of these variations, which could lead to some possible confusion, represents a kind of combination of these two methods: an author announces a controlling idea, gives several supporting ideas, then concludes by **restating** the controlling idea in a slightly different form. This method is even clearer than "pure deduction" since it reinforces the controlling idea by placing it both at the beginning and at the end. The following diagram symbolizes this arrangement of ideas.

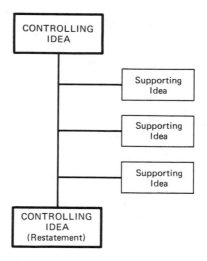

The text which follows represents the same information used to demonstrate deductive and inductive arrangement. It has been rewritten to exemplify deduction/restatement.

In addition to the words which a speaker uses to convey meanings in a conversation, the hearer has to deal with certain kinds of nonverbal clues. The first is body movements. A body position or movement does not by itself have a precise or universal meaning, but when it is linked with spoken language, it gives fuller meaning to a sender's words.

5   Intonation, too, influences the hearer's perception of what is being said. Intonations can actually change the meaning of a verbal message, adding information which is not contained in the words themselves. The facial expression of the speaker conveys still another kind of nonverbal message. Facial expressions can show many of the speaker's characteristics that would not be obvious in a written transcript of the conversation. The

10   final kind of unspoken signal which every speaker sends has to do with the way he spaces himself, in terms of physical distance, from the hearer. What is considered proper spacing in various kinds of situations is largely dependent on cultural norms. How the speaker respects or disregards those norms always has meaning for the hearer. Thus, these four types of nonverbal signals play a great role in creating the *total content* of a spoken

15   message.

1–7
VISUALIZE

Directions: Visualize the arrangement of controlling and supporting ideas in the preceding text by constructing and labeling a diagram of your own.

Coherence Device: SUBSTITUTES*

An author sometimes uses a *substitute* to refer back to an idea announced in a previous sentence. Substitutes are, in reality, special kinds of repetition: instead of repeating an item, the author uses a substitute form which refers back to it. Substitutes include such things as the following:

• NOUN SUBSTITUTES
she, them, it, one, etc. *(personal pronouns)*
who, whom, which, that, etc. *(relative words)*
himself, themselves, etc. *(reflexive pronouns)*

• VERB SUBSTITUTES
do, does, did

• ADVERB SUBSTITUTES
then *(time)*
there *(place)*
thus, so, this way, that way *(manner)*

• ADJECTIVE SUBSTITUTES
whose *(possessive relative word)*
this, that, these, those *(demonstratives)*
such

• PHRASE AND CLAUSE SUBSTITUTES
mine, yours, ours, his, etc. *(possessives)*
many, a few, some, etc. *(quantifiers)*
such, so

Notice some of the instances of substitution in the sample text used to demonstrate deduction/restatement.

In addition to the *words* which he uses to convey meanings in a conversation, the speaker always sends the hearer certain kinds of nonverbal clues. The first is body movements. A body position or movement does not by itself have a precise or universal meaning, but when it is linked with spoken language, it gives fuller meaning to a sender's
5   words. Intonation, too, influences the hearer's perception of what is being said. Intonations can actually change the meaning of a verbal message, adding information which is not contained in the *words* themselves. The facial expression of the speaker conveys still another kind of nonverbal message. Facial expressions can show many of the speaker's characteristics that would not be obvious in a written transcript of the
10 conversation. The final kind of unspoken signal which every *speaker* sends has to do with the way he spaces himself, in terms of physical distance, from the hearer. What is considered proper spacing in various kinds of situations is largely dependent on cultural norms. How the speaker respects or disregards those norms always has meaning for the hearer. Thus, these four types of nonverbal signals play a great role in creating the total
15 content of a spoken message.

---

* The charts in this book which list various structures—coherence devices in Chapter 1, thought relationship signals in Chapter 2, etc.—are not intended to be complete reference lists. They are included only to serve as reminders.

1–8
EXEMPLIFY / VISUALIZE / DISCUSS

A. Find other examples of substitute forms in the preceding text. Circle or box them, and draw arrows to their referents. (Do they all refer backward to something, or do some of them refer *forward* to something?)

B. Which substitute form refers back not to a preceding word, phrase, or clause, but rather to an entire section of the text?

Implied Controlling Idea

Still another variation—less frequent perhaps in textbooks, where the purpose is to inform, than in certain other kinds of writing such as short stories and novels—is the case where the controlling idea is never stated directly, but only **implied**. In this kind of arrangement, the reader must synthesize all the supporting ideas and draw a conclusion as to what the unifying principle behind them is. When the writer does not explicitly state the controlling idea, the reader must make an *inference*.

The following diagram symbolizes this kind of organization. The absence of an explicit relationship is shown by the dotted lines.

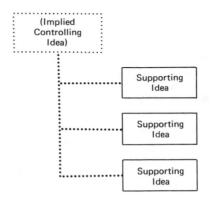

The paragraph below represents an example of an implied controlling idea. Notice that four different kinds of things are being discussed, but we are never told explicitly what the more general term is. *The reader must infer it.*

> Although a position or movement of the body does not by itself have a precise or universal meaning in a conversation, when it is linked with spoken language, it gives fuller meaning to the speaker's words. Intonation, too, influences the hearer's perception of what is being said. An intonation can actually change the meaning of a verbal message,
> 5 adding information not contained in the words themselves. The facial expression of the speaker can show many of the speaker's characteristics that would not be obvious in a written transcript of the conversation. And the way the speaker spaces himself from the hearer, in terms of physical distance, has meaning. What is considered proper spacing in various kinds of situations is dependent largely on the norms of the culture. How the
> 10 speaker disregards or respects those norms adds to the total content of the message.

In some instances, particularly in textbooks, the controlling idea may best be thought of as an implied one, related in some way to a word or phrase which is printed in **boldface**, *in italics*, or <u>underlined</u>. Although the author does not make such a statement, the implication is that the text which follows will be a discussion of that word or phrase. That discussion might include such things as the precise meaning of the word or phrase, its function, a physical description of the item in question, its uses, its practical manifestations, its types or kinds—almost any aspect which the author feels is important. Because the controlling idea is not explicitly stated, these kinds of words or phrases may be thought of as suggesting the presence of implied controlling ideas. The following text illustrates this special kind of controlling idea:

> *Facial expressions* are the most obvious indicators. We can tell a lot about a person's emotional state by observing whether he is laughing, crying, smiling, or frowning. Many facial expressions are innate, not learned; children who are born deaf and blind use the same facial gestures to express the same emotions as normal children do. Charles Darwin observed that most animals share a common pattern of muscular facial movements—for

5 example, dogs, tigers, and men all bare their teeth in rage. Some human facial expressions of emotion are universal; others are unique (Izard, 1971).

In his study of facial movements, Ray Birdwhistell (1952) has determined that the most expressive emotional signals are transmitted by the shape and disposition of the mouth, nose, and eyebrows. While most people can recognize widely differing emotions in facial
10 expressions, they do tend to confuse some emotions with others, such as fear with surprise (Tomkins & McCarter, 1964). Thompson and Meltzer (1964) designed an experiment to see if certain emotions were easier to express facially than others. They found that most people have no trouble expressing love, fear, determination, and happiness, but suffering, disgust, and contempt are significantly more difficult to express—and to recognize. In
15 another experiment with male and female subjects, Drag and Shaw (1967) found that women were better than men at recognizing happiness, fear, love, and anger in facial expressions. (*Psychology*, pp. 408–409.)

Note, in the preceding text, that the phrase *facial expressions* has been given in italics. In the first sentence, the author indicates that facial expressions are "the most obvious emotional indicators," and the material which follows gives examples of facial expressions and explains their function as indicators of emotions. However, it does not confine itself exclusively to their being "obvious," as the first sentence might seem to suggest. A comparison is suggested between humans and animals. In addition, the question of innate versus learned facial expressions is raised briefly. In the second paragraph, the author indicates the parts of the face which play a key role in communicating emotional messages, but he does not pursue the matter. Instead, he shifts to the *confusion* which can stem from facial expressions as indicators of emotion: he relates certain experiments which tend to show (1) that facial expressions are *not* always reliable indicators of emotion, and (2) that they are even less reliable in the case of men than they are in the case of women.

All things considered, then, the phrase *facial expressions* can be thought of as only the *general topic* of the text. The implied controlling idea is, in effect, the following: "The text which follows is a discussion of certain aspects of the topic *facial expressions*." Although this is a common pattern of organizing ideas in textbooks, do not expect that this will be the case with every italicized word that you encounter; only a careful reading of the text in question will determine whether or not you are dealing with this special type of implied controlling idea.

Coherence Device: THE DEFINITE ARTICLE the

An important—but very subtle—function of the definite article *the* in written discourse is to identify certain nouns so that readers can follow a writer's progression of ideas with a minimum of effort and confusion. The writer, by his use of *the*, promises the reader that help, established either by words in the text or by the signaling that certain information is shared and understood by both the reader and the writer.

There are basically six cases in English which are considered proper types of such identification. They are listed below, then exemplified in the text which follows.

• EXPLICIT STRUCTURAL IDENTIFICATION

1. A special adjective:*

THE	+	special adjective	+	noun

EXAMPLE: *The* first kind is body movements.

* "Special" adjectives include:
(1) superlative adjectives (the *most interesting* topic, the *largest* group);
(2) sequential adjectives (the *first* category, the *next* item);
(3) spatial adjectives (the *top* shelf, the *middle* seat, the *upper righthand* corner);
(4) uniqueness adjectives (the *only* survivor, the *other* suggestion, the *same* reason).

2. The rule of "previous mention": the noun—or a synonym—has already been mentioned in the text.

noun or synonym	+	*THE*	+	noun

EXAMPLE: *A* speaker in a conversation uses certain kinds of nonverbal clues in a conversation. For example, *the* speaker uses certain body movements to convey meanings.

3. A structure following the noun (usually a full or reduced adjective clause):

THE	+	noun	+	relative clause, phrase

EXAMPLE: *The* words which a speaker uses convey meaning.

• IMPLIED (UNDERSTOOD) IDENTIFICATION

4. Implied by the situation in the text:

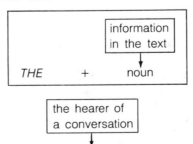

EXAMPLE: Intonation, too, influences *the* hearer's perception of what is being said.

5. Implied by the nature of the noun (one of a kind, common knowledge, no other meaning possible, etc.):

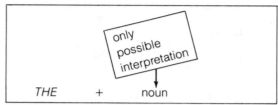

EXAMPLE: A position or movement of *the* body does not have a universal meaning.

6. Generic meaning.* When the previous five rules all fail to explain the use of *the*, then the noun might refer to the *entire class* of such items, that is, to the idea in a very general sense.

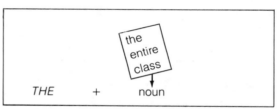

EXAMPLE: Before the invention of *the* tape recorder, it was impossible to study conversations.

* This is a fairly limited use of *the*, restricted mostly to:
(1) plant and animal species (*the lion, the tomato*);
(2) technological inventions (*the atomic bomb, the telephone*);
(3) professionals (*the physicist, the musician*);
(4) certain adjectives (*the rich, the poor, the disabled*).

1–9
EXEMPLIFY / DISCUSS

A. Explain the use of each of the italicized articles in the following text:

> In addition to the words which a speaker uses to convey meanings in a conversation, the hearer has to deal with certain kinds of nonverbal clues. Before the invention of the tape recorder and *the* camera, it was difficult, if not impossible, to study and classify these clues, since there could be no record kept of a conversation
> 5 between two people. Since the invention of these two instruments, however, modern linguists have been able to classify these important communicative clues. The first is body movements. A position or movement of the body does not by itself have a

precise or universal meaning, but when it is linked with spoken language, it gives fuller meaning to the sender's words. A shrug of *the* shoulders, for example,
10 sometimes indicates indifference. Intonation, too, influences the hearer's perception of what is being said. An intonation can change the meaning of a verbal message, adding information not actually contained in the words themselves. The facial expression of the speaker conveys yet another kind of nonverbal message. Facial expressions can show many of the speaker's characteristics that would not be obvious
15 in *a* written transcript of the conversation; *the* transcript might not, for instance, indicate aggression, fear, joy, arrogance, or shyness. *The* final kind of unspoken signal which the speaker sends has to do with *the* way he spaces himself, in terms of physical distance, from the hearer. What is considered proper spacing in various kinds of situations is largely dependent on the norms of *the* culture. How the speaker
20 respects or disregards those norms always has meaning for the hearer.

B. What is the general organizational pattern of this text? Locate the controlling idea and tell how many sentences comprise it.

C. What seems to be the function of the second and third sentences?

1–10
EXEMPLIFY / VISUALIZE / DISCUSS

Directions: Referring to the introduction to Resource Chapter A ("Motivation"), pp. 229–30, find examples of all four kinds of coherence devices.

A. In the first two paragraphs, locate examples of *repetition*, either exact repetition or use of a related form of the same word.

B. In the third paragraph, find all the examples of *substitute forms* used by the author to avoid repetition. (Note that all refer to something previously mentioned in the text except one. Which is it?)

C. In the third and fourth paragraphs, explain the following uses of the definite article *the*:

- *Paragraph 3:*
  "*the* family"
  "*the* next-door neighbor"
  "*the* parlormaid"
  "*the* poodle"
  "*the* tragedy"
- *Paragraph 4:*
  "*the* network of motives"
  "*the* set of factors"
  "*the* same thing"
  "*the* local crime ring"

D. In the final paragraph of the introduction, which two *synonymous* words or phrases have been used to mean *triggers*? In the third paragraph, what synonymous phrase has the author used to mean *a detective story*?

1–11
EXEMPLIFY / DISCUSS

Directions: After studying each of the selections below, do the following:

A. Underline the controlling idea.
B. Indicate, in the space provided after each selection, which general method of arrangement has been used:
  • deduction
  • induction
  • deduction/restatement
  • implied controlling idea

1. You will remember that the degree of effort an individual exerts depends on his or her perception of the effort-performance, performance-reward, and reward-goal satisfaction linkages. If individuals are not given the data necessary to make the perceived probability of these linkages high, motivation will be less than it could be. If rewards are
5 not made clear, if the criteria for determining and measuring performance are ambiguous, or if individuals are not relatively certain that their effort will lead to satisfactory performance, then effort will be reduced. So communication plays a significant role in determining the level of motivation. (From *Organizational Behavior*, p. 232.)

METHOD: _____

2. To understand the autonomic nervous system it is necessary to make one more division. The autonomic nervous system consists of two branches—the **sympathetic** and **parasympathetic** divisions. These two divisions act in almost total opposition to each other, but both are directly involved in controlling and integrating the actions of the
5 glands and blood vessels within the body.
The nerve fibers of the sympathetic division pathways are busiest when you are frightened or angry. They carry messages that tell the body to prepare for an emergency, to get ready to act quickly and strenuously. In response to messages from the sympathetic division, your heart pounds, you breathe faster, your pupils enlarge, digestion stops. The
10 sympathetic nervous system also tells the adrenal glands to start producing epinephrine, which further intensifies these reactions. Sympathetic nerve fibers connect to every internal organ in the body, which explains why the body's reaction to sudden stress is so widespread.
Parasympathetic nerve fibers connect to all the same organs as the sympathetic nerve
15 fibers, but the messages they carry tell the organs to do just the opposite of what the sympathetic division has directed. The parasympathetic division says, in effect, "Okay, the heat's off. Let's get back to normal." So the heart goes back to beating at its normal rate, the stomach muscles relax, digestion begins again, breathing slows down, and the pupils of the eyes get smaller. Thus the parasympathetic division compensates for the
20 sympathetic division and lets the body take a rest after a period of stress. (From *Psychology*, p. 38.)

METHOD: _____

3. Reports are often late or not timely because the proper inputs were not available for computer processing when they should have been. Or the inputs were available but they were so inaccurate that they were returned to data preparations for further checking and corrections. Then by the time they are actually available, the report is late. (From
5   *Essentials of Management*, p. 185.)

METHOD: _____

4. Shortly after their introduction to the business world, it became obvious that computers could produce substantial cost savings in areas where large volumes of repetitive paperwork were required. Payrolls, order recordings, shipping documents, invoice preparation, accounts receivables, and many other high-volume operations, such
5   as loan processing in banks, provided ample justification for early computers. In other words, the production of operational information was the initial impetus for computer acquisition by commercial firms. (From *Essentials of Management*, p. 174.)

METHOD: _____

5. The complex cable of nerves that connects the brain to most of the rest of the body is known as the **spinal cord**. The spinal cord is made up of bundles of long, nearly round nerve fibers. The inside of the spinal cord has a grayish color, while outside the coverings of myelin sheaths give it a whitish appearance. The spinal cord has two basic functions.
5   The first is to carry messages to and from the brain. The second is to cause reflex movements—a message signaling pain from touching the thorn on a rose, for example, comes into your spinal cord, and an impulse is sent out to cause the almost instantaneous response of pulling your hand away. Because of the way the neural circuits are arranged, the same incoming message produces the same responses every time. The message does
10   travel to the brain, but by the time it gets there you have probably already reacted. Most of these spinal reflexes are protective; they enable you to avoid damage to the body. Some other reflexes, which are not protective ones, do pass through circuits in the brain before action is taken. One reflex that involves the brain is a sneeze—you generally know when you are about to sneeze and sometimes you can control it. (From *Psychology*, p. 39.)

METHOD: _____

6. The force theory of the origin of state embraces two schools of thought. The original school goes back to ancient times. In it the state was created by conquest and force; it grew out of the forceful imposition of the strong over the weak. Therefore the state was an evil thing that could be resisted in a righteous cause. As one might imagine, this particular
5   attitude has been dogma to revolutionary groups through the ages: to the early Christians resisting the Roman Empire, to medieval theologians trying to make temporal authority subject to the spiritual sword, to democratic insurrectionists leading the struggle against monarchical tyranny, and so forth.
   The second school of thought based on the force theory developed in Germany during
10   the nineteenth century. At that time almost every West European area had developed into a nation-state except Germany and Italy. Internal political divisions and external pressures had prevented the consolidation of these areas into modern political units. A nationalistic spirit had been growing in Germany, however, since the Napoleonic wars. It became exaggerated as a result of the frustration encountered by its proponents.

15   The theory of the forceful origin of the state was developed mainly by Georg Hegel (1770–1831) and Friedrich Nietzsche (1844–1900). Their theories form the basis of what is now called *statism*. They argued that the state was indeed created by force, but that rather than being evil this feature dignified the state. Force was *not* something to be avoided. On the contrary, it was the primary value in society. It was its own justification.
20 The state, institutionalizing the power of the strong over the weak, simply arranged affairs as they should be. According to force theorists, the weak should be ruled by the strong.
     Students of Hegel and Nietzsche have argued that the state is the most powerful form of human association. As such, it is above any ordinary moral or ethical restraint, and it is greater than any individual. It is not limited by something as insignificant as the
25 individual's rights. (From *Political Ideologies*, p. 44.)

METHOD: _____

    7. People have often lamented the fact that we spend a third of our lives asleep. Think what we must be missing! What we are actually missing by being able to sleep are the following: visual, auditory, and tactile sensory disorders; vivid hallucinations; inability to concentrate; withdrawal; disorientation of self, time, and place; lapses of attention;
5 increased heart rate and stress hormones in the blood; and the onset of psychosis. This alarming list, of course, refers to extreme instances—people who have stayed up, on a bet or for a television marathon, for over 200 hours. But if you have been up all night, you may be slower in taking notes or answering questions on an exam the next day, or you may even fall asleep in class. In short, the human body needs **sleep** to function, just as it needs
10 food and water. (From *Psychology*, p. 358.)

METHOD: _____

    8. **Computer storage** takes many forms, but the most common element is the ability to record and retain information such as letters and numbers. The main storage of a computer is composed of a large number of storage locations, each with a unique address and each possessing the ability to hold a specific number of letters or numbers. These
5 storage locations are analogous to post office boxes, each with an address, each with storage capacity. The analogy is extremely close. The storage can hold names, addresses, part numbers, account balances, or even literary works. In short, any combination of letters, numbers, or special characters which can be written can be stored in computer storage. These kinds of information are referred to as **data**. Of course, computers with
10 larger storage capacities are accompanied by larger price tags. (From *Essentials of Management*, pp. 177–78.)

METHOD: _____

    9. The **hindbrain**, since it is found in even the most primitive vertebrates, is believed to have been the earliest part of the brain to evolve. The part of the hindbrain nearest to the spinal cord is the *medulla*, a narrow structure about an inch and a half long. The medulla controls breathing and many important reflexes, such as those that help us maintain our
5 upright posture. The medulla is also the point where many of the nerves from the higher parts of the brain are crossed—the nerves from the left part of the brain travel to the right side of the body, and vice versa.
    Above the medulla lies the *pons*, a slightly wider structure that serves as a pathway that

connects the cerebral cortex at the top of the brain to the topmost section of the hindbrain,
10   the *cerebellum*.

The cerebellum is composed of two circular hemispheres. It performs quite a number of chores—it handles certain reflexes, especially those that have to do with balance, and it coordinates the body's actions to make sure that movements go together in efficient sequences. The cerebellum also has an important role in organizing eye movements. It
15   allows you to keep your eyes fixed on a particular point while your head and body are moving, and it controls the eye movements that are important in following an object in motion (Llinas, 1975). (From *Psychology*, pp. 40–41.)

METHOD: _____

10. The manager must make decisions for future actions and thus must forecast future demand. Forecasting may be oriented to estimating economic conditions in the near future, or it may be directed toward estimation of specific quantities that will be purchased in various markets. This section summarizes the first of these problems; the
5   latter problem will receive attention in Chapter 14.

We have seen that the individual demand for a given firm depends upon the health of the total demand in the economy; therefore, a first step is to forecast the conditions of the economic environment.

A second step in forecasting the demand for a given product usually concentrates on the
10   total demand for the industry. Large firms keep close contact with all factors affecting the industry because they have a large stake in the problem. Smaller firms may accept the opinions of business economists of these large firms. The demand for the industry can be analyzed by individual components such as: (1) sales of products to new customers (for example, the sale of autos or television sets to people who do not own the product);
15   (2) sales of additional products to old customers (for example, a second auto or television set); (3) replacement sales for products that have worn out; and (4) sales affected by recent technological developments. Each company may wish to concentrate on a particular segment of the industry and forecast sales in these segments more carefully, for example, sales to farmers, the retired workers, teenagers, and so on.
20   A third step in forecasting the demand for a given company is the estimate of the market share of the particular company. Past share of the market may serve as the base for this step. Adjustments, however, should be made by forecasting the effect of new programs planned by the company, expected reactions of competitors to the company's actions and to industry conditions, and detailed reports by salesmen in different localities.
25   (From *Essentials of Management*, pp. 119–20.)

METHOD: _____

A SPECIAL CASE: INTRODUCTIONS

While it is generally true that the beginning of a text is a good place to look for a controlling idea, there are some situations, particularly when you are dealing with longer texts, in which you must be careful: *Beginning* is a relative term, and it does not necessarily mean the first sentence of the first paragraph. One of these special situations is **introductions.** This term is used here to include at least three different kinds of introductory sections: (1) the beginning of a book, (2) the beginning of a chapter, and (3) the beginning of a chapter section or subsection.

Deductive Introductions

Authors are free, of course, to introduce their material in a straightforward, deductive fashion. In such an introduction, the reader quickly becomes aware, perhaps even from the first sentence, of the author's approach—what the material will be about, how it relates to previous material in the book, and perhaps even the general way in which the book/chapter/section will be organized. A good example is the following text, which is the introduction to a chapter of a textbook on management (the controlling idea of the chapter is in italics):

Two closely related functions of management will be discussed together in this chapter. Planning looks to the future; controlling checks the past. The two, thus, jointly serve as perspectives for the manager who makes decisions in the present. Both have been the subjects of considerable research and both have developed separate theories. (From *Essentials of Management*, p. 85.)

Nondeductive Introductions

Introductions will often use other kinds of techniques—many of them longer and more complicated, some of them more inductive in nature—all of which require greater attention on your part until you have become more familiar with them. A good example is the introduction to Resource Chapter A ("Motivation," pages 229–30). From reading the chapter title, you already know that the main subject of the chapter is motivation; and since this is a psychology textbook, you have already guessed that it will approach motivation from the psychologist's point of view.

However, as you read the introduction to this chapter, notice that if you looked at the first paragraph expecting to find some kind of deductively organized chapter plan, you would be misled by what you found. Like the chapter title, the first paragraph establishes the context—motivation. It does this, however, in a very specific way, by mentioning an example of "motivation manipulated at a very sophisticated level": a detective story. A murder has been committed, and the police are wondering who had a strong enough motive to have committed it. This, of course, is not the precise controlling idea of the chapter. Nor are you any closer to a controlling idea or a chapter plan in the second paragraph, which examines the possible motives each of the characters in the story may have had for killing Miss Jones. It is only in the *third* paragraph that the author begins to fit all these details together into a total picture by beginning to focus in on the chapter organization. He does not do this, however, until the *end* of the paragraph, and only after having offered many other examples of specific kinds of motives the characters may have had for doing many different things. It is this very last sentence which finally shows us how the author has used all these examples to give an idea of his chapter plan. Notice the clever use, in this last sentence, of the coherence devices *these* and *this*:

relates the previous examples to his statement of the chapter's main focus

In all **these** less spectacular forms of behavior, motivation is also present. In **this** chapter, *we will discuss all **these** motives, from the most basic to the most complex.*

In the remainder of the introduction—which another writer might have set off in a separate section—the author of this text proceeds to give a general description of motivation as a process consisting of five stages; this description will apply to all the particular forms of motivation to be presented subsequently in the chapter. (A quick skimming of the chapter will show you that, as he has promised, the author has divided motives into several main types and subtypes and has examined them one by one, defining and describing each.)

This is only one of many different and interesting nondeductive ways of introducing a subject. The list is practically endless, even in the most formally written academic textbook, for the techniques are as numerous as there are authors. However, most nondeductive introductions have certain elements in common:

1. They begin by *establishing a context* which introduces the reader to the content area, in either a very general or a very specific way. That is, the author "sets the stage" in the way he or she feels will be most interesting to the reader—quotations, examples, historical background information, rhetorical questions, reference to a previous chapter, and so on.
2. The author is eventually led to *focus further* on the content area in a way which will orient the reader in the right direction. Authors do this through description, through definition, or through more specific exemplification.
3. The author is finally led to focus, in very clear terms, on the exact subject matter of the text—that is, the *controlling idea*.

In other words, the basic movement of a nondeductive introduction is a function of the degree to which the author focuses clearly on the controlling idea:

UNFOCUSED INFORMATION: interesting and/or informative matter designed to *catch readers' attention and orient their thinking*

FOCUSED INFORMATION: the author's *controlling idea* stated very clearly

Note that the movement from unfocused to focused does not correlate with how general or how specific each part of the introduction is. A nondeductive introduction can move from the general to the specific, or it can do just the opposite. An example of a *general-to-specific* introduction would be one in which the author begins by announcing a broad category or general statement, breaks it into parts or subdivisions, and concludes by limiting the discussion in that chapter or section to only one of those parts. In a *specific-to-general* pattern, on the other hand, an author might well begin with one or several striking examples, or even an attention-getting quotation; the remainder of the introduction will then broaden into the more general statement or category that corresponds to the controlling idea.

In either of the above cases, the author may of course decide to present a more detailed look at the organization of the text which follows, indicating, for example, the topics of various subsections. At this point the introduction has become *deductive*. Nondeductive introductions thus can be fairly confusing, and you should exercise great care in reading them until you have become accustomed to the most common variations.

1–12
EXEMPLIFY / DISCUSS

Directions: Read the following introductions to textbook chapters and sections. As you examine each, consider the following:

A. Where has the author indicated what the main emphasis of the chapter or chapter section will be?
B. Does the author "outline" the chapter organization for the reader?
C. In cases where the controlling idea is not immediately stated, what techniques does the author use to "get there"—for example, rhetorical questions,[2] reference to another chapter or section, quotations, background information, definition, description, analogy,[3] examples, limiting the subject.

1. An early argument in personality research was whether an individual's personality was the result of heredity or environment. Was the personality predetermined at birth or was it the result of the individual's interaction with his or her environment? Clearly, there is no simple "black-or-white" answer. Personality appears to be a result of both
5 influences. Additionally, there has recently been an increased interest in a third factor—the situation. Thus, an adult's personality is now generally considered to be made up of both hereditary and environmental factors, and moderated by situational conditions. (From *Organizational Behavior*, p. 63.)

2. The first major coordinating and integrating mechanism of the body that we will look at is the **nervous system**. The more we learn about the nervous system, the more certain we are that all of its parts work together, all the time, to integrate the extraordinarily intricate activities of the body. Yet its parts are so many, so various, so

---

[2] A *rhetorical question* is a special kind of question used to emphasize a point; no immediate answer is expected.

[3] An *analogy* is a special kind of comparison in which the writer explains a complex term by comparing it to something which is likely to be more familiar to the reader. See pages 40–41.

5   complex, and, to a large extent, still so mysterious that it is easier to approach the nervous
system by looking first at its various parts. We will start with the smallest part, the
individual neuron. Multiplied many billions of times, this single cell underlies the activity
of the entire nervous system. (From *Psychology*, p. 32.)

3. Economics and business management have always been closely related; in fact,
most schools of business have their origins in departments of economics. Yet the
viewpoints of the economist and the manager have, until recently, been different. The
economist has been concerned chiefly with the functioning of the economy as a whole and
5   social issues such as monopoly and competition, tax policy, the pricing system, and the
distribution of income. The manager has been concerned primarily with maximization of
profits, from the viewpoint of the individual firm, and with such company policies as
pricing, wage payments, market share, and employment of resources. Both the economist
and the manager, nevertheless, face similar problems of using scarce resources in the
10 satisfaction of human wants. Both concentrate on the analysis of demand characteristics
and supply factors, but the manager must orient his thoughts to making decisions in
business operations. **Managerial economics**, therefore, may be defined as the management's application of economic principles in the decision-making process.
This chapter will deal with those economic questions in which a manager's discretion is
15 of greatest importance. It will not deal with those economic questions over which the
manager has little control. Of course, all managers should have a knowledge of the
economic system in which they operate and should understand the institutional setting and
the environment of the industry to which they must adjust. This broader subject, however,
is not within the scope of this book. (From *Essentials of Management*, pp. 109–110.)

4. Problems of communication directly retard the success of managers in the
performance of their functions. If messages are poorly transmitted, or if the action is not
effected, management cannot plan or control activities properly. The barriers to good
communication require constant attention. Some of these barriers and remedies will now
5   be considered. (From *Essentials of Management*, p. 98.)

5. Management is confronted with two general types of propositions: those of a factual
nature, which accurately describe the observable world, and those of an ethical nature,
which assert that one course of action is better than another. According to this
classification, a **factual proposition** can be tested and proved to be *true* or *false*, but an
5   **ethical proposition** can only be asserted to be *good* or *bad*. Ethical matters pertain to
what conditions "ought to be." The ethical elements of a proposition are subject to
varying opinions and value judgments. To date, no philosophical system has been
developed that can be called a "science of ethics." The problem is that there is no way to
prove ultimate values. Value systems can be constructed only if we assume what is good;
10 for example, one school of thought may assume that "happiness" is an ultimate good, and
another school may assume that custom and tradition determine "right."
Management must meet problems involving varying mixtures of factual and ethical
elements. A useful approach is to segregate the factual elements from the ethical ones and
to use different methods for handling each group. A great part of the remainder of this
15 book involves methods by which the factual elements can be analyzed. In this section, we
concentrate on the ethical elements. (From *Essentials of Management*, p. 30.)

6. Disasters—floods, droughts, epidemics, and war—cause drastic changes in people's lives. Accidents happen. People we love die. A change in government policy or a sudden shift on the stock market puts people thousands of miles away out of work and threatens the most carefully planned lives.

5   A young mother talks about her child's "adjustment" to nursery school. A 66-year-old man seeks counseling because he is unable to "adjust" to retirement. A couple who have been childless for 7 years find it hard to "adjust" to the restraints and demands of their newborn. In each of these examples, *adjustment* refers to the individual's successful or unsuccessful adaptation to change. The need to adapt to change is a constant factor in all
10   our lives.

How we adapt to these changes, and how we relate to our environment generally, are the subjects of this chapter. Adjustment is the precarious and ever-changing balance between our needs and desires on the one hand and the demands and restraints of the environment on the other. Like adaptation in biology, adjustment implies changing in
15   order to survive.

People adjust to change in a variety of ways. The flood victim who has lost all possessions, for example, may call an insurance agent, look for a second job, move to a mountaintop, or simply collapse and end up in a hospital. All of these reactions—including collapse—are adjustments. Some, however, are obviously more effective than
20   others.

We begin this chapter with a description of the kinds of problems people face. We then consider various ways people may cope with these problems. In the final section we turn to the question of how psychologists determine whether someone is "well adjusted." (From *Psychology*, p. 457.)

2 Recognizing Major Thought Relationships

EXEMPLIFICATION
Textual Coherence Through Exemplification Signals

CONTRAST
Textual Coherence Through Contrast Signals

COMPARISON
Textual Coherence Through Comparison Signals

PRE-PARAPHRASING

ENUMERATION
Textual Coherence Through Enumeration Signals

CHRONOLOGY
Textual Coherence Through Chronology Signals

PROCESS

CAUSALITY
Textual Coherence Through Causality Signals

SPATIAL ORDER
Textual Coherence Through Spatial Signals

UNDERSTANDING A TEXT GOES BEYOND MERELY IDENTIFYING ITS CONTROLLING IDEA. You must also be able to recognize the way in which pieces of information—that is, the text's supporting ideas—are related. Major supporting ideas usually represent one or more of what we will call **major thought relationships**. These are the various ways in which speakers and writers of English give order to their ideas. There are eight of these relationships:

1. Exemplification
2. Contrast
3. Comparison
4. Enumeration

5. Chronology
6. Causality
7. Process
8. Spatial order

These relationships are not always clearcut and mutually exclusive, but rather are often combined in various ways. Moreover, each can be mentioned only briefly in a text, or it can become a kind of general focus for the entire text.

Each of the major thought relationships has its own set of **relationship signals**—words and phrases by which the writer shows the reader, in an *explicit* way, that the relationship exists. You can expect to find these signals used fairly frequently by most authors, depending of course upon the length and complexity of the text in question. However, if a writer feels that the relationship is made evident by the content itself, he or she can choose not to use any signals, leaving it to you, the reader, to perceive the relationship. In this case, the relationship is called *implicit*, and the text requires a more careful reading on your part.

EXEMPLIFICATION

Examples are ideas which represent *specific realizations* of more general ideas. Since less abstract ideas are recognized and understood more immediately than more abstract ones, authors use examples to make their more abstract ideas clearer to their readers. In a text which classifies things, for example, the name of the class is the most general idea, the names of subclasses are less general, and the actual members of the subclasses are the most specific of all. Thus, the term *human motivation* can be divided into three general types, one of which is physiological motives (or primary drives). However, this type, even when defined as "basic unlearned motives by which humans and other animals maintain life," could remain a bit abstract until we learn that hunger, thirst, and sleep are all specific instances of primary drives. The fact that we have all felt hungry, thirsty, and sleepy brings the abstract notion much closer to our understanding.

Examples can themselves be relatively abstract, as are the words *hunger*, *thirst*, and *sleep*, concepts that apply to all animals, including humans, in any place and at any time. A more *concrete* example would be the personal experience you had last night when, responding to your body's signals, you felt the need to sleep, whereupon you went to bed.

The following text—a variation of the one used in the first chapter—classifies nonverbal behavior into four types and provides many examples of each:

> In addition to the words which a speaker uses to convey meanings, the hearer has to deal with certain kinds of *nonverbal clues*. The first is body movements. When a body position or movement is linked with spoken language, it gives fuller meaning to a sender's message. For example, we lift one eyebrow for disbelief, rub our noses for puzzlement,
> 5 shrug our shoulders for indifference, and slap our forehead for forgetfulness. Intonation, too, influences the hearer's perception of what is being said. A smooth, soft tone creates a different meaning than an intonation that is abrasive. The facial expression of the speaker also conveys meaning. Facial expressions can show certain characteristics of the speaker that would never be communicated in a written transcript of the conversation—
> 10 such things as arrogance, aggressiveness, fear, and shyness. The final kind of message which a speaker sends has to do with the way individuals space themselves in terms of physical distance. What is considered proper spacing in various kinds of situations is largely dependent on cultural norms. How a speaker respects or disregards those norms always has meaning for the hearer. If someone stands closer to you than is considered
> 15 appropriate, for instance, it may indicate aggressiveness or sexual interest. If farther away than usual, it may mean disinterest or displeasure.

A special type of example used by many writers is what we will call a *hypothetical example*. Usually signaled by the use of an *if*-clause (or what we commonly refer to as a "conditional" structure), an example of this kind can be relatively abstract *or* concrete, depending on the intentions of the writer. The writer of a textbook on organizational behavior, having defined the term *coercive power* as a kind of power which depends on fear of punishment, might then exemplify this term in the following hypothetical manner: "At the organizational level, A has coercive power over B if A can dismiss, suspend, or demote B, assuming that B values his or her job."

Exemplification is rarely used as the major organizational pattern of a longer text; thus, do not expect to see an entire chapter composed of a generalization followed by examples. However, you can expect smaller sections of text to be devoted chiefly to either one long example or several shorter ones. And be aware that well chosen examples are frequently used in combination with any of the other major thought relationships presented in this chapter. Note, too, the presence of examples as you read the sections of this chapter on contrast, comparison, enumeration, causality, process, chronology, and spatial order.

Textual Coherence Through Exemplification Signals

The author of the preceding sample text has used certain structures to make parts of his text cohere, or hold together, in the relationship of exemplification. There follows a list of the most common such structures in English. Note, under the heading "Implicit

Exemplification," that the relationship has obviously been suggested by the author, but no formal structures signal its presence to the reader.

Structures of Explicit Exemplification

- **NOUNS**

An | illustration / example | of this might be lifting one's eyebrow for disbelief.

- **VERBS**

This is best | illustrated / exemplified | by facial expressions.

- **PHRASE MARKERS**

Facial expressions can show characteristics | such as | fear and arrogance. . . .
  or: . . . | such | characteristics | as | . . . .
Body movements have meaning— | e.g. |, the lifting of an eyebrow for disbelief.
Body movements have meaning (| for example |, the lifting of an eyebrow for disbelief).

- **SENTENCE LINKERS (CONJUNCTIVE ADVERBS)**

Body movements have meaning. Take, | for example / for instance |, the lifting of one eyebrow for disbelief.

Body movements have meaning. | For example / For instance |, we lift one eyebrow for disbelief.

Implicit Exemplification

- **HYPOTHETICAL EXAMPLES (THE WORD IF)**

Body movements have meaning. | If | the speaker shrugs his shoulders, it might indicate indifference.

- **NO SIGNAL (SEPARATE SENTENCES OR PARAGRAPHS)***

Intonations have meaning. A smooth, soft tone does not "say" the same thing as an abrasive tone.

   * Here readers are left to perceive the relationship for themselves. The example may occur in the following sentence, or it may constitute the entire next paragraph.

- **PUNCTUATION**

Body movements have meaning—a shrug of the shoulders might indicate indifference.
Intonations have meaning (a smooth, soft tone does not "say" the same thing as an abrasive tone).

2–1
VISUALIZE

Directions: Visualize the use of examples in the preceding sample text (types of nonverbal behavior in a conversation) by labeling the boxes of the diagram with words and phrases from the text.

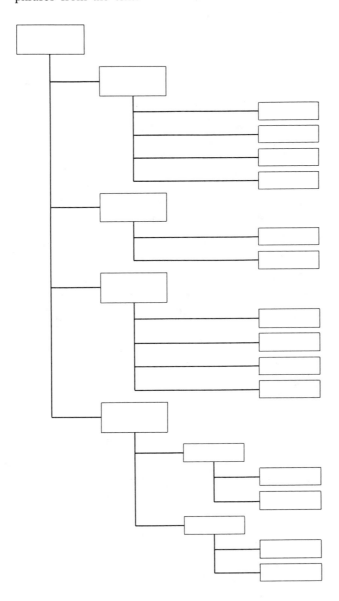

2–2
EXEMPLIFY / DISCUSS

A. In the preceding sample text:
   1. Identify the controlling idea.
   2. Find and underline the signals of exemplification used in this text.
B. Refer to the section entitled "Coercive Power" in Resource Chapter B (page 246). How many examples can you find? Which seem the most concrete? Are any of them hypothetical?

2–3
WRITE DOWN

Outside Research: In a textbook which you are using in another course, find a one- or two-paragraph section of text which contains examples.

1. Copy the text.
2. Underline all signals of exemplification.
3. In the margin, indicate whether each example is concrete—that is, something which can be perceived by the senses, or which actually happened in time—and whether it is hypothetical or not.

2–4
WRITE

Directions: Reread the sample text on nonverbal communication. Then, develop a text of your own based on the topic and guidelines below.

Topic

Write a paragraph of 200–300 words in which you *describe and give specific examples of nonverbal communication as it is found in your native culture.*

Controlling Idea

Your controlling idea will be "_____ people use certain nonverbal clues which add meaning to the words they say." (Fill in the blank with an adjective indicating your own native culture: "Turkish people," "French people," "Venezuelan people," etc.)

Guidelines

1. Use at least two (2) of the categories suggested in the sample text—i.e., body movements, intonations, facial expressions, and physical spacing (you may use 3, or even all 4).
2. Your paragraph should contain at least six (6) examples.
3. Use any appropriate "relationship signals" of Exemplification.
4. Avoid the personal pronouns (*I, my, our,* etc.).

CONTRAST

An author is using **contrast**[1] when he or she points out the differences which exist among things. Like other thought relationships, contrast can be mentioned briefly, or it can become the central focus of an entire paragraph, a series of paragraphs, or even a much longer text.

In order to truly understand a contrastive relationship in a text, you must be able to determine the *basis* of the contrast—the area or the sense in which the items are shown to be different (in their physical appearance or structure, in the way they function, in their historical development, in the effects which they produce, and so on). Thus, contrast, by its very nature, usually encompasses one or more of the other thought relationships we are about to examine in this chapter. Like these other relationships, contrast can be explicitly stated or only implied. As a reader, you must be able to specify what is involved in a contrast. Textbook writers of course are obligated to make this clear; if they do not, the text is either poorly written or intended for someone who already understands much of what is being discussed.

In practical terms, this means that you should probably be able to visualize a well-written contrast in graphic terms. The following simple two-level branching diagram represents one such possible visualization:

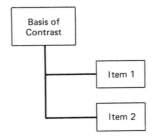

The sample text that follows focuses mainly on contrast—in this case, certain differences between two forms of national government. Note, as you read, that all the differences which are mentioned refer to the basis of contrast which is announced in the controlling statement.

The parliamentary-cabinet system differs from the American system by centralizing power in Parliament and making each of the other two branches dependent, at least technically, on the legislature. The only popular elections held in this system are elections to Parliament. Parliament chooses its leader, who is either the chief of the majority party or the head of a coalition; the head of state then appoints the majority leader to the office of prime minister. The head of state, acting on the advice of the prime minister, appoints other MPs to the cabinet, creating a plural executive in contrast to the singular executive system of the United States. The cabinet creates policy as a unit, and it takes collective responsibility for the consequences. The parliamentary-cabinet system is less stable than

[1] This section concentrates on *adversative contrast*. For a discussion of concessive contrast, see pp. 150–52.

10   the presidential-congressional system, especially if a majority must be achieved through a coalition, but party loyalties tend to be much more binding in the British system. (From *Political Ideologies*, p. 144.)

2–5
VISUALIZE

Directions: Fill in the boxes in the following diagram with phrases of your own to show the basic contrastive relationship contained in the preceding text. Be sure to label the top box (the basis of contrast) accurately. Note that this is a very *general* diagram; no specific differences need be mentioned. Note also that you will have to infer a certain amount of information to fill in the box which refers to the American system.

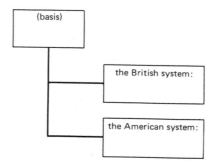

Textual Coherence Through Contrast Signals

The author of the preceding sample text has used certain structures to make his entire text cohere in the relationship of contrast. Following is a list of the most common such structures in English. Note, in the section "Implicit Contrast," that the author has suggested the relationship but has used no formal structure of contrast to signal its presence to the reader.

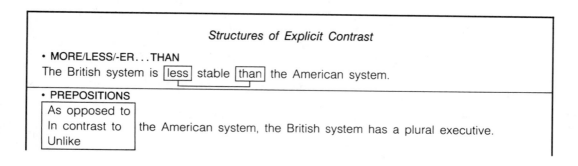

Structures of Explicit Contrast

• MORE/LESS/-ER...THAN
The British system is [less] stable [than] the American system.

• PREPOSITIONS
As opposed to
In contrast to   the American system, the British system has a plural executive.
Unlike

- VERBS

The British system | contrasts with / differs from | the American system in that it has a plural executive.

- NOUNS

There are many | differences / contrasts | between the two systems.

- ADJECTIVES

The British system is | different from / dissimilar to | the American system.

- SENTENCE LINKERS

Coordinate Conjunctions
The British system has a plural executive, | but | the American system. . . .

Conjunctive Adverbs*

The British system has a plural executive. The American system, | however / in contrast / on the other hand | , has

a singular executive system.

* Note that when a conjunctive adverb is used, it is also possible to place a *semicolon* between the two sentences.

Subordinate Conjunctions†

| While / Whereas | the British system has a plural executive, the American system has a singular one.

† Note that the subordinate conjunction can be placed *between* the two clauses.

Implicit Contrast

- TERMS WHICH POTENTIALLY SUGGEST CONTRAST
. . . a | singular | executive . . . a | plural | executive system.

(adjectives)

. . . a | democracy | . . . a | dictatorship | .

(nouns)

. . . are | elected | . . . are | appointed | .

(verbs)

- SEPARATE SENTENCES‡
The British system has a plural executive. The American system has a singular executive system.

(*or*: The British system has a plural executive; the American system. . . .)

‡ Note that the presence of potentially contrasting terms—*British system* and *American system*—and parallel sentence structure do much to indicate the contrast.

- SEPARATE PARAGRAPHS:
The British system _____

_____

_____

The American system _____

_____

_____

_____

2–6
EXEMPLIFY / DISCUSS

A. In the text used to illustrate contrast:
  1. Identify the controlling idea. Do any key words or phrases indicate that contrast will be dealt with?
  2. How many specific points are contrasted?
  3. What contrastive signals can you find in the text? (Find and underline them.)
  4. Does the word *this* (line 3) refer to the British system or to the American system?
B. Refer to Resource Chapter B, to the section entitled ''A Definition of Power'' (page 245). How has contrast been used? Are there any signals?

2–7
EXEMPLIFY / WRITE DOWN

Outside Research: In a textbook which you are using in another course, find a section of text (*at least* one paragraph) which exemplifies the relationship of contrast as a main organizational technique.

A. Copy the text.
B. Underline all contrast signals which you find. (Remember that contrast can be implicit.)
C. At the end of the text, construct a simple list of the specific contrasts you were able to find.

COMPARISON

A relationship often associated with contrast is that of **comparison**, in which an author attempts to point out the *similarities* between or among things. Like contrast, comparison can be mentioned only briefly, or it can receive great emphasis in a text. Also like contrast, comparison can involve other relationships. It is often combined, as a matter of fact, with contrast since things being compared/contrasted usually share certain characteristics but not others.

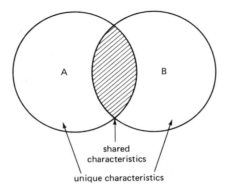

Which aspect—similarities or differences—the author chooses to emphasize depends, of course, on his or her purpose. In either case, however, it is important for you to be able to discern the precise nature or basis of both the similarities and the differences.

This "double relationship" can be symbolized by the following diagram.

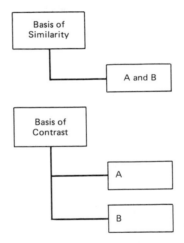

The sample text below exemplifies this comparative/contrastive relationship.

Behaviorism was thriving when the Gestalt psychologists reached America. Among its leading advocates was psychologist B. F. Skinner. Like Watson [an earlier behaviorist], Skinner believes that psychology should restrict itself to the study of observable and measurable behavior. Also like Watson, Skinner explains behavior in terms of the
5   stimulus-response formula. He too is primarily interested in changing behavior through conditioning—and discovering natural laws of behavior in the process. But his approach is subtly different from that of his predecessor.

Watson changed behavior by changing the stimulus. Skinner adds a new element— **reinforcement**. He rewards his subjects for behaving the way he wants them to. For
10   example, an animal (rats and pigeons are Skinner's favorite subjects) is put in a special cage (called a **Skinner box**) and allowed to explore. Eventually the animal will reach up

and press a lever or peck at a disc on the wall. A food pellet drops into the box. Gradually the animal learns that pressing the bar or pecking at the disk always brings food. Why does the animal learn this? Because it has been reinforced, or rewarded. Skinner thus
15 makes the animal an active agent in its own conditioning. (Adapted from *Psychology*, pp. 11–12.)

2–8
VISUALIZE

Directions: Visualize the information in the preceding text by labeling the diagram with the suggested phrases (ordering them correctly, of course).

Phrases:

the fundamental formula of study

changing the stimulus

the stimulus–response formula (conditioning)

the limits of psychological study

changing the stimulus + positive reinforcement

observable and measurable behavior

implementation of the formula

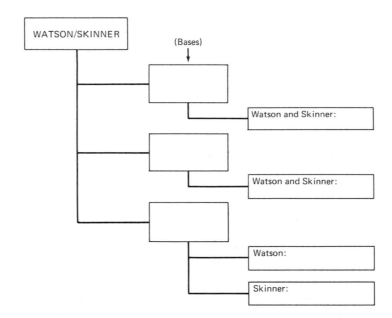

Textual Coherence Through Comparison Signals

The author of the preceding sample text has used certain structures to make parts of his text cohere in the relationship of comparison. Following is a list of the most common such structures in English.

Structures of Explicit Comparison

- **AS...AS**

  Skinner is as interested as Watson in changing behavior.

- **PREPOSITIONS**

  Like Watson, Skinner believes in changing behavior.

- **ADJECTIVES**

  Skinner is similar to Watson in that they believe in changing behavior.

  Both men believe that behavior can be changed.

- **NOUNS**

  There are several similarities between Skinner and Watson.

- **VERBS**

  Skinner resembles Watson in that they both believe in changing behavior.

- **ADVERBS**

  Skinner, too, believes in changing behavior through conditioning.

- **SENTENCE LINKERS**

  Coordinate Conjunctions*

  Watson explained behavior in terms of stimulus-response, and so does Skinner. (*two affirmative sentences*)

  Watson did not focus on behavior which could not be measured, and neither does Skinner. (*two negative sentences*)

  Watson explained behavior in terms of stimulus-response, and Skinner does, too. (*two affirmative sentences*)

  Watson did not focus on behavior which could not be measured, and Skinner doesn't, either. (*two negative sentences*)

  Correlative Conjunctions

  Just as Watson believed in stimulus-response, so Skinner is interested primarily in changing behavior through conditioning.

  Conjunctive Adverbs*

  Watson believed in stimulus-response.

  | Similarly |
  | Likewise |
  | Correspondingly |
  | In the same way |
  | In like manner |

  , Skinner is interested primarily in changing behavior through conditioning.

  * Note that with these correlative conjunctions and conjunctive adverbs expressing similarities, the second sentence should be more than a simple repetition of the first. Remember, too, that when you use a conjunctive adverb, you can place a *semicolon* between the two sentences instead of a period.

2–9
EXEMPLIFY / DISCUSS

A. In the preceding sample text (comparison/contrast):
  1. Identify the controlling idea. Do any key words or phrases indicate comparison and/or contrast?
  2. How many specific points are compared? contrasted?
  3. What relationship signals are used? (Find and underline them.)
  4. In the second paragraph, how could you explain the use of *the* in line 12 ("*the* wall")?
B. Refer to Resource Chapter B, to the section entitled "Reward Power" (page 246). How have comparison and contrast been used? Are there any signals?

2–10
WRITE DOWN

Outside Research: In a textbook which you are using in another course, find a section of text (*at least* one paragraph) which exemplifies either the relationship of comparison or the combined relationships of comparison and contrast as a main organizational technique.

A. Copy the text.
B. Underline all contrastive and/or comparative signals.
C. At the end of the text, construct a simple list of the specific comparisons and/or contrasts which you were able to find.

Analogy is a special type of comparison between items which, at first glance, do not seem similar. It is often used when there is a complex term to be explained; in addition to giving a definition—which sometimes turns out to be as complex as the term itself—the writer then proceeds to explain the term by comparing it to something which is more familiar. The idea behind this device is to graphically demonstrate the unfamiliar by using something familiar as a point of reference.

The same signals are often used. In addition, the writer might specify analogy by using the expressions *an analogy, analogous to,* or *by analogy.*

Analogy, like literal comparison, is often combined with contrast. When writers attempt to show similarities by means of an analogy, they frequently make a special effort to point out the *limits* of their analogy—that is, the point where the similarities end and real differences begin. Even when these limits are not explicitly stated, they are always assumed to exist, for no analogy is perfect. Such is the case, for example, in the following text, where the author has attempted to explain a rather complex idea (the organization of human long-term memory) in terms of a more familiar one (the card catalog of a library or the index of a book):

How is long-term memory organized? There is considerable debate on this point, but most often long-term memory is compared to a library and its card catalog, or to a

book and its index. Material is categorized or indexed, and the card catalog or book index is used to find any given item that is needed. Similarly, information entering long-term
5   memory is categorized or indexed according to its meaning, and we can "call up" a piece of information by using the indexes. We may get to the word "Iowa" through thinking of corn, or hearing "Cedar Rapids" mentioned, or reading the word "Ionic" and recognizing the similarity of the initial sounds. The more indexes or associations an item has, the easier it will be to remember, just as it is easier to find a certain passage in a book if many
10   of its key words and terms, rather than just one or two, are indexed.

Although most of what we select for permanent storage is organized or categorized on the basis of its meaning, it is possible that some of the information in long-term memory is encoded in terms of sound (*acoustic* or *phonetic coding*) or visual images. For example, do you know what a bassoon sounds like? Can you describe what your bedroom looked
15   like when you were 7 years old? Most of us would probably say yes to both questions. Because we are able to recognize sounds we may not have heard for a long time and describe things we saw long ago, it seems that at least some long-term memories must be coded in terms of sight and sound as well as meaning. (*Psychology*, p. 192.)

2–11
EXEMPLIFY / DISCUSS

A. In the preceding text:
1. Identify the controlling idea. Do any key words or phrases suggest an analogy?
2. What specific similarities are mentioned? What specific differences? How are they distributed between the two paragraphs?
3. What relationship signals of comparison and contrast have been used? (Find them and underline them.)
4. What are the referents for the following?

it (line 9)
it (line 9)
its (line 10)
its (line 12)
it (line 17)

5. What are *corn, Cedar Rapids,* and *Ionic* examples of? *Bassoon*?

B. Refer to text No. 8 of Exercise 1–11. What is being compared? What limits has the author placed on his analogy?

PRE-PARAPHRASING

Paraphrasing—expressing someone else's ideas in your own words—is essential to most types of academic writing assignments. Although it is a complex task involving thinking, reading, and writing, as well as a good knowledge of English structure, it is something which can be learned if a student is willing to devote to it the required time, effort, and patience. To facilitate the learning of this multifaceted skill, we have divided it into a certain number of specific techniques. We will present and demonstrate these techniques at various points throughout the book. In this chapter, for example, we will concentrate on a form of restatement which is related to the thought relationships under discussion: relationship signals.

Pre-paraphrasing Technique: Alternating Sentence Linkers

In the two boxes that follow, you are given pairs of sentences and several ways of linking them so as to preserve the relationship between them. In the first box, the relationship in question is that of contrast; in the second, comparison.

Be aware, however, that although each of the variations expresses the same idea in a different way, this particular technique, used by itself, *does not constitute a true and complete paraphrase.*

Pre-Paraphrasing Technique:
Alternating Sentence Linkers (Contrast)

• ORIGINAL SENTENCES
1. Hunger, thirst, and sleepiness cause a person to seek food, drink, or sleep.
2. Pain leads to escape or avoidance rather than to seeking.

• PRE-PARAPHRASES (SENTENCE LINKERS)

But
Hunger, thirst, and sleepiness cause a person to seek food, drink, or sleep, <u>but</u> pain leads to escape or avoidance rather than to seeking.

However, On the other hand, In contrast
Hunger, thirst, and sleepiness cause a person to seek food, drink, or sleep; pain, <u>on the other hand</u>, leads to escape or avoidance rather than to seeking. (*A period may be used instead of a semicolon.*)

Whereas, While
<u>While</u> hunger, thirst, and sleepiness cause a person to seek food, drink, or sleep, pain leads to escape or avoidance rather than to seeking. (*The order may be reversed: "...while...."*)

(Implicit Contrast)
Hunger, thirst, and sleepiness cause a person to seek food, drink, or sleep; pain leads to escape or avoidance rather than to seeking. (*A period may be used instead of a semicolon.*)

Pre-Paraphrasing Technique:
Alternating Sentence Linkers (Comparison)

• ORIGINAL SENTENCES
1. When you are hungry, your stomach growls.
2. When you are thirsty, your mouth is dry, and your throat is scratchy.

• PRE-PARAPHRASES (SENTENCE LINKERS)

Similarly, Likewise, Correspondingly, In the same way, In like manner
When you are hungry, your stomach growls; similarly, when you are thirsty, your mouth is dry, and your throat is scratchy. (*A period may be used instead of a semicolon.*)

Just as...so
Just as your stomach growls when you are hungry, so your mouth is dry and your throat is scratchy when you are thirsty.

(Implicit Comparison)
When you are hungry, your stomach growls; when you are thirsty, your mouth is dry, and your throat is scratchy. (*A period may be used instead of a semicolon.*)

And so, And...too, And neither, And...either
The above sentences cannot be joined by any of these linkers, which all require that the vocabulary and structure of the two sentences be practically identical: "Hunger causes a reaction in the human body, and so does thirst" (that is, "Thirst causes a reaction in the human body.")

2–12
PRE-PARAPHRASE

Directions: Write partial paraphrases of each of the following sentences. Do each in two ways, using the suggested structures of comparison or contrast. (Note: Remember that the result is *not* a complete paraphrase of the original.) You may have to reorder some of the elements in some of the sentences.

1. While a first generation computer with a specified set of capabilities rented for $800 per month, a similar second generation machine rented for less than half that amount.

   (but) A first generation computer with a specified set of capabilities rented for $800 per month, but a similar second generation machine rented for less than half that amount. (on the other hand) A first generation computer with a specified set of capabilities rented for $800 per month. A similar second generation machine, on the other hand, rented for less than half that amount. *(Note that a semicolon could be used in place of a period.)*

2. The economist and the manager face similar problems of using scarce resources in satisfaction of human wants. (and so) (and...too)

3. While the primary focus of the psychologist is on the employee as an individual, the sociologist focuses on that individual employee's interactions with others formally and informally. (but) (however)

4. Neither the hunger mechanism nor the thirst mechanism has yet been fully understood. (and neither) (and...either)

5. Positive reinforcement is the presentation of an attractive stimulus following the desired behavior whereas negative reinforcement is the *removal* of an aversive or unpleasant stimulus following the desired response. (*implicit contrast*) (on the other hand)

6. Much of what we eat is influenced by learning, and learned factors can affect how we respond to the thirst drive. (just as...so) (similarly)

7. Unlike the short-term hunger mechanism, which regulates day-to-day intake of food, the long-term hunger mechanism seems to regulate the body's weight. (whereas) (*implicit contrast*)

8. When a manager operates primarily through *force*, his employees will usually comply with his wishes only when in his presence or when they feel he is monitoring them. A manager who is respected and obeyed because of his *knowledge or skill* will usually have to do much less monitoring of his employees. (while) (in contrast)

2–13
WRITE

Directions: Reread the sample text used to illustrate contrast (the differences between the British parliamentary-cabinet system and the American system) and the one used to illustrate comparison/contrast (the similarities and differences between Skinner and Watson). Then develop a text of your own based on the topic and guidelines below.

Topic:

Write a composition of 200–300 words in which you *compare and/or contrast the distribution of power in your country's governmental system with the American system as described in the chart which follows.*

Guidelines:

1. Study the chart before you begin to write.
2. You do not have to use all the information in the chart. Select only what you need; do not try to write an exhaustive comparison or contrast—limit yourself to three or four key similarities and/or differences.
3. Use any appropriate "relationship signals" of comparison and/or contrast.
4. Avoid the personal pronouns (*I, my, our,* etc.).

The United States Government:

Power distributed among three branches; a system of "checks and balances" (aim: no one branch too powerful)

	EXECUTIVE BRANCH	LEGISLATIVE BRANCH—THE CONGRESS (BICAMERAL: 2 HOUSES)		JUDICIAL BRANCH (THE SUPREME COURT)
		The Senate	The House of Representatives	
Title(s) + *Number*	President; 1	Senators; 2 per state	Congressmen; number based on population per state (total number = 433)	Supreme Court Justices; 9
Term of Office	4 years; limit = 2 terms	6 years; no limit	2 years; no limit	lifetime
Method of Obtaining Power	nominated by political party (1 candidate per party) or may run as independent candidate; elected by the Electoral College, based on popular vote	nominated by political party through primary elections or may run as independent candidate; elected by popular vote		nominated by President; confirmed by Senate
Roles	formulates government policy; implements laws passed by Congress, or can reject (veto) them; can propose new legislation to Congress; can nominate Supreme Court Justices; almost total control of foreign affairs	total control of fiscal policy; initiate legislation; accept or reject policy proposed by President; accept or reject presidential nominees (Senate); can override President's veto; can impeach any member of Congress or President		cannot propose legislation; can declare laws constitutional or unconstitutional

ENUMERATION

One of the most common means of relating ideas is by **enumerating** them—in other words, by taking items which refer to the same general idea and arranging them one after the other. In its loosest form, enumeration can be a simple list of any number of related items—for example, a list of adjectives used to describe some object. We will call this type *informal enumeration*.

There is, however, a more formal kind of list extremely common to all branches of academic writing, a list which combines enumeration with at least two other thought relationships and which presupposes a more analytical and disciplined thought process. This kind of "closed" list represents a set number of items which comprise a formal class. It thus attempts to divide a general category into its total number of natural parts, whatever that number is currently taken to be by reputable scholars in the field. We will call this type of enumeration *classification*. When a linguistics textbook states, for example, that the language family known as "romance languages" is made up of eight specific languages, the writer is arranging his ideas according to classification. This kind of formal enumeration is sometimes called *partition* when it lists not the members of a class, but rather the parts of a single object (for example, when the human brain is divided into its three component parts—the forebrain, the midbrain, and the hindbrain).

A well-written classification usually consists of three parts: the *class* to which the members belong, the *members* themselves (all or as many as the writer can or cares to list), and the *basis* on which they have been grouped together as members of the class. Classification thus involves, by its very nature, the two other thought relationships previously mentioned: comparison, since it is on the basis of some fundamental similarity that the items have been put into the same class; and contrast, since it is on the basis of significant differences that the items remain individual members.

Enumeration—either informal listing or classification—can appear in combination with any of the other thought relationships presented in this chapter. It is possible, for example, to construct a formal or informal list of the *causes* or the *effects* of something, the *similarities* or the *differences* between things, the *steps* in a process, *examples*, and so on.

The abstract branching diagram presented here, with its numbered boxes at the second level, represents a possible way of visualizing this important thought relationship in all its various forms.

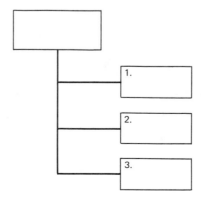

Notice how the author of the following sample text has avoided, in his first paragraph, an open-ended, overly informal list. By narrowing his discussion to the ideas of a particular expert in the field, he more closely approaches a list which resembles a formal classification.

> The characteristics of a good manager may be described in broad terms of initiative, dependability, intelligence, judgment, good health, integrity, perseverance, and so on. The trouble with this broad approach is that it is not very useful in describing how a given individual can develop into a better manager. Two more useful approaches provide
> 5 conceptual help to those aspiring to managerial position.
> One approach, suggested by Robert Katz, is to explain the *skills* which can be developed. In this approach three skills are fundamental: (1) technical, (2) human, and (3) conceptual. **Technical skills** relate to the proficiency of performing an activity in the correct manner and with the right techniques. This skill is the easiest to describe, because
> 10 it is the most concrete and familiar. The musician and the athlete must learn how to play properly and must practice their skills. The executive, likewise, develops skills in such areas as mechanics, accounting, selling, and production that are especially important at lower levels of an organization. As he rises to more responsibility, other skills become relatively more important. A second required skill involves **human relationships**. The
> 15 executive deals with people and must be able to "get along" with them. Human relations concentrates on developing this skill of cooperating with others. However, if colleagues notice that the executive has read a book on "how to win friends" and is consciously attempting to manipulate them, trouble develops. A third skill involves **conceptual ability**: to see individual matters as they relate to the total picture. This skill is the most
> 20 difficult to describe, yet it is the most important, especially at higher levels of an organization. Much of this skill can be learned, and is not "just born into a person." Conceptual skill depends on developing a creative sense of discovering new and unique ideas. It enables the executive to perceive the pertinent factors, to visualize the key problems, and to discard the irrelevant facts. (From *Essentials of Management*, pp. 8–9.)

Note that in this text the three skills have been arranged in a special order: from the simplest to the most difficult, and also from the lowest level to the highest. This kind of order is called "climactic" or "ascending" order. The opposite would be "anticlimactic" or "descending" order.

2–14
VISUALIZE

Directions: Construct a simple 2-level diagram which represents the basic thought relationship of the preceding text. The second level should consist of three boxes. Do not include any details.

Textual Coherence Through Enumeration Signals

The author of the preceding sample text has used certain structures to make his text cohere in the relationship of enumeration. In the following display you will find a list of the most common such structures in English.

Structures of Explicit Enumeration

• *AND* (OFTEN USED WITH LETTERS AND NUMERALS)

technical, human, | and | conceptual skills

or: (1) technical, (2) human, | and | (3) conceptual skills

or: (a) technical, (b) human, | and | (c) conceptual skills

• NOUNS (OFTEN USED WITH NUMBERS AND/OR QUANTITY WORDS)

There are | three / several / etc. | | kinds / types / etc. | of managerial skills.

• VERBS

Managerial skills can be | classified / divided / etc. | into three types.

The first category | is composed of / is comprised of / consists of | necessary techniques.

• THERE IS / THERE ARE

| There are | three types of managerial skills.

• LISTING STRUCTURES

Conjunctive Adverbs

| Third / Finally / In addition / Then | , there are conceptual skills.

Adjectives

| The *third* category / Still *another* type / The *final* kind | is conceptual skills.

Implicit Enumeration

• PARALLEL STRUCTURES WHICH IMPLY

A CERTAIN NUMBER OF TYPES, KINDS, OR CATEGORIES

...| technical | skills, | human | skills, and | conceptual | skills....

(adjectives)

• SEPARATE SENTENCES OR SEPARATE PARAGRAPHS

For the form, refer back to "Implicit Contrast." It is not unusual that both contrast and enumeration may be expressed implicitly in these two ways, since enumeration presupposes both contrast and comparison.

2–15
EXEMPLIFY / DISCUSS

A. In the sample text for enumeration:
   1. Identify the controlling idea. Do any key words or phrases suggest enumeration?
   2. How many items are enumerated?
   3. What signals have been used? (Find and underline them.)
   4. How has enumeration been used *within* enumeration? Are there any signals?
   5. How has comparison been used? Is it explicit or implicit?
   6. Locate a hypothetical example in the text.
   7. What synonym has been used in place of the word *manager* to add coherence?
   8. What probably follows this text in the book from which it is taken?
   9. How would the text have been different, in terms of length and complexity, if the author had based its organization on the first sentence of the *first* paragraph?
   10. How do you know whether the text is written in *ascending* or *descending* order?
B. Refer to Resource Chapter A, to the section entitled "Achievement" (p. 240). After a careful reading of the entire section for the main ideas, discuss the use of enumeration in the following paragraphs, indicating what is being enumerated and any signals which have been used:
   1. "From psychological tests and personal histories,..." (p. 240, paragraph 2)
   2. "Once we know..." (p. 240, paragraph 4)

2–16
WRITE DOWN

Outside Research: In a textbook which you are using in another course, find a section of text (*at least* one paragraph) which uses the relationship of enumeration as a main organizational technique.

A. Copy the text.
B. Underline all enumerative signals which you find.
C. At the end of the text, construct a simple list of the items being enumerated. Give your list a title which indicates *what* is being enumerated.

2–17
WRITE

Directions: Reread the sample text used to illustrate enumeration (the skills which can be developed in a manager). Then, develop a text of your own based on the topic and guidelines suggested.

Topic

Write a composition of 200–300 words in which you *enumerate and explain three or four skills necessary for success in the field which you intend to enter.*

Guidelines

1. Use appropriate enumeration signals if necessary.
2. Be sure, in the course of your explanation, to discuss *why* each skill is important. Give specific examples, if necessary, to illustrate your point.
3. Avoid the personal pronouns (*I, my, we, our*).
4. Arrange the skills in any of the following orders:

   Ascending order: The most important, the most difficult, or the easiest is *saved until last.*

   Descending order: The most important, the most difficult, or the easiest is *given first.*

   Equal order: No one item is treated by the writer as being significantly more important, more difficult, or easier than any other item.

(Be sure to indicate, at the end of your text, which order you have used.)

CHRONOLOGY

When a list consists of events arranged according to a *time sequence*, the relationship among these pieces of information is called **chronology**, or **chronological order**. This kind of arrangement of ideas is most common in fiction—novels and short stories—but it is frequently encountered in textbooks as well: history textbooks, to be sure, and any section of any kind of textbook which attempts to give historical background information. Chronology is really a kind of enumeration in which an author orders the content around a list of events or periods of time. Chronology becomes recognizably enumeration when time is formally divided into measurable periods, for example, the Middle Ages, the Renaissance, the Reformation, and so on.

Although chronology is usually combined with other relationships, in its purest form it can be symbolized in the following manner. Note that the boxes are numbered and that the arrows suggest a necessary time sequence.

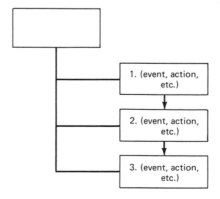

Notice how chronology has been used in the following text, taken from a textbook on management:

In spite of the fact that administrative problems received attention in ancient times, no important managerial tools of analysis developed until the end of the Dark Ages, when commerce began to grow in the Mediterranean. In the thirteenth and fourteenth centuries, the large trading houses of Italy needed a means of keeping records of business
5   transactions. To satisfy this need, the technique of *double entry bookkeeping* was first described by Pacioli in 1494. The roots of modern accounting, therefore, were planted four centuries before they were to form an important field of knowledge for the modern manager.

Not until after the rise of the capitalistic system did students rigorously give attention to
10   the field of economics. In 1776, Adam Smith wrote *The Wealth of Nations*, in which he developed important economic concepts. He emphasized the importance of *division of labor*, with its three chief advantages: (1) an increase in the dexterity of every workman; (2) the saving of time lost in passing from one type of work to the next; and (3) the better use of new machines. The development of the factory system resulted in an increased
15   interest in the economics of production and the entrepreneur. (From *Essentials of Management*, p. 14.)

Textual Coherence Through Chronology Signals

The author of the preceding sample text has used certain structures to make his text cohere in the relationship of chronology. A list of the most common such structures in English follows. Although we include a category covering implicit chronology, the most usual function of chronology in textbooks and articles is to give historical background, and when doing this, most authors are generally careful to clearly mark all chronological relationships. Note also that since chronology can actually be considered a type of enumeration, some previously encountered enumeration signals recur in the following display.

Structures of Explicit Chronology

- PREPOSITIONS (+ SPECIFIC TIMES)
  [in] ancient times, [on] March 1, [in] 1864, [at] the end of the war

---

- ADJECTIVES*
  the [first] tools, [later] attempts

  * Note the presence of enumerative "listing structures."

- TENSES AND "ASPECTS" OF VERBS
  Present (Basic) Tense: grows, belongs
  Past Tense: grew, belonged
  Continuous (Progressive) Aspect[†]: is growing, was growing
  Perfect Aspect: has grown, had grown, has belonged, had belonged

  [†] There is no continuous aspect to stative verbs such as "belong."

- NOUNS
  a [period], a [century], a [decade]

• SENTENCE LINKERS

Conjunctive Adverbs

(action or time)	;‡	then at that point after that afterwards thereafter before that meanwhile during this time	(action) .

‡ Remember that the two sentences can also be separated by a *period*.

Subordinate Conjunctions§

While Before After When By the time As	(action) ,	(action) .

§ Remember that the order of the sentences can be reversed; in that case, the conjunction *and* the sentence which it introduces come last.

Implicit Chronology

• *AND*

Pacioli felt the need for keeping records of business transactions, and he decided to describe the technique of double entry bookkeeping.

• PARTICIPIAL PHRASES

Having felt the need for keeping records of business transactions , Pacioli decided to describe the technique of double entry bookkeeping.*

* This sentence can be considered a shortened form of "*When* Pacioli felt....." or "*After* Pacioli felt...".

2–18
EXEMPLIFY / DISCUSS

A. In the preceding sample text:
  1. Identify the controlling idea. Do any key words or phrases suggest chronological order?
  2. How many distinct periods of time are mentioned in the text?

3. What chronological signals have been used? (Find and underline them.)

4. How has enumeration been used outside the chronological relationship? Is it implicit or explicit?

5. Discuss the use of repetition in the text—either of the same word or of a different form of the word.

B. Refer to text No. 6 of Exercise 1–11. Discuss the use of chronology. Are there any signals?

2–19
WRITE DOWN

Outside Research: In a textbook which you are using in another course, find a one- or two-paragraph section of a text whose organization is mainly chronological.

1. Copy the text.
2. Underline all chronological signals.
3. At the end of the text, construct a simple list of events and/or time periods.

PROCESS

When a text lists the *steps or stages* by which some action is accomplished, the relationship among these various steps or stages is usually referred to as **process**. In all of its forms, process is intimately connected with chronology, since the steps or stages follow each other in time. In some of these forms, such as the sample text that follows, we can isolate clearly defined steps or stages which are relatively independent of each other. This kind of process is common both in *instructions* and in texts which describe how something is or was done. In this case, process more or less coincides with formal enumeration. (In other cases, such as in the description of a biological process, the steps or stages are less clearly defined and follow each other in close succession; since this is quite intimately connected with causality, we will save our discussion of this type of process until the next section.)

You will note that the diagram representing the enumerative type of process closely resembles the diagrams for both enumeration and chronology, except that the boxes at the second level all represent steps or stages.

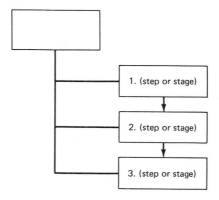

The following text is typical of enumerative process. As you read it, note that the signals used by the author are a combination of enumerative and chronological signals.

After the problem to be solved by the computer is defined, a **system definition** and a **system design** are written which define the goals, objectives, and specifications relating to the problems to be solved and precisely how the system is to operate when it becomes operational. There are five basic steps involved: (1) A **flow chart** (a graphical explanation
5   of the problem-solving procedures) is prepared to ensure efficient processing. (2) A program is written in one of the general programming languages, which can then be translated by the machine into the machine language used by the specific computer. (3) Forms are designed and needed reports finalized. (4) After the programs have been written, they are **debugged** (the process by which all evident errors are removed).
10   (5) Documentation is prepared to describe how the programs and the system are to operate.
   Next the system goes into *production*, whereby the actual work is performed. If an obsolete, existing system was in operation prior to this step, **parallel operations** are often performed, in which the old and new systems operate concurrently and the results are
15   compared to detect errors in the new system. Finally, the system enters a **maintenance state**, in which minor modifications and corrections are made from time to time. (From *Essentials of Management*, p. 182.)

2–20
VISUALIZE

Directions: Visualize the information in the preceding text by labeling the diagram with the suggested phrases (ordering them correctly, of course).

Phrases

documentation
maintenance state
writing the program
system definition/design
debugging
defining the problem
writing a flow chart
production
designing forms, finalizing reports

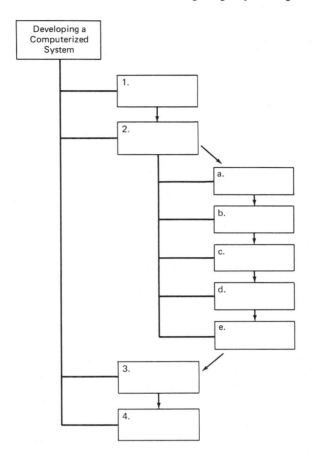

2–21
EXEMPLIFY / DISCUSS

A. In the preceding sample text:
   1. Identify the controlling idea. Do any key words or phrases suggest process?
   2. How many major steps are enumerated? Are any subdivided?
   3. What enumerative and chronological signals have been used?
   4. Explain the use of *the* in line 7 ("the machine").
B. Refer to Resource Chapter B, to the section entitled "Who Wants Power" (pages 248–50). Read the two paragraphs beginning with "Those 'in power' will resist attempts...." How has process been used? How many steps are indicated?

2–22
WRITE DOWN

Outside Research: In a textbook which you are using in another course, find a one- or two-paragraph section of the text (longer if necessary) which uses process as a main organizational technique.

1. Copy the text.
2. Underline all chronological and enumerative signals.
3. At the end of the text, construct a simple list of steps. If the author has indicated major steps with substeps, you should do the same; otherwise, a simple list will suffice. Give your list a title which is descriptive of the process in question.

2–23
WRITE

Directions: After rereading the previous sample text (Developing a Computerized System), write a composition of 300–500 words on one of the suggested topics, following the suggested guidelines.

Topic 1

Describe the process by which *power usually changes hands in your country's government (elections, successions, etc.).* If there are many small steps, try to divide them into several large steps, as was done in the previous sample text.

Topic 2

Describe the process by which *a man and a woman get married in your country.* If there are many small steps, try to divide them into several large steps, as was done in the previous sample text.

Guidelines
1. Review the sample text and the diagram before you write your composition, in order to fully understand the technique of grouping several smaller steps into one larger one.
2. Use any appropriate "relationship signals" of enumeration and chronology to make your process clear to the reader.
3. Avoid the personal pronouns (*I, my, our*, etc.).

CAUSALITY

As was mentioned earlier in this chapter, chronology takes two items and relates them in time by specifying that one comes before the other. **Causality**, in similar fashion, creates a time relationship between two actions, events, or happenings—with, however, an important additional element: the notion that one will, might, or should *lead to the other by causing it*. Thus, organizing information in terms of causality can mean explaining either the reasons, causes, sources, motives, or objectives of something or—proceeding in the opposite direction—it can mean explaining the effect or result of something, either actual (that is, a real result in time) or intended (objective or purpose).

It is assumed—in academic thought, at least—that nothing just happens "by accident," even though the expression does exist in English. There is *always* a presumed reason or cause of some sort, human or otherwise, conscious or unconscious. Serious thinkers in all fields of study are always expected to ask, and feel justified in asking, *why?*, even if they do not expect to easily find the answer to their question. The search for causes or explanations of phenomena is the *cornerstone of academic research*.

Like other thought relationships, causality is often mentioned only in passing. However, it can sometimes become the main organizing principle of a paragraph or of a much longer text. When it is combined with enumeration, for example, the resulting text will be a list of either causes or effects. But whether combined with enumeration or not, causality is almost always related to chronology, since causes and effects always occur in time, the former always preceding the latter.

The following text, which describes certain barriers to effective communication in an organization, is an example of information related causally.

> Organizations, because they have formal structures, cannot help but create barriers to effective communication. The existence of excessive hierarchy creates physical distance between people. Additionally, the reliance in organizations upon having clear lines of authority in a structured hierarchy requires that formal communications follow prescribed
> 5 channels through the organization. As a result, messages must frequently pass through many layers of the organization, each offering a potential for distortion. Remember the parlor game of "Telephone," where one person makes up a story that is passed around the group until it reaches the final member, who relates, in his own words, the message that he has received? Anyone who has played that game can see the distortion that can occur as
> 10 information is passed between levels in an organization. (From *Organizational Behavior*, p. 228.)

2–24
VISUALIZE

Directions: Visualize the information in the preceding text by placing each item from the following list in its correct box in the diagram which follows the list.

Phrases

distortion of communication at each layer
semantic barriers
physical distance between people
many layers through which communications must pass
communication barriers created by organizations
prescribed channels for communications
excessive hierarchy
the need for clear lines of authority
physical barriers

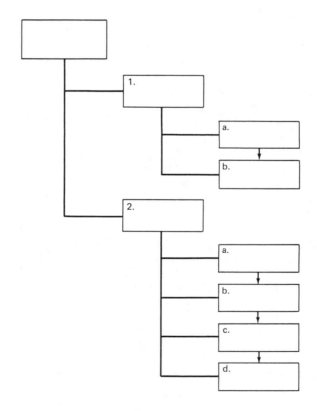

Textual Coherence Through Causality Signals

The author of the preceding sample text has used certain structures to make his text cohere in the relationship of causality. There follows a list of the most common such structures in English.

Structures of Explicit Causality

• NOUNS

a | cause | of, a | reason | for, a | result / consequence | of,

• VERBS

Organizations | cause / lead to / create / result in / produce / contribute to | communication barriers.
(cause) | | *(result)*

Communication barriers | result from / stem from | the formal structures of organizations.
(result) | | *(cause)*

• ADJECTIVES

to be | responsible | for, a | causal | relationship, a | resultant | condition, a | contributing | factor

• SENTENCE LINKERS

Coordinate Conjunctions

Organizations create barriers, | for | they have formal structures.
        (result)   *(cause)*

Organizations have formal structures, | so | they create barriers.
        (cause)   *(result)*

Conjunctive Adverbs*

...formal structures; | therefore / consequently / as a result / because of this / for this reason / hence | , they create barriers.
    (cause) | | *(result)*

   * The two clauses may be written as two sentences separated by a period.

Subordinate Conjunctions

Because / Since / Etc. | organizations have formal structures, they create barriers to communication.
                               (cause)   *(result)*

There are | so | many layers | that | the message gets distorted.[†]
        (cause)   *(result)*

  [†] Remember that several combinations are possible using *so...that* and *such...that*.

Noun Clause Introducers
The fact that they have formal structures explains <u>why they create</u>. . . .
             (cause)   *(result)*

Implicit Causality

• ANY VERB WHICH IMPLIES A CAUSAL RELATIONSHIP
The existence of many layers | means | that messages tend to get distorted.
       (cause)   *(effect)*

• SOME CHRONOLOGICAL RELATIONSHIPS (INCLUDING PARTICIPIAL PHRASES)
| As | messages pass through many layers, they tend to get distorted.
          (cause)   *(effect)*

• MANY CONDITIONAL STRUCTURES
| If | messages have to pass through many layers, they tend to get distorted.
           (cause)   *(effect)*

• SOME ADJECTIVE (RELATIVE) CLAUSES
Messages | which pass through many layers | tend to get distorted.
             (cause)   *(effect)*

• APPOSITIVE SENTENCES*
| The more | layers there are, | the more | messages get distorted.
       (cause)   *(effect)*

  * Many combinations are possible—*the more . . . the more, the more . . . the less, the less . . . the more, the less . . . the less*, and so on. Whatever the combination, the definite article *the* and a *comparative form* must be present.

• PARTICIPIAL PHRASES
| Having to pass through many layers |, messages tend to get distorted.[†]
         (cause)   *(effect)*

  [†] This sentence can be considered a shortened form of "*Because* messages have to pass through many layers, . . .".

2–25
EXEMPLIFY   /   DISCUSS

A. In the preceding sample text:
   1. Identify the controlling idea. Do any key words or phrases suggest causality?
   2. Why are there no arrows connecting boxes 1 and 2 in the diagram?
   3. What causal signals have been used? (Find and underline them.)
   4. What other relationships are present (enumeration, chronology, exemplification)? Are there any signals?
   5. Explain the use of *the* in line 7.

B. Refer to the paragraph beginning, "Once we know . . ." in Resource Chapter A, p. 240. How has causality been used? Are there any signals?

Although enumeration is involved in the preceding sample text, it is obvious in the description of the second barrier that there is more than just a single cause leading to a single result (refer back to the series of arrows in the previous diagram). In certain kinds of processes, an extremely close and immediate causal reaction is implied among the steps. This is particularly apparent in texts describing biological processes or chemical reactions, but it is typical of other types of texts as well, such as those dealing with human behavior from a psychological point of view. Such texts usually rely heavily on the relationship of causality and use both causal and chronological signals (and perhaps terms like *step* or *stage* as well). We call this kind of process a **chain reaction**. Each action closely follows the preceding one as its result, becoming, in turn, the cause of the next action, step, or stage of the sequence. Indeed it is sometimes almost impossible to tell where one ends and the next begins, and we therefore use the words *step* or *stage* with reservation to describe such a process.

In the diagram symbolizing chain reactions, the arrows flow freely through the walls of the boxes, indicating that each event is closely interconnected with other events in the process.

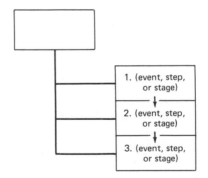

The following sample text, which describes the hunger mechanism in human beings, demonstrates the organization of thoughts in chain reaction. The description centers around the element of *glucose* and its role, or function, in the process—that is, what parts of the causal chain it dominates.

Laboratory experiments demonstrate that the hunger drive is set in motion by a chemical imbalance in the blood. A simple sugar called *glucose*, which forms the basis of carbohydrates, can be stored in the liver only in small quantities and for a short time. When the amount of glucose in the blood (the blood-sugar level) falls below a certain

5 point, an area in the hypothalamus is activated, signaling you to eat and replenish your glucose supply. After eating, when the blood-sugar level has risen, the hypothalamus seems to turn off the hunger drive. When the blood of an animal that has eaten is transferred to an animal that has been deprived of food, the animal will refuse to eat, even though it still needs food (Davis, Gallagher, & Ladove, 1967). Similarly, when hungry

10   people are injected with glucagon, a hormone that raises the blood-sugar level, they cease
to eat, even though they still need food (Schulman et al., 1957). (From *Psychology*,
p. 356.)

Note that the text represents a special kind of chain reaction—a continuous or *cyclic* one
in which the "last" element of the chain leads back to the "first," and the sequence begins
again.

2–26
VISUALIZE

Directions: Visualize the information in the preceding text by placing each item from the
list in the correct box of the diagram. Notice that the form of the diagram indicates a *cyclic*
chain reaction.

Sentences and Phrases

An area in the hypothalamus is activated.   A person eats.
An area in the hypothalamus is activated.   A person stops eating.
The glucose level rises.   The hunger mechanism
The glucose level falls.

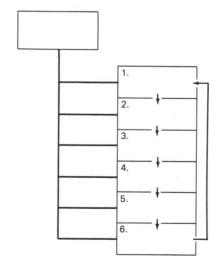

2–27
EXEMPLIFY / DISCUSS

A. In the preceding sample text:
   1. Identify the controlling idea. Do any key words or phrases suggest chain reaction?
   2. What is the first cause in the chain reaction? the final result? Does it matter which is
      placed first and which is placed last?

3. What is the difference between this text and the one used to exemplify enumerative process (p. 54)?
4. What causal or enumerative signals have been used in this text? (Find and underline them.)
5. Is contrast or comparison present in the text? How do you know?
6. Find an instance of the "first mention" rule for using the article *the*.

B. Refer to text No. 5 of Exercise 1–11. Explain the use of chain reaction causality. What signals have been used?

2–28
WRITE DOWN

Outside Research: In a textbook which you are using in another course, find a one- or two-paragraph text which exemplifies chain reaction or enumerative causality, or a combination of both.

1. Copy the text.
2. Underline all appropriate signals.
3. At the end of the text, construct either a list of causes or effects (enumerative causality) or a diagram (chain reaction).

2–29
PRE-PARAPHRASE

Directions: Paraphrase each of the following pairs of sentences using the suggested structures. If necessary, refer back to the lists of structures for chronology and causality to refresh your memory. Remember that the result is *not* a complete paraphrase of the original.

1. When the sympathetic nervous system sends a message, your heart pounds, you breathe faster, your pupils enlarge, and digestion stops.

   (if) *If the sympathetic nervous system sends a message, your heart pounds, you breathe faster, your pupils enlarge, and digestion stops.*

   (at that point) *The sympathetic nervous system sends a message. At that point, your heart pounds, you breathe faster, your pupils enlarge, and digestion stops. (Or: ...; at that point, ...)*

2. Computers were introduced to the business world; shortly thereafter, it became obvious that they could produce substantial savings in areas where large volumes of repetitive work were required.   (shortly after)   (and...soon)

3. Rewards are sometimes not made clear in an organization; in that case, it is difficult to measure the performance of an employee.   (if)   (the less...the more)

4. Reports were often late or not timely; proper inputs were not available for computer processing when they should have been. *(Note: the first sentence is the result.)*
   (so)   (for)

5. With the advent of the transistor, the second generation computers were born.   (at that point)   (when)

6. Sympathetic nerve fibers connect to every internal organ in the body; this explains why the body's reaction to stress is widespread.   (because)   (so)

7. Social factors can make a meal a ceremony, and elaborate rituals have grown up around offering and accepting food.   (because of this)   (since)

8. If our personal daily rhythm is upset, we may feel tired to the point of becoming ill.   (whenever...so...that)   (whose)

9. A person feels pain; he knows he is in some sort of danger and seeks to escape from it.   (who)   (if)

10. The level of sodium chloride in the blood reaches a certain point, indicating that the tissues need more water. A thirst center in the hypothalamus is stimulated, thus activating the thirst drive.   (after)   (at that point)

SPATIAL ORDER

When information is organized according to *physical location or spatial sequence*—that is, the information moves from one place to another, or from one part of a thing to another, describing how those places or parts are related to each other in space—the relationship is called **spatial order**. This kind of arrangement of ideas is particularly common in cases where a writer wants to give a physical description of something. Spatial order, like other thought relationships, appears frequently in combination with other relationships. Such is the case in the following text, where the writer lists the various parts of the neuron and mentions their various "jobs" or "roles" (their particular *functions* in the causal chain).

The number of nerve cells, or **neurons**, that make up the nervous system has been estimated at 100 to 200 billion. Although neurons come in many different shapes and sizes, they are all specialized to receive and transmit information.

5 In common with all other cells, a neuron has a nucleus, a cell body where metabolism and respiration take place, and a cell membrane, which encloses the whole cell.

What makes a neuron different from other cells are the tiny fibers that extend out from the cell body (see Figure 2–1). These extensions are what enable the neuron to perform its special job—to receive messages from surrounding cells, carry them a certain distance, and then pass them on to other cells. The short fibers branching out around the cell body

10 are called **dendrites**. Their role is to pick up incoming messages from their surroundings and carry them to the cell body. The single long fiber extending from the cell body is called an **axon**. The axon fiber is very thin and usually much longer than the dendrites. In adults the axons that run from the brain to the base of the spinal cord can sometimes be as long as 3 feet, but most axons are only an inch or two in length. The axon's job is to carry

15 outgoing messages—either to pass them on to the next neuron in a series or to direct a muscle or gland to take action. When we talk about a **nerve**, we are referring not to a single fiber but to a group of axons bundled together like parallel wires in an electrical cable.

The axon shown in Figure 2–1 is surrounded by a fatty covering called a *myelin sheath*.

20   One of the purposes of the myelin sheath seems to be to speed up the transmission of neural impulses. The sheath is not continuous, but is pinched in at intervals, which makes the axon look somewhat like a string of microscopic sausages. Not all axons are covered by myelin sheath, but myelinated axons can be found in all parts of the body. (From *Psychology*, pp. 32–33.)

Notice how the author of the preceding text has arranged his details. He takes the cell body as his point of departure, then proceeds outward from it. If you compare his description with the diagram which accompanies it in the text, you will be able to visualize the direction of movement more easily:

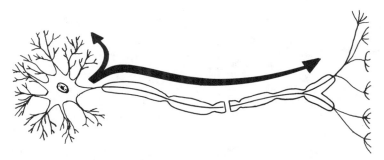

Figure 2–1
A typical neuron

Some of the most common ways of organizing spatial details are based on the following *polar opposites*: left/right, top/bottom, east/west, north/south, clockwise/counterclockwise, toward/away from, innermost/outermost. No one way is better than another in all situations; much depends on what is actually being described.

2–30
VISUALIZE

Directions: Locate and label the following parts of Figure 2–1 above, basing your labeling on the preceding sample text.

cell body	dendrites
myelin sheaths	axon
terminal branches	cell nucleus

Textual Coherence Through Spatial Signals

The author of the preceding sample text has used certain structures to make his text cohere in the relationship of spatial order. In the following display you will find a list of the most common such structures in English.

Structures of Explicit Spatial Order

- NOUNS (PARTS OF SOMETHING)

the edge , the center , the lower stratum

- VERBS

...the tiny fibers that [extend / stretch / move / run] outward from....

- PREPOSITIONS

The short fibers branching out [around / from / through / outside] the cell body....

- POLAR OPPOSITES

south / north, top / bottom, right / left, internal / external

- PRECISE MEASUREMENTS

...the axons that run from the brain to the base of the spinal cord can sometimes be as long as 3 feet , but most axons are only an inch or two in length .

2–31
EXEMPLIFY / DISCUSS

A. In the preceding sample text:
  1. Identify the controlling idea. Do any key words or phrases suggest spatial order?
  2. How are enumeration and spatial order interwoven in the description of the neuron? Are there signals for each? If so, find and underline them.
  3. Find examples, if you can, of the following relationships: contrast, comparison, causality, and process.
  4. Could the writer have chosen to organize his text by moving in a different way (that is, choosing a different set of "polar opposites")? If so, what might he have done? If not, why not?
B. Refer to text No. 9 of Exercise 1–11. Discuss spatial order in reference to this text. Are there any signals? Are any other relationships present (enumeration, comparison, contrast, causality)?

2–32
WRITE DOWN

Outside Research: In a textbook which you are using in another course, find a one- or two-paragraph section of text (longer if necessary) which uses spatial order as a main organizational principle.

1. Copy the text.
2. Underline all spatial signals.
3. At the end of the text, indicate what strategy the writer has used to order his spatial details—from north to south or from top to bottom, for example.

2–33
DISCUSS / EXEMPLIFY

Directions: Study "The Fat of the Land," Resource Chapter A, p. 231. After reading through the text, look for examples of the major thought relationships:

Contrast   Process
Comparison   Causality
Enumeration   Spatial order
Chronology   Exemplification

Remember that these often occur in combination with each other. Remember, too, that a relationship can exist without signals (that is, in an *implicit* form).

Be prepared to defend your choices.

2–34
WRITE

Directions: Reread the following sample texts:

p. 54 (developing a computer system)
p. 61 (the hunger drive)
p. 64 (a description of the neuron)

Then, develop a text of your own based on the topics and guidelines which follow.

Topic

Write a composition of 200–300 words in which you describe a *basic process* with which you are familiar, perhaps from another course which you are taking or have taken. Possibilities include processes like the following:

• a biological process such as photosynthesis
• a political process, such as how a person is elected to a certain office in a particular country
• an economic process such as inflation
• a process from some branch of the arts, such as how film is developed in a laboratory

Guidelines

1. Your text should include the thought relationships of chronology and causality, and it may include various kinds of enumeration as well. It should also include spatial order if your process is a physical one.
2. Be sure to use clear examples if they are necessary.
3. Avoid the use of personal pronouns (*I, my, our*, etc.).

3 The Short Paper

THE TERM "SHORT PAPER" CAN BE APPLIED TO ANY NUMBER OF WRITING ASSIGNMENTS and, for this reason, is particularly difficult to define. It is generally three to five pages in length, although a paper of six, seven, or eight pages can also be considered a short paper. The short paper is *not* a formal research paper, even though some sort of research may be required. Thus, in assigning a short paper, a professor usually specifies the subject matter and the manner in which students should approach it. By contrast, a longer research paper is developed from a thesis based on the student's own investigation.

Although each short paper will require a unique approach and format according to the nature of the assignment, there are some elements which are common to all types of short papers. (1) All short papers begin by explicitly stating the controlling idea or thesis. Therefore, all are developed *deductively*. (2) All require that *evidence or examples from some objective source be provided* to support the generalization made at the beginning. (3) Finally, all are written *objectively*, unless the professor specifically asks for a personal response to the subject matter.

Before we focus our attention on the actual writing of the short paper, however, it would be a good idea to turn briefly to the term *thesis*.

THESIS VERSUS CONTROLLING IDEA

In persuasive writing, where the author is trying to convince the reader of something, a special type of controlling idea called a **thesis**[1] is most often used. A thesis is a controlling idea in that it limits and predicts the kinds of information which are most likely to follow. However, another element is added: An interpretation or judgment is made about the information under discussion—a judgment upon which not everyone will agree. In other words, in addition to limiting and predicting what will follow, a thesis makes a statement about a subject which the writer will support by providing evidence of the "truth" of the statement.

In point of fact, the question of whether there is such a thing as absolute objectivity or truth can be raised in every field of academic study. The search for truth is, of course, the goal of all academic pursuit. However, what one person sees as truth about a subject may be quite different from another person's view. In Research Chapter A, for instance, the author describes the controversy surrounding *aggression*: While some reputable psychologists subscribe to one particular interpretation of aggression, others most definitely do not.

---

[1] A thesis is sometimes called a *thesis statement*, an *argument*, or a *predication*.

Expository writing such as that found in most introductory textbooks is usually more informative than persuasive in nature. This is to be expected, since the purpose of the writer of such a textbook is almost always to give the student an overview of the field in all its diversity and complexity. Introductory texts attempt to explain, in the most general way, the state of *accepted knowledge* in the field. What is "true" at any one time in any one field is likely to turn out to be nothing more than that which is convincing evidence to the *greatest number of reliable experts in that particular field*. Thus, the writer of an introductory textbook will usually make a great effort to indicate, in very honest fashion, the dividing line between "truth" and "opinion." If there are competing theories about some aspect of the subject, they will most likely be presented side by side and given an appropriate degree of emphasis according to the most recent research in the field. Look, once again, at the discussion of aggression in Resource Chapter A. On pages 238–39, the author has been very careful to point out the existence of at least three different interpretations of aggression, none of which is considered indisputably "true" by all "qualified experts": (1) the "innate drive" concept, which suggests that aggression is inborn; (2) the humanistic approach, in which cooperation seems as noteworthy as aggression; and (3) the "frustration-aggression hypothesis," according to which aggression is not a motive at all, but rather a form of behavior caused by specific stimuli.

A thesis, on the other hand, evaluates and judges, and it is supported by any evidence which the writer can provide to convince the reader that the judgment or interpretation is "true." The most likely places for you to encounter such thesis statements are in the "outside reading" assigned in many courses (journal articles, for example) and in nonintroductory textbooks, where controlling ideas will often take the form of theses which reflect the writers' own interpretations of factual information.

What, then, are the characteristics of a good thesis statement? One of the most important is that a thesis *avoids the obvious*. When most professors give you an assignment to develop your own thesis in a particular area, their purpose is most often to see how capable you are of coming up with the various thought relationships which exist within a subject. Thus, in developing a thesis statement, you should avoid a simple restatement of what most experts already consider obvious in the subject area and thus needs no proof. The following types of information, for example, would not be thought of by most professors as theses since they are either self-evident or are likely to be clearly stated in some textbook:

Simple Enumerative Statements

There are three basic kinds of human motives.
Traffic accidents occur for several reasons.
There are many kinds of barriers which inhibit communication between people.

Statistical or Descriptive Information

There are thousands of traffic accidents in the United States each month.
More International students attend American universities today than thirty years ago.

Historical Facts

Simon Bolivar is considered the liberator of certain South American countries. Alexander Graham Bell was responsible for the invention of the telephone.

Any of these statements might appear as the controlling idea of a paragraph or a chapter section in a textbook, but none qualifies as an acceptable thesis statement. Remember that a thesis identifies important thought relationships—it talks about causes and results or it suggests important similarities and differences—and evaluates information according to the perceptions of the writer. In the examples just listed there is nothing to argue, nothing to evaluate.

Thus a thesis dealing with the subject of barriers to good communication, in contrast to a simple controlling idea on the same subject, will go beyond the presentation of self-evident or commonly accepted information about this subject and make a judgment about some particular aspect—a judgment which is not self-evident and which will therefore have to be proved to the reader. Notice how this has been illustrated in the following two generalizations:

There are three types of barriers which inhibit good communication: physical, human, and semantic.
(Controlling idea)

Of the three barriers to communication—physical, human, and semantic—perhaps the most difficult to remedy is that of human limitations.
(Thesis)

In the thesis statement, the writer has decided that the three barriers to communication do not have equal value. He has made the point that one of these—human limitations—creates more of a problem than do the others. The text which would follow such a statement would probably define all three barriers and then take the direction imposed by the key phrase in the thesis: evidence to explain *why* that particular barrier is more difficult to remedy than the others.

3–1
EXEMPLIFY / DISCUSS

Directions: Read the section of Resource Chapter A entitled "The Power Motive" (page 241). Then, basing your answers on an analysis of that text, do the following: (1) decide whether each of the following statements is a simple controlling idea or a thesis; (2) try to predict the thought relationship(s) which would be used to support or develop each statement.

1. Democratic presidents are high in the need for power.
   (1) *Thesis* (The statement is an interpretation based on the text. The data reported in the text are not conclusive.)

(2) Possible thought relationships:
  • causality (that is, *why* they are high in the need for power)
  • exemplification (specific instances of Democratic presidents who were found to be high in the need for power)

2. Researchers have defined the power motive as the need to influence others.
3. Presidential policy decisions have always been influenced a great deal by a president's need for power.
4. Presidents who have a high need for power have been highly rated by historians.
5. Winter's analysis of U.S. presidents' need for power was based on how this need was demonstrated in the inaugural addresses of the presidents in question.
6. Of all the social motives, the need for power is the most insignificant.
7. During his presidency, Richard Nixon did not demonstrate the need for power in any of his actions.
8. Both Jimmy Carter and Theodore Roosevelt were found to be about the same in the need for power and the need for achievement.
9. We should think of the need for achievement in terms of specific skills.
10. The voter should always consider whether or not to vote for a candidate in terms of the candidate's demonstrated need for power.

PRE-PARAPHRASING TECHNIQUE: ALTERNATING ACTIVE AND PASSIVE VERB FORMS

In general, academic writing aims at being "objective" in its expression of ideas, and thus tries to avoid specific reference to personal opinions. Your academic writing should imitate this style by eliminating first-person pronouns ("*I* propose...," "In *my* opinion...," "It seems to *me*...") as far as possible. The passive form of the verb ("passive voice"), which is fairly common in academic writing, can sometimes help you to delete these particular pronouns from your writing.

Moreover, the ability to alternate between active and passive structures is an extremely useful paraphrasing technique. There are, of course, situations in which the passive is preferred to the active—when the performer of the action (1) is not known, (2) is not important, (3) is perfectly obvious, or (4) refers to the writer.

1. No one knows the exact period when language *was* first *spoken*.
   (The actual performer of the action is not known.)
2. This sweater *was made* in England.
   (The identity of the industrial worker who made the sweater is not important.)
3. French *is spoken* in France.
   ("By the French people" is obvious.)
4. It *can be concluded* that further research is necessary.
   (It is the *writer* who is drawing the conclusion: "I conclude that....")

However, there are many cases where the passive and the active substitute equally well for each other without any noticeably harmful effect on the meaning of the sentence, and it is in these cases that the technique can be of enormous help in paraphrasing. In the following box, you are given two such possible active-passive alternations. (Be sure to note, however, the cases where the alternation is *not* possible.)

A last word of caution: Be aware, as you read the information in the display, that even in situations where the technique is possible this kind of active-passive alternation *does not by itself constitute a true and complete paraphrase.*

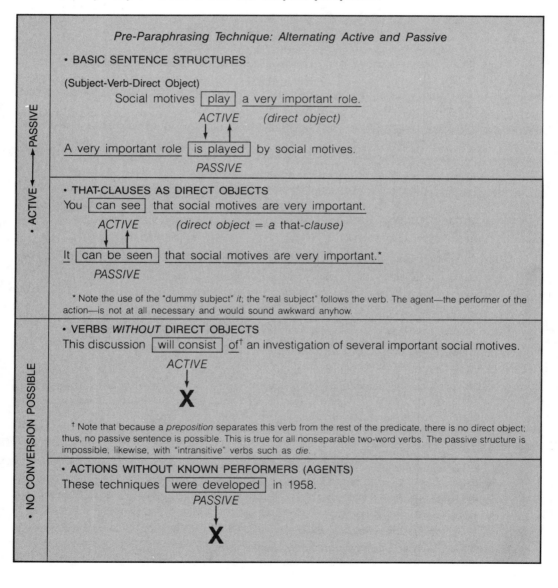

Pre-Paraphrasing Technique: Alternating Active and Passive

• BASIC SENTENCE STRUCTURES

(Subject-Verb-Direct Object)
    Social motives [play] a very important role.
          ACTIVE   (direct object)

A very important role [is played] by social motives.
          PASSIVE

• THAT-CLAUSES AS DIRECT OBJECTS
You [can see] that social motives are very important.
    ACTIVE   (direct object = a that-*clause*)

It [can be seen] that social motives are very important.*
    PASSIVE

* Note the use of the "dummy subject" *it*; the "real subject" follows the verb. The agent—the performer of the action—is not at all necessary and would sound awkward anyhow.

• VERBS *WITHOUT* DIRECT OBJECTS
This discussion [will consist] of† an investigation of several important social motives.
          ACTIVE

X

† Note that because a *preposition* separates this verb from the rest of the predicate, there is no direct object; thus, no passive sentence is possible. This is true for all nonseparable two-word verbs. The passive structure is impossible, likewise, with "intransitive" verbs such as *die*.

• ACTIONS WITHOUT KNOWN PERFORMERS (AGENTS)
These techniques [were developed] in 1958.
          PASSIVE

X

(left margin: • ACTIVE ⟷ PASSIVE • NO CONVERSION POSSIBLE)

3–2
PRE-PARAPHRASE

Directions: Wherever possible, change the active sentences to passive sentences and vice versa. (Some cannot be changed.) When you convert an active sentence to a passive sentence, decide whether or not it is necessary to include *agent* (*by* + a noun or noun phrase); if not, leave it out.

1. Social motives *play* an important role in people's lives.
   An important role is played in people's lives by social motives. *(The phrase "by social motives" is necessary. Why?)*
2. People seek achievement for many reasons.
   Achievement is sought (by people) for many reasons. *(The phrase "by people" is not essential to the sentence. Why not?)*
3. In all kinds of activities, you *can see* that the desire to perform with excellence is certainly present.
4. It is this interest in achievement for its own sake that *leads* psychologists to suggest a separate achievement motive. (Hint: "...by which...")
5. The need for achievement (*nAch*, as it *is abbreviated*) *varies* widely from one person to another.
6. Techniques *have been developed* by David C. McClelland to measure *nAch* experimentally.
7. It *has been discovered* by psychologists that high-*nAch* individuals *function* best in competitive situations and are fast learners; moreover, psychologists *have found* that the need to live up to a high self-imposed standard of performance *drives* these people.
8. In 1965, it *was found* that 83 percent of the subjects with high *nAch* scores *chose* "entrepreneurial occupations" such as sales and management consulting.
9. Such things as a high degree of risk and challenge, decision-making responsibility, and objective feedback on job performance *characterize* these "entrepreneurial occupations."
10. Two major causes for a high need for achievement *have been suggested.*
11. For one thing, children who *are exposed* by their parents to high standards for excellence will soon learn that their parents will *praise* them for achievement and *punish* them for lack of it.

WRITING AN INTRODUCTION

Like other introductions, the introduction to the short paper should have as its main goal to familiarize the reader with the subject and to give a clear indication of the contents of the discussion to follow. You will remember, from the brief discussion of nondeductive introductions in Chapter 1 (pages 22–24), that an introduction does this in the following ways: (1) It establishes a *context* which introduces the reader to the content area or subject; (2) it provides *further focus* on the content area in a way which will orient the reader in the right direction; and (3) it establishes very clearly the exact subject matter of the text by announcing a *controlling idea or thesis*.

Establishing the Context

The purpose of putting the subject in context is to establish a "link" with your reader. The most common way of doing this is to use certain techniques which assist the reader in identifying the subject or content area of the paper. In a short paper, this can usually be done in one or two sentences.

Assume, for instance, that you are taking a course in organizational behavior. The professor of that course has just assigned the following short paper on the general subject of *social motives*:

Short Paper Assignment

There seems to be a relationship between two of the "social motives"—*the need for achievement* and *the need for power*—in determining a person's success within an organization. In a short paper (3 to 5 pages), discuss this relationship in terms of the characteristics typical of people with a high need for achievement and those of people with a high need for power.[2]

Let us further assume that from your reading in a psychology course, you remember that the term *social motives* refers to a class of learned motives or needs "which centers around our relationships with other people," that these kinds of needs "play a very great part in our lives," and that they "are numerous and complex."[3] Drawing on this information, you might make use of any of the following techniques to begin your introduction in a way which will help your reader to "get a feel" for the subject of social motives:

Shared Knowledge

Because of the complexity of our relationships with others, social motives play an important role in everyday behavior.

A Rhetorical Question[4]

What person who has ever been a part of an organization can deny the influence of social motives on our relations with others?

_____

[2] Before going on, it would be a good idea to glance briefly at the two sections of the resource chapters which deal with these terms, since the need for achievement (abbreviated *nAch*) and the need for power (abbreviated *nPwr*) will be used to illustrate the techniques of writing a short paper. The texts in question are (1) Resource Chapter A ("Achievement" and "The Power Motive," pp. 240–41 and (2) Resource Chapter B ("Who Wants Power," pp. 248–50).

[3] Resource Chapter A, p. 239.

[4] A *rhetorical question* is one in which the writer emphasizes a point by asking a question to which no answer is expected. Thus, the rhetorical question in the example is equivalent in meaning to the following: "*Nobody* who has ever been a part of an organization can deny the influence of social motives on our relations with others."

Background Information

It has only been within the last twenty-five years that social scientists have begun to study the importance of social motives in determining group behavior.

A Quotation

"The principle that individuals are motivated by their personal self-interest," claims Stephen P. Robbins, "underlies almost every economic theory and is contained, explicitly or implicitly, in all theories of motivation."

The first sentence of the introduction, then, draws attention to the topic and helps to make that topic meaningful to the reader. This is an important first step, and it can provide a smooth approach which puts the reader at ease by demonstrating that you are clearly in control of the paper—all the more important if that reader is your professor!

Providing Further Focus

After you have introduced the reader to the content area of the paper in rather general fashion, you must begin to focus more clearly on the aspect of that subject which you intend to emphasize. This is usually done through description, definition, or more specific exemplification. In practical terms, this usually means that techniques like the following can be used, either singly or in combination:

1. *Defining/describing*: Briefly define and/or describe the subject itself, or clarify one or two central terms relating to the eventual controlling idea or thesis.
2. *Establishing chronological perspective*: In the case of background information, some kind of transition between past and present is often useful (indicating, for example, how the approach to the subject has changed over the last ten or twenty years).
3. *Establishing the relevance of a quotation*: You may want to point out how the quotation leads you around to the precise controlling idea or thesis if the link is not immediately apparent. A useful "trick" is to use a quotation with which you can disagree, so that you can then move closer to the point of view you will eventually adopt.
4. *Limiting the subject*: You may want to restrict the general subject to one or two examples or categories, which will then become the precise aspects upon which you will concentrate in the paper.

In terms of the imaginary paper on social motives, let us assume that you have chosen for your first sentence the technique of using a quotation, for example, the statement by Stephen P. Robbins that self-interest is a basic motivating force. A link is needed to tie this quotation to social motives in general and to the two particular social motives with which you are concerned—the need for achievement and the need for power as they affect a person's success within an organization. This might well be accomplished in the following way:

Model Introduction (Partial)

"The principle that individuals are motivated by their personal self-interest," claims Stephen P. Robbins, "underlies almost every economic theory and is contained, explicitly or implicitly, in all theories of motivation." This element of self-interest is particularly obvious in the case of the "social motives," which play an important role in our behavior toward others. Two of these motives—the need for *achievement* (that is, the need for excellence of performance) and the need for *power* (that is, the need to control others)—are especially important in terms of success within an organization. Although such success is no doubt the result of a combination of many motives, the need for achievement and the need for power appear to be very important contributing factors.

Establishing the Relevance of the Quotation: the quote is linked to the general subject of "social motives"

Limiting the Subject: 2 motives

Defining/Describing: brief definitions

Limiting the Subject: (1) a particular result—success; (2) a particular context—organizations; and (3) a particular relationship between the 2 motives

---

Thus, three of the four techniques have been used to get the reader from the beginning quotation to the point where the writer's approach begins to seem apparent. All that remains is for the writer to make a final transition into the controlling idea or thesis.

3–3
EXEMPLIFY / DISCUSS

Which ideas are "carried" from one section to another by means of the coherence devices of *repetition* and *substitute forms*?

Providing Final Clarification: The Controlling Idea or Thesis

The purpose of the paper—in the form of a controlling idea, if the paper is dealing strictly with factual information, or in the form of a thesis statement, if the paper is presenting an argument—is expressed in the *concluding sentence(s) of the introduction*. While there is no "law" which says that this is the only place for a controlling idea or thesis,[5] it is such a standard technique that you should learn to structure your introductions in this way.

In terms of the paper which we are using to demonstrate the techniques in this chapter, you will remember that you have already done the following things: (1) focused the reader's attention on the general subject area—social motives, (2) limited your scope to two of those motives—the need for power and the need for achievement, and (3) suggested that there is a probable relationship between the two in a particular context—

---

[5] Remember that introductions can be *deductive*. Such introductions were described in Chapter 1 (p. 22).

success within an organization. All that remains is for you to develop a controlling idea or thesis statement which controls the information which is to follow in the paper. After careful study of the texts which you believe to be relevant—the section entitled "Achievement" from Resource Chapter A and the section entitled "Who Wants Power?" from Resource Chapter B—let us assume that you decide on a generalization which is a thesis statement rather than a simple controlling idea, since what you have decided to argue falls outside the generally accepted body of knowledge in this field. This, then, is what your completed introduction will look like:

Model Introduction (Complete)

"The principle that individuals are motivated by their personal self-interest," claims Stephen P. Robbins, "underlies almost every economic theory and is contained, explicitly or implicitly, in all theories of motivation." This element of self-interest is particularly obvious in the case of the "social motives," which play an important role in our behavior toward others. Two of these motives—the need for *achievement* (i.e., the need for excellence of performance) and the need for power (i.e., the need to control others)—are especially important in terms of success within an organization. Although individual success is no doubt the result of a combination of many motives, the need for achievement and the need for power appear to be very important contributing factors. **This paper will propose that, in terms of the personal characteristics associated with each of these two motives, a strong need for power would seem to be most effective when a strong need for achievement is also present.**

Thesis Statement

Textual Coherence Through Purpose Signals

In academic prose, the controlling idea or thesis statement is usually presented in a direct way so that the reader has a clear idea of what the writer of the paper is attempting to do—that is, the *purpose* of the paper. Thus, whether you use a "structure of explicit purpose" or a sentence with no obvious purpose structure, you should remember to place your controlling idea or thesis statement *at the very end of the introductory paragraph*. Note that any of the thesis statements in the following boxes can replace the one in the model introduction.

Structures of Explicit Purpose

• THE WORD *PURPOSE*

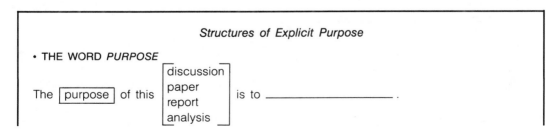

EXAMPLE: The purpose of this paper is to show that there is a probable relationship between the need for power and the need for achievement in terms of characteristics found in those persons who rank high in both of these social motives.

- CLAUSES OF PURPOSE

| _____(Sentence)_____ | so that
in order that | _____(Sentence)_____ . |

EXAMPLE: This paper will examine the characteristics of those persons having a strong need for power and those having a strong need for achievement so that a dependency relationship may be drawn between these two social motives.

- PHRASES OF PURPOSE

| In order to | _____(verb +)_____ , | _____(Sentence)_____ . |

EXAMPLE: In order to demonstrate that a relationship exists between the need for power and the need for achievement, this paper will analyze the characteristics of those persons ranking high in these two social motives.

- *WILL* + ACTIVE VERB

| This | discussion
paper
report
analysis | will | propose
analyze
suggest
describe
examine
discuss
show | that _____ |

EXAMPLE: This paper will propose that persons having a strong need for power are more likely to achieve success if a strong need for achievement is also present.

- *WILL* + PASSIVE VERB

| In this | discussion
paper
report
analysis | it | will be | argued
proposed
suggested
shown | that _____ . |

EXAMPLE: In this paper, it will be proposed that persons having a strong need for power are more likely to achieve success if a strong need for achievement is also present.*

* Notice how the use of the "dummy subject" *it* shifts the main idea of the sentence to the end.

Implicit Purpose

- A DECLARATIVE SENTENCE WITH NO PURPOSE CLUES

It seems quite likely that those individuals who exhibit both a high need for achievement and a high need for power are those who will have the highest degree of success.

3–4
WRITE

Directions: Carefully read each of the three texts that follow. Assume that these three texts about power are the only sources of information you have on this particular subject.

A. Using the information in all three texts, formulate two new controlling ideas about the subject of power. Your controlling ideas should be completely different from the controlling ideas in the three source texts. Express each of the controlling ideas in a different way, referring back to the preceding list of structures of explicit purpose if necessary.
B. Indicate whether each is a simple controlling idea or a thesis.
C. Choose one of your generalizations and write an introduction to a short paper based on it. In your introduction you can also make use of information from any of the source texts.

    1. While the concept of authority remained important from its emphasis in classical theory and influence received special attention in participative approaches, the concept of power has only recently been emphasized. **Authority** is the right to act as indicated in the organizational hierarchy; **influence** is the effect of one person on the behavior of others.
5 **Power** is the potential force that others perceive a person to possess that gives the capacity to influence actions of others. Power, then, is a psychological force that identifies the potential of a person as perceived by others. The design of structure helps to identify one's authority and the interrelationship for influencing others, but power is a more general term that includes other sources of potential force in the organization. For example, a
10 person may be low in the hierarchy of authority and yet have significant power as a result of personal characteristics, associations with family or political connections, expert knowledge or strategic duties, or physical location at a particular time. Thus recognition of power centers is essential to effective organization design. (From *Essentials of Management*, pp. 79–80.)

    2. Different people place different values on the gain and exercise of power. The evidence suggests that the amount of power an individual exercises is dependent largely on the strength of his or her power motive. Those people with a high need for power (*nPwr*) are attracted to jobs that provide latitude for defining their roles; selecting their
5 actions; and advising, evaluating, and controlling the behavior of others. It is not our purpose to investigate why people differ in *nPwr*—for example, arguments have been made that power seeking is a neurotic behavior based on childhood deprivations. Rather, we are concerned with establishing whether or not people differ.
    Research indicates that there are indeed differences in *nPwr* among people and that
10 individuals who score high on *nPwr* tend to purchase prestige objects so as to cause envy in others, seek jobs such as business managers or teachers that provide considerable opportunity to exercise influence, are more likely to run for political office, and seek to dominate others in group discussions. So we can conclude that while most people strive for power, some seek it considerably more than others. (From *Organizational Behavior*,
15 p. 268.)

3. Winter (1973) studied the power motives of 12 American presidents, from Theodore Roosevelt through Richard Nixon. His technique was to score the concerns, aspirations, fears, and ideas for action of each president as revealed in his inaugural speech. The highest scorers in terms of power drives were Theodore Roosevelt, Franklin Roosevelt,
5 Harry Truman, Woodrow Wilson, John Kennedy, and Lyndon Johnson. Except for Theodore Roosevelt, all were Democrats and all six men are known as action-oriented presidents. All also scored high in need for achievement. By contrast, Republican presidents (such as Taft, Hoover, and Eisenhower) are known more for restraint and tend to score much lower in power motivation and in need for achievement. Richard Nixon
10 scored quite high in need for achievement but relatively low in power motivation. According to Winter, the effect of this is a tendency toward vacillation and hesitancy when faced with a power-oriented issue. Winter (1976) studied Jimmy Carter when he was still a presidential candidate and found his power motive to be about average and his need to achieve somewhat above average (about the same as Theodore Roosevelt's).
15 Winter suggests a number of interesting relations between the power motive and specific presidential policy decisions and actions:

Those presidents in power when the country entered wars tended to score high on power motive.

Power scores of presidents seem significantly related to the gain or loss of territory
20 through wars, expansion, treaties, and independence struggles.

Presidents with high power scores tended to have the highest turnover in cabinet members during their administrations. (From *Psychology*, pp. 372–373.)

PROVIDING EVIDENCE

Once you have defined the subject matter and stated your controlling idea or thesis in the introduction, you must then structure the rest of your paper to achieve that purpose by providing information to support your controlling idea or prove your thesis. Ordinarily you will combine supporting information from two or more sources so that your reader can easily follow your argument. The information you choose as support or proof must meet three criteria.

First of all, the information must be **relevant** to the point you are making. If you are drawing a relationship between the need for power and the need for achievement, you will search your sources specifically for data which illustrate or prove that relationship. In other words, you will *ignore* much of the information in your source texts if it does not relate in a direct way to your purpose.

The information you choose must also be **convincing** to your reader. Perhaps the best way to convince your reader that your thesis is correct is to report on *research* which demonstrates the validity of your thesis. Another type of convincing support is to quote directly from an *expert* in the field.

Finally, your support or proof must be **specific**. The research you choose to report as evidence, and particularly the examples you choose to illustrate your point, must speak directly to the point.

A Note on Specificity and Language Use

One of the most frequent faults in student writing is the tendency to *overgeneralize* when exemplifying and drawing conclusions. A few suggestions in each of these areas will no doubt help you to avoid this annoying practice.

EXAMPLES. In order to provide strong support or proof for your controlling idea or thesis, you must learn to choose very specific instances to illustrate its validity. For instance, to exemplify the fact that the need for achievement and the need for power are frequently found together, you might choose to use an example from politics. The Winter study in Resource Chapter A (page 241) reports a study made of certain U.S. presidents. Weak support for your thesis would be the following very general example:

Nonspecific Example

Among the U.S. presidents studied by Winter, many were found to be high in power as well as high in achievement.

A far more convincing example would be to choose one of the presidents studied and to show precisely how the need for power and the need for achievement were combined in the behavior of that particular president. Notice how much more clearly the following example illustrates the thesis:

Specific Example

More specifically, in a study of power needs among U.S. presidents (Winter, 1973), John F. Kennedy was identified as one of the presidents with a high need for power. Kennedy, one of the most popular presidents, was well known for his energy, self-confidence, competitiveness, and sense of perseverance.

The first example, it is true, might have its use in a paper—as a lead-in to a more focused discussion, for example; only the second, however, has the specificity required of a good example.

CONCLUSIONS. Because of the nature of academic writing, you must guard against allowing your conclusions to "presume too much"—that is, to be too general. Most of what is written in all areas of academic pursuit is very carefully worded so as to indicate that what is being said is *tentative or uncertain*—i.e., "true" only according to the best available evidence. Thus, in your reading, you will find heavy use of such structures as modal auxiliaries (*may, might, could*, and *would*), conditional structures (*if-* and *unless-*clauses), adverbs indicating uncertainty (*possibly, perhaps, conceivably, probably*, etc.), and clauses of concessive contrast (*although-*clauses, *while-*clauses, etc.).

As a student writer, you too should make use of this kind of language in your writing. Otherwise, the conclusions you draw or the support you offer will be open to criticism from your professors and classmates as not being intellectually honest in that you are not "leaving the door open" for other points of view. For this reason, it is wise to avoid the use of such "absolute terms" as *all, always,* and *never.*

Notice in the following examples the impression which is made by the overgeneralized statements, as opposed to that made when more tentative language is used.

Overgeneralizations	*Tentative Statements*
Research shows that persons who have a high *nPwr* have a need to dominate group discussions.	Research *tends to demonstrate* that persons who have a high *nPwr* have a need to dominate group discussions.
Thus, in order to be able to satisfy the need for power, the need for achievement is a prerequisite.	Thus, *although it is clear that a number of social motives are at work at any one time in determining the behavior of individuals,* in order to satisfy the need for power, the need for achievement *would seem* to be a prerequisite.
The desire to do things well and those personal traits which enable a person to do so serve as the foundation for assuming positions of leadership and the ability to control and influence others.	The desire to do things well and those personal traits which enable a person to do so *could* serve as the foundation for assuming positions of leadership and the ability to control and influence others.

3–5
EXEMPLIFY / DISCUSS

Directions: Below is a thesis based on the three texts in Exercise 3–4. Using this thesis as an indication of the direction the paper might take, evaluate the statements which follow it as to the validity each offers as proof of the thesis. To do this, decide whether each statement is

a. not relevant (statement does not belong),
b. overgeneralized (statement does not belong), or
c. adequate support (statement relevant and to the point)

   POSSIBLE THESIS: "As indicated by some recent research, a career likely to be chosen by a person high in the need for power is politics."

1. According to the Winter study, Theodore Roosevelt, Franklin Roosevelt, and Harry Truman all scored high in the need for power.
2. Democratic presidents all have a high need for power.
3. The positive way in which a candidate is perceived by others seems to be a critical factor in gaining political office.
4. Authority can be defined as the right to act according to the hierarchical structure of an organization.

5. Action-oriented presidents always have a high need for power.

6. For example, people who have a high need for power tend to purchase prestige items.

7. When there are frequent changes in cabinet members during an administration, the president usually has a high need for power.

8. Only politics offers an opportunity for high-*nPwr* individuals to exercise real influence over others.

9. Thus, we can see that politicians have a high need for power.

10. Among other behavioral characteristics, it has been suggested that persons who score high in the need for power seek positions where they can control others.

Preliminaries: Assembling the Data

Because your controlling idea is usually defined in part by the writing assignment itself in the shorter paper, your search for supporting evidence or illustration will be *deductive*—that is, you will seek support for a generalization early in the process, rather than having to collect all the evidence on your own before finally being in a position to make your own generalization (induction). In the model introduction, for example, the thesis statement is the following: "This paper will propose that, in terms of the personal characteristics associated with each of these two motives, a strong need for power would seem to be most effective when a strong need for achievement is also present." To find evidence to support this predication, we will look at the appropriate sections of two of the resource chapters in this book—the sections entitled "Achievement" and "The Power Motive" from Resource Chapter A (pages 240–41) and the section entitled "Who Wants Power" from Resource Chapter B (pages 248–50).

In such a paper, the need for power and the need for achievement will be discussed in terms of *characteristics*. Therefore, a likely place to begin would be to discover which characteristics are found in persons with a strong need for achievement and which are found in persons with a strong need for power. On page 240 of Resource Chapter A, there is a paragraph listing the traits found in the former; on page 249 of Resource Chapter B, a paragraph listing the traits found in the latter. We will first list these traits and attempt to find some relationship among them:

Preliminary Work List of Traits

High nAch

1. functions best in competitive situations
2. learns fast
3. has high self-imposed standards
4. is self-confident
5. is responsible
6. can resist outside pressure
7. is energetic
8. perseveres in achieving goals
9. is prone to tension and to psychosomatic illnesses

High nPwr

1. purchases prestige objects to create envy
2. seeks jobs that provide opportunity to influence others
3. is likely to run for political office
4. tries to dominate in group discussions

Remember, as you do this, that only *relevant* data can be used. Not all of the traits in the preliminary list offer support for the idea that the need for power is dependent in some way on the need for achievement. Therefore, it is best to begin by "selecting out" that information which you will not make use of. In this case, point No. 9 from the first column does not have any apparent relationship to the traits in the second column, so it can be eliminated. Similarly, point No. 1 in the second list does not seem to relate to the traits in the first list. Thus, deleting these two items gives us the following revised work list:

Revised Work List of Traits

High nAch

1. functions best in competitive situations
2. learns fast
3. has high self-imposed standards
4. is self-confident
5. is responsible
6. can resist outside pressure
7. is energetic
8. perseveres in achieving goals

High nPwr

1. seeks jobs that provide opportunity to influence others
2. is likely to run for political office
3. tries to dominate in group discussions

Deciding on the "Plan of Attack"

The next step is to organize the information so that it will support the controlling idea. This is best done by preparing a plan (an outline or even a simple list) to clearly demonstrate the relationship between the two sets of traits. Because the thesis states that "a strong need for power would seem to be most effective when a strong need for achievement is also present," let us take each of the three points of the "high *nPwr*" list and attempt to organize the paper in terms of three main correlations with the "high *nAch*" list.

When assembling our evidence, we must be aware that our evidence may not always support our thesis. If that turns out to be the case, there are two possible alternatives. (1) If we feel sure, based on what we have read, that our thesis can be adequately supported, we can start over and approach the evidence in a different way, hoping for better results. (2) If, however, we come upon strong evidence which *contradicts* the thesis, we will have to revise our original thesis. For example, if our thesis had proposed that a high need for achievement always presupposes a high need for power, the example of Richard Nixon (Resource Chapter A, p. 241—"Richard Nixon scored quite high in need for achievement but relatively low in power motivation") would have made us consider revising the thesis.

Let us begin, then, with the first point of the "high *nPwr*" list: persons with a strong need for power *seek jobs where they can have influence over others*. In order to get such a job, what other characteristics must high *nPwr* people have? It is logical to assume that such individuals must also possess virtually all of the traits in the revised "high *nAch*" list:

nAch Traits Necessary to Get and Maintain Positions of Leadership

- competitiveness
- ability to learn fast
- high self-imposed standards
- self-confidence
- responsibility
- resistance to outside pressures
- high energy level
- perseverance

Certainly, a person who does not demonstrate these characteristics would have little chance of assuming and successfully maintaining a position of influence within an organization. This information, then, can probably serve as the first paragraph of the body of the paper.

To further convince the reader that this correlation is a valid one, a good technique is to find *documentation from an expert in the field*, which can now be quoted to support the point. The quote is from the article by Maccoby, which follows Resource Chapter B (pp. 258–59). It is a long quote describing the "new manager":

His main interest is in challenge, competitive activity where he can prove himself a winner. Impatient with others who are slower and more cautious, he likes to take risks and to motivate others to push themselves beyond their normal pace. He responds to work and life as a game. The contest hypes him up and he communicates his enthusiasm, thus energizing others.

Indeed, because of the very length of the quote, we will probably give it a separate paragraph in the paper, with its own introductory comment.

Following this lengthy illustration, the paper can now proceed to a second important correlation: the second trait found among those possessing a strong need for power is *the need to dominate in group discussions*. Going back to the revised list of high *nAch* traits, we can draw further parallels to support the relationship between achievement and power:

nAch Traits Necessary to Dominate in Group Discussions

- competitiveness
- ability to learn fast
- self-confidence
- high energy level

The correlation between these traits and the person's behavior in a group will become the next paragraph in the body of the paper.

The final correlation of the paper—based, once again, on information in the resource chapters—concerns the remaining trait from the "high *nPwr*" list: *the likelihood of running for public office*. Our approach here might well be to illustrate the relationship between the need for power and the need for achievement in U.S. presidential politics. On page 241 of Resource Chapter A, a study of the power motivation of twelve U.S. presidents is cited. From this study one president who combines the traits mentioned earlier can be chosen. Perhaps the most obvious example, in terms of the controlling idea, is John F. Kennedy:

Political Success of John F. Kennedy

• Winter study: high need for power
• personal traits: high need for achievement

CONCLUDING THE PAPER

Before going into the mechanics of writing a conclusion, we would like to point out that a conclusion is not always necessary. Since the purpose of a good conclusion is to leave the reader with a comfortable sense that the paper has been completed, if a paper has done this by the end of the body—particularly a short paper, where the reader has probably not had time to forget the information—a conclusion really adds nothing, especially if it is simply a repetitious summary of what has been said.

If, however, you feel that your paper does not end on a particularly final note and therefore needs a conclusion, you should know that there is no one "correct" way to conclude. There are probably as many types of conclusions as there are authors who write them. From all possible methods, we can suggest three which you are likely to find helpful and fairly easy to use: (1) restating/summarizing, (2) drawing additional implications, and (3) using a short, relevant quotation. These techniques, like the techniques of "further focus" in introductions, can be used alone, but are often used in combination with one another.

Restating/Summarizing

If you feel that your arguments are complicated enough, that the facts you have presented are detailed enough, or that the final section of the paper is undramatic enough to warrant reminding the reader of the contents of your paper, summarize this information, by all means. But do it in slightly different form—that is, *paraphrase*. More will be said on the subject of summarizing in a later chapter. For now, be aware that it is not necessary to restate every single idea, particularly in the case of a short paper; restrict yourself to the *most important points* so that the reader is led to reinterpret the thesis or controlling idea in terms of the evidence which has been provided.

Drawing Additional Implications

You may wish, as a method of concluding, to suggest certain implications of your thesis or controlling idea, or allude to some aspect of the subject which you did not touch upon in your paper. This may mean one or more of the following:

• possible applications of a theory
• predictions for the future
• tentativeness or limits of your conclusion or of your controlling idea
• reference to ongoing research in the field

However, what you do in the conclusion should definitely *conclude the paper*. Do not, by any means, express these implications in a way which contradicts your thesis, or opens up an entirely new area of the subject—this will only confuse the reader! Thus, in concluding the paper on social motives, it would be perfectly acceptable to admit that power and achievement motivation are still being studied by researchers in the field, and that the "final word" on the subject has not yet been written. At that point, however, you should shift the focus back to what you have been arguing. In other words, you should reemphasize that there seems to be a strong positive relationship between the two motives in terms of success within an organization (your thesis). It would not be wise to reverse the order, ending on a suggestion that further research will probably prove this correlation to be false. Nor would it be a good idea at this point to introduce a third important social motive—the need for affiliation (*nAfl*)—and to suggest that it plays an even more important role in organizational behavior. If *nAfl* was of such importance, you should have included it in your thesis statement!

Using a Quotation

Although the technique of using a quotation in introductions and conclusions should not be abused, a relevant quotation from a qualified expert in the field is always useful in a short paper assigned for a course. It is likely that this technique is best combined with one of the two other techniques presented above:

Restating/Summarizing + Quotation

If you wish to summarize your arguments but wish to avoid sounding repetitious, a well-chosen quote can give needed variety—and emphasis—to your summary; it can also, when placed at the end, add a sense of completion.

Drawing Additional Implications + Quotation

If you have indicated that your conclusions are valid, but only within certain limits, you can at that point shift the attention of the reader back to the validity of these conclusions by the choice of an appropriate quotation from some expert in the field, thus ending the paper on a positive note.

A final word of warning concerning this technique is in order. To be effective in an argument, a quotation must be to the point—that is, relevant. Make sure that it says what you want it to say; if not, don't use it. Additionally, make quite sure that the person you are quoting is a recognized authority in the field; this means, of course, someone who is *currently* recognized, not a person whose views have been seriously called into question by recent trends in the field.

WRITING AN OUTLINE

It will now be relatively easy to organize our various lists into a formal outline (if one is required by the professor) to indicate the total organization of the paper. More detailed practice in outlining will be provided in the next chapter. For the moment, notice the arrangement in the outline, paying particular attention to the alternation of *roman numerals* (I, II, III, etc.), *capital letters* (A, B, C, etc.), and *arabic numerals* (1, 2, 3, etc.).

The Short Paper: A Topic Outline

I. INTRODUCTION / THESIS: a strong need for power would seem to be most effective when a strong need for achievement is also present.
II. *nAch* traits necessary for *leadership positions* (*nPwr*)
    A. Competitiveness
    B. Ability to learn quickly
    C. High self-imposed standards
    D. Self-confidence
    E. Responsibility
    F. Resistance to outside pressures
    G. High energy level
    H. Perseverance
    I. Maccoby's description of the "new manager"
III. *nAch* traits necessary to *dominate discussions* (*nPwr*)
    A. Competitiveness
    B. Ability to learn quickly
    C. Self-confidence
    D. Resistance to outside pressures
    E. High energy level
IV. Illustration of the *nPwr/nAch* correlation in *politics* (*nPwr*)
    A. Necessity of possessing most *nAch* traits
    B. Political success of John F. Kennedy
        1. Winter study: high need for power
        2. Personal traits: high need for achievement

We are now ready to put all parts of the paper together in its final form. Notice how the plan suggested in the outline has been implemented and how supporting data have been integrated from various sources.

Model Short Paper

Psychologists are quick to observe that because of the complexity of our relationships with others, "social motives play a very great role in our lives" (Morris, 1979, p. 370). Two of these social motives—the need for *achievement* (i.e., the need for excellence of performance) and the need for *power* (i.e., the need to control others)—are especially
5 important in terms of success within an organization. While individual success is no doubt the result of a combination of many motives, the need for achievement (*nAch*) and the need for power (*nPwr*) appear to be very important contributing factors. This paper

will propose that, in terms of the personal characteristics associated with each of these two motives, a strong need for power would seem to be most effective when a strong
10 need for achievement is also present.

One of the most obvious traits found in those people who have a high *nPwr* is their tendency to seek positions in which they are able to exert control over others—i.e., positions of leadership (Robbins, 1979). These positions may be in any domain (business, education, government, and so on), but in all these areas, in order to
15 successfully maintain a position of leadership, a person must also have certain other personal characteristics. To get the position in the first place, the individual must be competitive. In order to assume a role of leadership within an organization, one must be able to "learn the ropes" quickly and to persevere in carrying out long-range plans. To accomplish this, a person must have a high level of energy and a sense of responsibility.
20 Moreover, since the individual is in a leadership position, success rests largely on the internal standards which have been set, as well as on some ability to resist outside pressure. Interestingly enough, these traits—competitiveness, the ability to learn quickly, perseverance, a high energy level, a sense of responsibility, the ability to resist outside pressure, and high self-imposed standards—are among those most commonly found in
25 persons who have a high *nAch* (Morris, 1979).

In the field of management, Maccoby (1971) describes the typical modern corporate executive. This "new manager" combines a high *nPwr* with a high *nAch*:

His main interest is in challenge, competitive activity where he can prove himself a winner. Impatient with others who are slower and more cautious, he likes to take risks
30 and to motivate others to push themselves beyond their normal pace. He responds to work and life as a game. The contest hypes him up and he communicates his enthusiasm, thus energizing others.

Further, research tends to demonstrate that persons who have a high need for power seek to dominate group discussions (Robbins, 1979). To assume and successfully
35 maintain a dominant position in a discussion group, an individual must possess characteristics which enable him/her to do so. These include the following: competitiveness, in order to dominate; a sense of self-confidence, in order to express opinions in a group; the ability to learn quickly, in order to respond appropriately; and a high level of energy combined with the ability to resist outside pressures, in order to maintain
40 dominance. Once again, these traits are those found in persons who have a high need for achievement (Morris, 1979).

Politics, one of the fields commonly chosen by those with a high need for power (Robbins, 1979, p. 268), provides a good illustration of the relationship between these two social motives. To achieve success in politics, a person must demonstrate most of
45 the characteristics of high-*nAch* personalities. More specifically, in a study done of the power motivation of certain U.S. presidents (Winter, 1973), John F. Kennedy was identified as one of the presidents with a high need for power. Kennedy, one of the most popular presidents, was well known for his energy, self-confidence, competitiveness, and sense of perseverance. In addition, self-imposed high standards and the ability to grasp
50 the essentials of a problem were qualities assigned to Kennedy. Kennedy's high *nPwr*, as determined by Winter in this study by ". . . the concerns, aspirations, fears, and ideas for

action of each president as revealed in his inaugural address" (Morris, 1979, p. 372), seems, for successful fulfillment, to be dependent on the possession of high *nAch* as well.

55   Thus, although it is clear that a number of motives are at work at any one time in determining the behavior of any individual, current research indicates that in terms of success within an organization, the need for power (*nPwr*) and the need for achievement (*nAch*) are among those most deserving of further consideration. And while there has been, to date, no definitive study which establishes an absolute correlation between
60   these two motives, a careful comparison of their respective component traits seems to suggest that a strong need for achievement is a prerequisite for the most complete satisfaction of a strong need for power. The desire to do things well—and those personal traits which enable a person to do so—would appear to constitute an excellent foundation for assuming and maintaining positions of leadership, providing a most
65   effective complement to the desire to control and influence others.

• REFERENCES

Maccoby, Michael. "The New Manager: A Game-Player Rather Than Power-Seeker." In Robbins, Stephen P. *Organizational Behavior*. Englewood Cliffs, N.J.: Prentice-Hall, Inc., 1979, pp. 282–83.

Morris, Charles G. *Psychology*. 3rd ed. Englewood Cliffs, N.J.: Prentice-Hall, Inc., 1979.

Robbins, Stephen P. *Organizational Behavior*. Englewood Cliffs, N.J.: Prentice-Hall, Inc., 1979.

Winter, D. G. "What Makes the Candidates Run." *Psychology Today*, July 1976, pp. 45–49.

3–6
EXEMPLIFY   /   DISCUSS

Directions: Discuss the preceding model short paper in terms of the following elements. (You might want to mark the paper and make notes in the margins prior to class discussion.)

A. The Introduction
   1. What technique has been used to *establish the context*?
   2. How has *further focus* been achieved?
   3. Why is this an example of a *nondeductive* introduction?
B. The Body
   1. How many major sections does the body of the paper contain?
   2. What is the purpose of the *first* major section? How many paragraphs make up this section? How many references to authoritative sources can you find?
   3. Discuss the use of enumeration in the second paragraph. What kind of items is being enumerated? How many items are there?
   4. What is the purpose of the third paragraph?
   5. What is the purpose of the *second* major section? How many paragraphs make up this section? How many references to authoritative sources can you find?

6. What two thought relationships dominate the fourth paragraph? Explain.

7. What is the purpose of the *third* major section? How many paragraphs make up this section? How many references to authoritative sources can you find?

C. The Conclusion

1. What concluding techniques have been used?

2. At what point might the conclusion have accidentally altered the focus of the paper? How has the writer avoided this?

D. What examples of "tentative language" has the writer included in the paper to avoid the impression of overgeneralizing? Do you see any other statements in the paper which might have been made more tentatively?

PRE-PARAPHRASING TECHNIQUE: ALTERNATING WORD FORMS

An obvious way of expressing an author's thought in your own words is to change the form of one word, from a verb to a noun, adjective, or adverb, for example. This technique, though effective, is not always as easy to use as it might first appear. This is due, first of all, to the sheer number of these forms in English—literally hundreds of thousands. You are no doubt familiar with the most common ones. As for the others, you will discover that certain recurring forms are of greatest use to you in your various courses; careful reading and frequent consultation of a good dictionary will allow you to continue perfecting your knowledge of these forms. Even with effort, however, this may take time, depending on the extent of your familiarity with this area of grammatical structure.

Another problem frequently encountered is the fact that certain words undergo a slight shift in meaning when they change forms, or that a word which has several meanings will undergo changes in word form in the case of only one of those meanings. Take, for example, the verb *to succeed*. Two possible meanings of this verb are (1) to accomplish the goals which one has set for oneself, and (2) to replace someone in a job or position. The first meaning gives the following forms, with which you are probably quite familiar:

Verb: to succeed
Noun: success
Adjective: successful
Adverb: successfully

The second meaning ("to replace someone in a job or position") gives only *one* of the forms associated with the first meaning, and it adds *two* forms which are never associated with the first meaning:

Verb: to succeed
   Reagan *succeeded* Carter as President of the United States.
Noun: successor ("the person who....")
   Reagan was Carter's *successor*.

Noun: succession ("the act of....")
   The United States Constitution provides for the peaceful *succession* of power.

A third and final difficulty is the fact that when you change the form of a word, this change involves *a structural change* in the sentence as well. The verb *to succeed* (in the second meaning) and the noun *successor* constitute a good case in point. The verb requires a direct object. The noun, in this case, can come either before or after the verb *to be*:

Noun: Reagan was Carter's *successor*.
   Carter's *successor* was Reagan.
Verb: Reagan *succeeded* Carter.

   Study the examples in the following box very carefully. They represent additional illustrations of the various structural problems with which you will have to deal when using this paraphrasing technique.

Pre-Paraphrasing Technique: Alternating Word Forms

to succeed (verb)	*to persevere* (verb)	*to manage* (verb)
success (noun)	*perseverance* (noun)	*manager* (noun)
successor (noun)		*management* (noun)
successful (adjective)	*persevering* (adjective)	*managing* (adjective)
succeeding (adjective)		*managerial* (adjective)
successfully (adverb)		*managerially* (adverb)

• ORIGINAL SENTENCE:
A *manager's* *success* is often due to *perseverance.*

• POSSIBLE PARAPHRASES
A *manager* often *succeeds* because of *perseverance.*
Perseverance often leads to *managerial* *success.*
A *persevering* *manager* is often *successful.*
Successful management is often a result of *perseverance.*
A *manager* who *perseveres* often *succeeds.*
Perseverance often causes a manager to achieve *success.*
Success is often the result of *perseverance* on the part of a *manager.*
If a *manager perseveres,* he or she often *succeeds.*
Perseverance often contributes to a *manager's* *success.*
The *success* of a *manager* often stems from *perseverance.*

3–7
PRE-PARAPHRASE

Directions: Paraphrase each of the following sentences by changing the italicized words or phrases in the suggested manner. Be careful: one suggestion is a "trick question" and cannot be changed as indicated; when you have decided which one it is, simply ignore it.

1. A variety of *definitions* of leadership have been proposed over the years.

   definition ———————→define
   (noun)   (verb)

   <u>Leadership has been defined in a variety of ways over the years.</u>

2. Leadership has long been considered one of the most important factors influencing *performance* in organizations.

   performance ——————→perform
   (noun)   (verb)

3. Early research focused on traits, or personality characteristics, *typically* found in leaders who had achieved *success*.

   typically ———————→typical
   (adverb)   (adjective)

   success ———————→successful
   (noun)   (adjective)

4. Later researchers recognized that leadership also involves the *relationship* between a leader and his or her subordinates.

   relationship ——————→relate
   (noun)   (verb)

5. Fred Fiedler *has suggested* that there are three such "situational factors"; this deserves our attention.

   suggest ———————→suggestion
   (verb)   (noun)

6. One factor of extreme *importance*, "leader-member relations," refers to the amount of *confidence* subordinates have in a leader.

   importance ———————→important
   (noun)   (adjective)

   confidence ———————→confident
   (noun)   (adjective)

7. *Secondly*, there is "task structure"—that is, the degree of routine which exists in carrying out assigned tasks.

   secondly ———————→second
   (adverb)   (adjective)

8. "Position power" is the *third* important factor; the term refers to how *authoritative* a leader's position *actually* is within the entire structure of an organization.

   third ———————→thirdly
   (adjective)   (adverb)

authoritative ⟶ authority
(adjective)   (noun)

actually ⟶ actual
(adverb)   (adjective)

9. Fiedler *believes* that no one leadership style is equally *successful* in all job *situations*.

believe ⟶ belief
(verb)   (noun)

successful ⟶ success
(adjective)   (noun)

situation ⟶ situate
(noun)   (verb)

10. Indeed, the effectiveness of a leadership style *depends* on the three "situational factors" and how they *relate* to the job in question.

depend ⟶ dependent
(verb)   (adjective)

relate ⟶ relationship
(verb)   (noun)

USING QUOTATION AS DOCUMENTATION

Quoting directly or indirectly, or referring to research done by another person, usually an expert in the field, is a common and effective technique for proving a thesis or supporting a controlling idea. You must always acknowledge the person you are quoting by mentioning the original source, whether the quote is direct (that is, the exact words of another person) or indirect (a paraphrase). This is called *crediting* or *citing* the source.

There are many methods of citing a source which are acceptable in academic writing. We will present the two most common methods: *footnoting*, which is formal and traditional; and *citation within a text*, which is less formal and traditional but which is gaining wide acceptance in academic circles.

Formal Footnoting

Resource Chapter B ("Power") follows formal footnoting conventions. Notice that in this chapter, each time the writer makes use of something written by someone else, a number appears after the material which is quoted or referred to, and a corresponding number appears at the bottom of the page. Following the number at the bottom of the page is *a complete identification of the exact source from which the material was taken*. The numbers run sequentially throughout the chapter. The advantage to this system of footnoting is that if the reader wishes to know the source of a quote, it can be found immediately because the complete publication information appears on the same page as the quoted material itself. The disadvantage is that the format is complicated and must be followed precisely.

In formal footnoting, the order in which the publication information appears and the punctuation of the footnote must follow certain academic conventions. This format varies slightly, depending on whether you are citing a book or an article. Thus, if you are not already familiar with these conventions, you should read this section very carefully.

FORMAL FOOTNOTES FOR BOOKS. There are four parts to this kind of footnote. Notice the order in which these parts are presented, as well as the order of the elements in each part; this is the order which is required, and it must be followed *exactly*! Notice, too, that like the first line of a paragraph, the first line of a footnote is *indented*. Footnotes, however, are *numbered*; paragraphs are not.

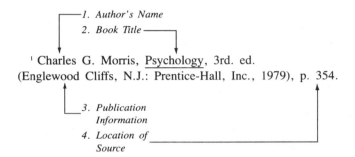

FORMAL FOOTNOTES FOR ARTICLES. There are five parts to this kind of footnote. Notice that footnotes for articles contain information which footnotes for books do not.

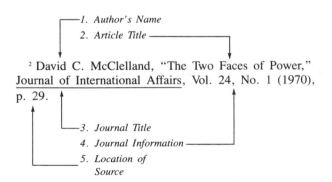

The format for the "author's name" and the "location of source" (page numbers) are the same as for a book footnote. The other parts, however, are different.

Capitalization and Punctuation in Titles

Notice the way article and book titles have been capitalized and punctuated in the model footnote forms. In compiling footnotes or a bibliography, or *whenever* you refer to a book or article in your writing, you will be expected to follow certain conventions of capitalization and punctuation. The conventions for capitalization are the same for all titles, but those for punctuation vary slightly between books and articles, plays, chapters, and so forth.

Punctuation in Titles

1. When book, magazine, play, movie, or newspaper titles are handwritten or typed, they are always completely <u>underlined</u>. (This may be somewhat confusing to you because when you see such titles in print they are italicized, not underlined.)

   <u>King Lear</u> (a play)

   <u>Paragraph Development</u> (a book)

   <u>Jaws</u> (a movie)

   <u>The New York Times</u> (a newspaper)

   <u>Time</u> (a magazine)

2. When titles of an article, a chapter or subsection of a book, a poem, or a TV show are handwritten, typed, or appear in print, they are completely enclosed in quotation marks ("/"):

   "Power" (Chapter 18 of the book *Organizational Behavior*)

   "Dallas" (a TV show)

   "The Two Faces of Power" (an article)

   "Poem in Prose" (a poem)

3. Any punctuation which appears in the title itself—a colon (:), a comma (,), an exclamation point (!), or a question mark (?)—is always included *within* the quotation marks:

   "Organizational Theory and Organizational Communication: A Communication Failure?"

Capitalization in Titles

1. Always capitalize the first letters of the first and last words in a title, and the first word after a colon (:):

   Nonverbal Communication: Readings with Commentary

2. Capitalize all other words in the title except for articles (*a, an,* and *the*), prepositions (*of, at, to, by,* etc.), and coordinating conjunctions (*and, but, or, nor, so, for,* and *yet*):

   A Biobehavioral Analysis of Consummatory Activities

   Pride and Prejudice

   A Practical Guide to the Teaching of English

   Viewpoints on English as a Second Language

3–8
CAPITALIZE / PUNCTUATE

Directions: Below are ten titles, each marked as to the kind of title it is. Capitalize and punctuate accordingly.

1. some extraordinary facts about obese humans and rats (article)
2. the psychology of affiliation: experimental studies of the sources of gregariousness (book)
3. does undernutrition during infancy inhibit brain-growth and subsequent intellectual development (article)
4. organizational politics: an integrating concept (chapter)
5. does group participation when using brainstorming facilitate or inhibit creative thinking (article)

6. desire under the elms (play)
7. of human bondage (novel)
8. the little house on the prairie (television show)
9. the search for the secret of fat (article)
10. whose life is it anyway (movie)

3–9
WRITE

Directions: Write sequentially numbered footnotes for the references in the following list. Note that the information has been scrambled; you must reorganize it and construct proper footnotes, numbering them from *1* to *5*. Refer back to the preceding descriptions of the proper formats for book and article footnotes. Follow the formats *precisely*!

1. an article entitled "Avoidance Behavior and the Development of Gastroduodenal Ulcers" in the first volume of *Journal of the Experimental Analysis of Behavior*; the date is 1958; the author is J. V. Brady; the quotation appears on page 70 of that issue of the journal
2. pages 77 to 79 of a book by David Kipnis called *The Powerholders*, published in 1976 by University of Chicago Press (located in the city of Chicago)
3. an article appearing in *American Sociological Review* (volume 27) in 1962; the quotation is on page 30 of the article; the author is R. E. Emerson; the title is "Power-Dependence Relations"
4. a reference to page 27 of a book entitled *Power and Poverty*, written by Peter Bachrach and Morton A. Baratz, published by Oxford University Press in the city of New York in 1970
5. a quotation appearing on page 427 of an article called "An Analysis of Control, Bases of Control, and Satisfaction in an Organizational Setting" by John Ivancevich; the article is found in the December 1970 issue of *Academy of Management Journal*

Citation Within a Text

Citation within a text is commonly used in the applied sciences and is presently accepted in the social sciences as well. Throughout the psychology textbook from which Resource Chapter A ("Motivation") is taken, for example, sources are credited informally.

DIRECT QUOTATIONS. When direct quotations are used, the source is ordinarily noted by giving only (1) the author's *family name*, (2) the *year* of publication, and (3) the *page number(s)*:

". . . there is a sense of being more substantial, of existing, of being real" (Davitz, 1970, 254–55).

If, however, the author's name is a necessary part of a sentence in the book—the subject or direct object of the sentence, for example—it is not repeated within parentheses, and *only the date and page(s)* are given. Moreover, when a direct quote by a certain author comes soon after the author's name has already been mentioned in a previous reference (that is, no other author has been mentioned in between), *only the page number* is given. Note how these two techniques are illustrated in the following sentence:

Thomas and Mayer (1973) feel that opportunities to be inactive are built into our automobile- and convenience-oriented culture. Their advice? "Walk, don't ride. Take the stairs, not the elevator" (p. 79).

INDIRECT QUOTATIONS. When indirect quotations are used, or when a source is simply referred to, the source is noted by giving only (1) the author's *family name* and (2) the *year* of publication. That is to say, no page number is given:

Although it is useful as a way of thinking about motives, Maslow's hierarchy of motives is a theory that is extremely difficult to test (Wahba & Bridwell, 1976).

If there are references to two sources written by the *same writer* in the *same year*, small letters are used to indicate this fact:

There are two fundamental theories as to why people become fat. One view, proposed by Stanley Schachter and his colleagues (1971a, 1971b), stresses the importance of food as a powerful stimulus affecting obesity.

In either case—direct or indirect quotations—at the end of the paper there is an alphabetical list of references to which the reader can refer if he or she wishes to pursue the reference. As you can see by comparing the two footnote forms, the advantage of the "citation within a text" system is its simplicity of form. The disadvantage is, of course, that the reader must turn to the end to find the full citation.

3–10
EXEMPLIFY / DISCUSS

Directions: In Resource Chapter A, refer to the last two paragraphs of the section entitled "Aggression," beginning at the bottom of page 239 with "Children's tendency to imitate aggressive behavior...". Discuss the following:

1. Why is only the date given in the first set of parentheses?
2. Does the second set of parentheses represent a direct or an indirect quotation? Why is only the page number given? Is this a different citation from that indicated by the first set of parentheses?
3. Does the third set of parentheses represent a direct or an indirect quotation?
4. Does the fourth set of parentheses represent a direct or an indirect quotation?
5. Does the fifth set of parentheses represent a direct or an indirect quotation? Why is only the page number given?

A final word of caution! While both of these methods for crediting sources—formal footnoting and citation within a text—are acceptable, it is always wise to check with your professor as to which method is preferred. Sometimes a specific guidebook is used as the standard form to be followed throughout a whole college or university. You will eventually have to refer to such a guidebook for the special format for citing unusual sources, such as unpublished papers or government documents.

Punctuating Quotations

The rules for punctuating quotations within the text of your paper depend on the length and thoroughness of the material taken from another source.

A SHORT DIRECT QUOTATION. If words, phrases, or even two to three short sentences are quoted directly from another source, they are incorporated directly into your paragraph and are enclosed in quotation marks. This is the case with the following short direct quotation, taken from Resource Chapter B:

Power is truly a neglected area of organizational behavior, and it may be correct to describe social scientists as having been "soft on power."[2]

A LONG DIRECT QUOTATION. If three or more long sentences are quoted, the material is *indented* and *single-spaced*. No quotation marks are used. The fact that this part of the paper is "set off" by indentation and different spacing is enough to indicate that it is quoted material. This is the case with the following long direct quotation, taken from Resource Chapter B:

Part of the problem lies in the connotation power has in a democratic society. Many believe that the overt desire for power is wrong.

In general, in American society at least . . . it is reprehensible to be concerned about having influence over others. . . . In our society in our time, and perhaps in all societies at all times, the exercise of power is viewed very negatively. People are suspicious of a man who wants power, even if he does so for sincere altruistic reasons. He is often socially conditioned to be suspicious of himself. He does not want to be in a position where he might be thought to be seeking power and influence in order to exploit others.[3]

AN INCOMPLETE DIRECT QUOTE. If, when you use a quotation, you leave out any part of it, even a single word, you indicate that the quotation is incomplete by using an *ellipsis* (. . .). This tells the reader that something has been omitted from the original quotation, and that the quotation you are using is not exactly the same as the original. If the omitted material includes the end of a sentence in the original, an extra dot should show this (. . . .).

Words, phrases, or even whole sentences may be omitted by using an ellipsis, but this may be done only when the quoted material *can be completely understood* without the omitted material and when that material *does not apply directly to the topic under discussion*. Note that ellipsis is used twice in the following incomplete direct quote, taken from Resource Chapter B:

The subject of Power has been described by Bertrand Russell as " . . . the fundamental concept in social science . . . , in the same sense in which Energy is the fundamental concept in physics."[1]

AN INDIRECT QUOTATION. An indirect quotation does not take any special punctuation. It is simply incorporated, *in paraphrased form*, into the text. If formal footnoting is used, the quote is followed by the number of the footnote. If informal crediting is used, the quote is followed by the citation in parentheses. In this example of an indirect quotation from Resource Chapter B (where formal footnoting is used), the footnote itself would cite the names of those researchers who have explored the power motive under discussion:

The evidence suggests that the amount of power an individual exercises is dependent largely on the strength of his or her power motive.[6]

Resource Chapter A, on the other hand, indicates an indirect quotation in the following manner:

It is important to remember that our standards of achievement are often biased by our culture (Maehr, 1974).

A NOTE ON PLAGIARISM

It is important for you to be aware that any time you use the words of another writer, *you must give credit to that writer by citing the work from which you have taken material* (either by formal or informal citation techniques). In addition, whenever you use even the *ideas* of another writer or even paraphrase those ideas, you must give credit to that writer. Those who do not credit their sources properly are guilty of the serious academic crime of *plagiarism*—that is, stealing the ideas, words, or research of someone else and representing them as their own. In many universities, students who are found guilty of committing plagiarism can be dismissed from the university.

In all fairness, it is sometimes difficult to decide what kind of information taken from other sources must be cited. This issue will be dealt with in the final chapter ("The Research Paper"). For the time being, keep in mind that any material you take from another source to develop your controlling idea or support your thesis *must be cited*!

LISTING REFERENCES

Whenever you use books or articles in writing a paper, you must list them at the end of the paper. This is true even if you have not quoted from them directly or indirectly. The purpose of this is to let the reader know what has influenced your thinking in the preparation of the paper. This list is called "References" if you have used the informal citation method; "Bibliography," if you have used formal footnoting. Once again, this list of source information must follow a particular format and must be arranged *in alphabetical order according to the authors' last (family) names*. Be aware, as you read the following book and article formats for bibliographic form, that unlike footnote formats, the first line is *not* indented; rather, it is the second and remaining lines which are indented. This is for the convenience of the reader, so that the family names can be easily identified. Note that the two formats present other differences as well.

Bibliographic Form—Book

Morris, Charles G. <u>Psychology</u>. 3rd ed. Englewood Cliffs, N.J.:
    Prentice-Hall, Inc., 1979.

Bibliographic Form—Article

McClelland, David C. "The Two Faces of Power." <u>Journal of International Affairs</u>,
    Vol. 24, No. 1 (1970), pp. 28–31.

Bibliographic Form—Chapter or Article by One Author
Reprinted in a Book by Another Author

Maccoby, Michael. "The New Manager: A Game-Player rather than a Power-Seeker." In
    Stephen P. Robbins. <u>Organizational Behavior</u>. Englewood Cliffs, N.J.: Prentice-Hall, Inc.,
    1979.

Once again, these forms are always acceptable in academic writing, whether you are compiling a list of References or a Bibliography, but you should check a *standard guidebook* for bibliographic forms for other types of sources (newspaper articles, unpublished articles, government documents, and so forth).

3–11
WRITE

Directions: Take the five footnotes you wrote for Exercise 3–9 and *write bibliographic entries for each of them*. Alphabetize your entries and arrange them in a list entitled *References*. In the case of two authors for a single source, alphabetize according to the family name which comes first in the alphabet.

3–12
WRITE

Directions: Following the suggestions in this chapter, *write a short paper* based on one of the following topics:

Topic 1

Choose the power base which you feel is the most effective (coercive power, reward power, expert power, legitimate power, or referent power). Discuss its effectiveness in terms of Maslow's needs hierarchy. Read Resource Chapter B (pp. 246–48) and Resource Chapter C (pp. 262–63) for information on this subject.

Topic 2

Different people place different values on the gain and exercise of power. Explain this statement in terms of motivational needs. Read Resource Chapter A (p. 241) and Resource Chapter B (pp. 248–50) for information on this subject.

Topic 3

Maccoby describes the new corporate executive as a "gamesman." Discuss this description in terms of Fiedler's research on situational factors that determine leadership. Read Resource Chapter B (the "counterpoint" article on pages 258–59 and Resource Chapter C (page 270).

Be sure to review the following guidelines before beginning your paper:

GUIDELINES FOR WRITING THE SHORT PAPER

1. Use one of the suggested introductory techniques.
2. Formulate a controlling idea (or thesis) and place it at the end of your introductory paragraph.
3. Search through the specified texts for information which will develop your controlling idea or support your thesis.
4. Feel free to use any of the other parts of the resource chapters with which you have become familiar.
5. When you quote directly or indirectly, use the techniques for "citation within a text"—i.e., do not use formal footnoting.
6. Use objective language.
7. Attempt to avoid overgeneralizing. Keep your language tentative.
8. Make sure that examples are well chosen and to the point.
9. Include a list of sources—*references*—at the end of the paper.

4 Coping with Longer Texts

IN THIS CHAPTER WE WILL CONCENTRATE ON SOME LONGER ORGANIZATIONAL PATTERNS common to most textbooks. After taking a closer look at the general organization of textbooks, we will examine formal and extended definitions. We will also introduce you to the basics of formal outlining.

TEXTBOOKS: GETTING AN OVERVIEW

The information in textbooks is arranged *deductively* for the most part. That is, the entire content of a textbook—particularly an introductory textbook of the type represented by the resource chapters at the back of this book—is divided systematically into progressively smaller units of information. Each of these units, or levels of generality, deals with a more limited amount of specific information. The highest, most general of these levels may be thought of as the entire book, as represented by the *title*; the lowest, as paragraphs or even sentences.

This progressive narrowing of focus is usually accomplished in a very orderly fashion. What an author actually calls the various levels differs somewhat from one textbook to another, but most authors use a system which resembles the following:

- a **book** is composed of *parts*
- **parts** are composed of *chapters*
- **chapters** are composed of *divisions* or *sections*
- **divisions** or **sections** are composed of *subdivisions* or *subsections*
- **subdivisions** or **subsections** are composed of *paragraphs*

This system may be visualized in terms of the same kind of "branching diagram" which we have been using up to this point.

It is important for you to realize that the notion of *controlling idea* can be applied to each of these units—from the entire book down to the paragraph. Each may be thought of as having a central idea, purpose, or aim which guides the arrangement of ideas at the next lowest level. The controlling idea of the book will, of course, be the most general and most complete; the controlling idea of a paragraph will be the most specific.

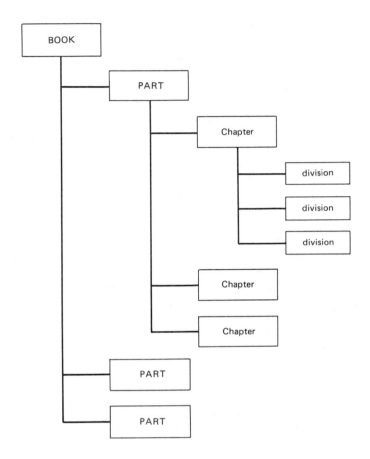

THOUGHT STRUCTURE VERSUS PHYSICAL STRUCTURE

A good way to gain an overview of a textbook's most general controlling ideas and their interrelationship is to make it a general practice, when you begin each of your course textbooks, to read the Preface from beginning to end and also to rapidly skim the Table of Contents. In the Preface, authors usually indicate the approach they have taken toward the subject matter, how they have organized material, and the most useful or original features of the book. Likewise, the Table of Contents, though it usually contains far too much material for you to assimilate at a glance, will at least give you a general idea of what to expect. Often the two will complement each other: the Preface will help prepare you for what you will find in the Table of Contents, or the Table of Contents will make more explicit what was only hinted at in the Preface.

Tables of Contents can, however, be misleading. Take, for example, the first page of Resource Chapter A, where the author gives the following small Table of Contents for the chapter:

Outline

Physiological Motives
   Hunger
   Thirst
   Sleep and Dreaming
   Pain
   Sex
   The Maternal Drive
Stimulus Motives
   Activity
   Exploration and Curiosity
   Manipulation
   Contact

Learned Motives
   Fear
   Aggression
   Social Motives
   Consistency
Unconscious Motives
A Hierarchy of Motives

Having read this "outline," an unsuspecting reader might expect four sections of the chapter to represent the thought relationship of formal classification (types of motives: physiological, stimulus, learned, and unconscious). No doubt the very physical arrangement of the titles and the four contrasting adjectives seem to be suggesting *implicit classification*. (The fifth section—"A Hierarchy of Motives"—by its very language, seems not to lend itself to the list.) Anyone who reads the chapter with this four-part classification in mind, however, will be impaired in understanding the author's intent.

4–1
EXEMPLIFY / DISCUSS

Directions: Referring to the chapter "outline," introduction, and section and subsection titles of Resource Chapter A, answer the following questions. Read only as much of the actual text as is necessary to be able to answer the questions.

A. Where does the author give a central description of the term *motivation* which can apply to the various kinds of motives presented in the chapter? What thought relationship dominates this description?

B. The author is using the device of implied classification in his "Outline" and chapter section titles and subsection titles. How many major units does he actually come up with? (In other words, how many major types of motives are there?)

C. Are *unconscious motives* a separate type? Why or why not?

D. How has the motive of "hunger" been subdivided? Do these subdivisions represent specific subtypes of hunger? If not, what do they represent?

E. Which of the "learned motives" have been subdivided? Do these subdivisions represent types, kinds, or specific members of a class? If not, what do they represent?

4–2
VISUALIZE

Directions: Using the information from the previous exercise, fill in the following general diagram of Resource Chapter A. As you work, note which of the major thought relationships of English are represented. Note, too, that the first "branch" of the diagram represents the important description of the motivation process given in the conclusion of the introduction; no other definitions or descriptions are represented.

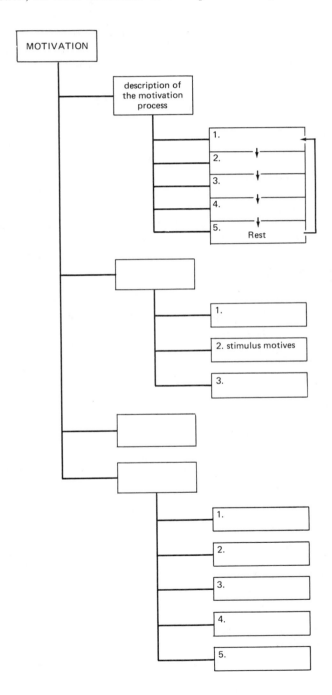

4–3
VISUALIZE

Directions: Construct a more detailed diagram of the first main section of Resource Chapter A ("Physiological Motives"). Include in your diagram the following terms:

Physiological mechanisms of hunger

Thirst

Physiological motives

Sex

Hunger

Learning and hunger

Sleep and dreaming

The maternal drive

Specific hungers

Pain

THE FORMAL OUTLINE

A formal academic outline, like the branching diagrams which we have been using, is a method of arranging ideas in a *visually meaningful way*. The main advantage of these kinds of graphic representations is that they are capable of representing levels of thought, as well as the thought relationships implied by those levels, in a manner which makes the multi-level structure immediately apparent to the reader. Thus, outlining and/or diagramming constitute excellent study tools in preparing for exams and other kinds of writing assignments.

There are basically two types of outlines, the **sentence outline** and the **topic outline**. In the first kind all items are written in complete sentences. More will be said about this type of outline in a later chapter; we will concentrate here on the topic outline.

Study the following topic outline. It represents a formal arrangement of the information which you have visualized in Exercise 4–2.

Motivation (Chapter 14)

   I. a description of the motivation process
      A. stimulus
      B. motive
      C. behavior
      D. goal attainment
      E. rest
  II. types of motives
      A. physiological
      B. stimulus
      C. learned
 III. unconscious motives
 IV. a hierarchy of motives
      A. physiological needs
      B. safety needs
      C. belongingness needs
      D. esteem needs
      E. self-actualization

Note the alternation of numerals and letters which has been used at the various levels: *roman numerals* (I, II, III, etc.) for the first level, *capital letters* (A, B, C, etc.) for the second level, *arabic numerals* (1, 2, 3, etc.) for the third level, and *small letters* (a, b, c, etc.) for the fourth level. If more levels are needed, the writer uses *arabic numerals in parentheses*—(1), (2), (3)—for the fifth level and *small letters in parentheses*—(a), (b), (c)—for the sixth level. Thus, a six-level outline might look something like this:

I. _____
  A. _____
     1. _____
     2. _____
     3. _____
        a. _____
        b. _____
           (1) _____
           (2) _____
              (a) _____
              (b) _____
           (3) _____
        c. _____
     4. _____
  B. _____
  C. _____
II. _____
  A. _____
  B. _____
  C. _____
(etc.)

Textual Coherence Through Grammatical Parallelism

Certain linking expressions in English (*and, or, but, either...or, not only...but also*, among others) require that the items they link be grammatically parallel. The structures thus joined may range from single words to whole sentences. Consider the following examples:

...other brain structures, such as *the limbic system* and *the temporal lobe*...
    (2 noun phrases)

...it is a physiological drive, just as *hunger, thirst,* and *pain* are....
    (3 nouns)

...elaborate rituals have grown up around *offering* and *accepting* food.
    (2 verbal forms having the same direct object)

...*visual, auditory,* and *tactile* sensory disorders....
    (3 adjectives)

The thirst drive *is controlled by delicate biochemical balances within the body,* and *has been linked to the level of salt (sodium chloride) in the blood stream.*
    (2 predicate structures, both in the passive construction)

Parallelism is, of course, partially a matter of stylistics. However, as can be seen in the preceding examples, it has another important function in written English. Like relationship signals, substitute forms, synonyms, and the other coherence devices we have studied, parallelism does much to insure textual coherence. It plays a subtle but crucial rule in letting the reader know how ideas have been organized and grouped together by the author.

Coherence Device: Parallelism

Note how parallelism helps the reader to perceive the relationship of enumeration in the following paragraph. Three members of the class "primary drives" are listed, followed by a partial definition of the terms, followed by three more members of the class.

For sheer survival, the body must have a certain amount of food , water , and sleep . Other basic physiological motives include the need to maintain proper body temperature , to eliminate wastes , and to avoid pain . We call these physiological motives *primary drives*. A primary drive is unlearned and common to every animal,
5 including humans. It expresses the need to sustain life. A certain physiological state—brought on by lack of food or sleep, cold, the presence of pain—activates these primary drives. How we behave once they have been triggered may be simply a reflex, like shivering when we are cold, or it may be the result of learning. Babies do not have to be taught to be hungry or sleepy, but they can learn to eat certain foods and to sleep at
10 certain times. All such behavior is aimed at reducing the state of arousal, but the patterns of that behavior may vary according to learning and experience.

Parallelism is also important in expressing certain relationships in outlines. To this end, all the items at a particular level of a topic outline can be put in grammatically parallel form to suggest such relationships as classification or process. In the chapter outline for "Motivation," for example, items A through E of Roman numeral I are all simple or compound nouns. Because of this similarity of form, these different *steps in a process* are more immediately apparent to the reader. These steps could, of course, have been expressed in a different but equally parallel form—abbreviated sentence form, for example. Compare the two versions that follow. Both express parallelism and, as such, both are of great help to the reader:

Parallel Noun Phrases	*Parallel Fragments*
A. stimulus	A. stimulus triggers motive
B. motive	B. motive activates behavior
C. behavior	C. behavior leads to goal attainment
D. goal attainment	D. goal attainment leads to rest
E. rest	

4–4
EXEMPLIFY / DISCUSS

A. Refer to the preceding sample text in the display.
    1. What examples of parallel structures do you find?
    2. What grammatical structures are involved?
    3. What thought relationships are involved?
B. Refer to the chapter outline for "Motivation."
    1. What grammatical structures are involved in the parallelism shown in Roman numerals II and IV?
    2. What thought relationships are involved?

4–5
VISUALIZE (OUTLINE)

Directions: Construct an outline based on your diagrams in the following exercises. Pay attention to *grammatical parallelism.*

A. Exercise 2–1
B. Exercise 2–20
C. Exercise 2–24

4–6
VISUALIZE (OUTLINE)

Directions: Using the information in Exercises 4–2 and 4–3, and the chapter outline for "Motivation," construct a general topic outline of Resource Chapter A ("Motivation"). You may use the following skeleton as your guide:

    I.

        A.

        B.

        C.

        D.

        E.

    II.

        A.

            1.

a.

b.

c.

2.

3.

4.

5.

6.

B.

1.

2.

3.

4.

C.

1.

2.

3.

a.

b.

c.

d.

4.

III.

IV.

A.

B.

C.

D.

E.

DEFINITIONS

Elements of Definition

To **define** a term is to give its meaning. Definition, by its very nature, involves at least three of the major thought relationships discussed in the second chapter: Since it deals with categorization, it implies classification, and this in turn implies both comparison and contrast.

Consider the word *psychology*, for example. In the first chapter of the psychology textbook from which the chapter "Motivation" has been taken, the author very carefully classifies this term so that it both resembles other members of its class and yet is different from them. First of all, psychology is a science—that is, it "seeks to *explain, predict*, and *control* what it studies."[1] In that sense, psychology is similar to every other science—physics, chemistry, biology, linguistics, sociology, and so forth. However, psychology is different from sciences like physics in that its focus is human behavior: it is a *behavioral* science, along with anthropology, sociology, and political science. And yet, though it is similar to these other behavioral sciences, it is still different from them in that the psychologist's outlook on human behavior can be distinguished from that of the sociologist, the anthropologist, or the political scientist. All this information can be stated fairly clearly in the following diagram:

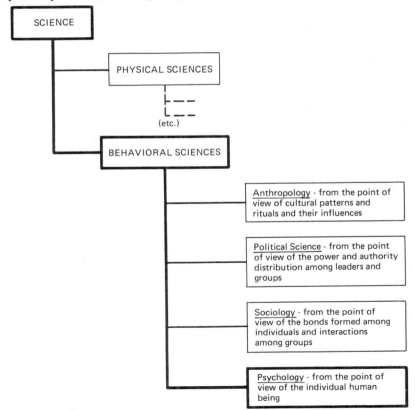

[1] *Psychology*, p. 5.

Formal Definitions

In the most formal kind of academic writing, the classic definition consists of three parts:

1. the *term* to be defined (in textbooks, this term is often printed in **boldface type**)
2. the *class* or *category* to which the term belongs (that is, what makes it similar to other members of the same class or category), and
3. the term's *distinguishing features*, including *subclasses* or *subcategories* (that is, what makes the term unique in its class, different from other members of the same class)

These three parts, or elements, are usually grouped together in the same sentence and stated for the reader in an obvious and predictable way:

TERM = CLASS + DISTINGUISHING FEATURES

In the following examples, note that between the term and the class, you usually find the verb *be*, or such alternative expressions as *can be defined as*, *may be described as*, *may be seen as*, *can be thought of as*, or *refers to*. Note also that the distinguishing features are phrased as full or reduced adjective clauses:

...psychology is a science that seeks to understand behavior and the factors involved in creating and influencing behavior.

...power-seeking is a neurotic behavior based on childhood deprivations.

A premise is a statement of the relationship between a cause and a consequence.

A committee may be defined as any group interacting in regard to a common, explicit purpose with formal authority delegated from an appointing executive.

Motivated forgetting refers to the inability to remember things that we do not want to remember.

Retrieval is the process by which we draw upon the information in memory.

Variations on the above pattern are numerous and range from a simple rearranging of elements to more implicit types of definitions. A few of the most common of these variations are presented for your analysis in the exercise which follows.

4–7
EXEMPLIFY / DISCUSS

Directions: Study the following definitions. All of them represent variations on the standard form. Which of the definitions represent the following:

- omission of the connecting word (the verb)
- reversal of elements (class + distinguishing features = term)
- omission of the class

Note, in particular, the use of *or*, dashes (—), commas, the expression *that is*, and *if*-clauses. Supply the class if it is missing.

1. Those psychologists who have applied basic knowledge in the subdisciplines of motivation, learning, and personality to an understanding of work behavior in organizations have identified themselves as industrial psychologists. . . . (From *Essentials of Management*, p. 136.)

2. Psychosurgery, operating on the brain to change a person's behavior, was introduced at the close of the nineteenth century. (From *Psychology*, p. 47.)

3. **Computer programmers** (people who write instructions for computers) and **systems analysts** (people who analyze problems and recommend solutions) designed and implemented the applications by studying the problems, designing new systems, and creating computer programs to perform essentially the same tasks that clerks previously performed. (From *Essentials of Management*, p. 174.)

4. When we use the phrase "systematic study," we mean looking at relationships, attempting to attribute causes and effects, and basing our conclusions on scientific evidence—that is, data gathered under controlled conditions and measured and interpreted in a reasonably rigorous manner. (From *Organizational Behavior*, p. 5.)

5. The function of memory is retention, or holding on to events and information from the past. (From *Psychology*, p. 184.)

6. A recent development in world business is the multinational or global company—a corporation which maintains world headquarters in one country but performs production, marketing, finance, and personnel functions within many nations. (From *Essentials of Management*, p. 46.)

7. Overlapping somewhat with the interests of industrial psychologists are the concerns of industrial sociologists, who have applied basic knowledge in the field of sociology to an understanding of the behavior of individuals in formal and informal groups. (From *Essentials of Management*, p. 136.)

8. If previous information or experience interferes with the retrieval of something we have learned more recently, we speak of proactive inhibition. . . . Retroactive inhibition, on the other hand, is caused by items that have been learned *after* what we are trying to remember. (From *Psychology*, pp. 198–99.)

4–8
WRITE

Directions: Six of the following items contain elements of definition, while four do not. (Remember that parentheses, dashes, and *if*-clauses are not always used in English to define.) Convert the six appropriate items to *formal definitions* by using the classic formula (term = class + distinguishing features).

Example: Still another kind of stress is frustration. In frustration an individual is somehow prevented from reaching a goal—something or someone is in the way.

Formal definition: Frustration is a kind of stress in which an individual is somehow prevented from reaching a goal.

1. Concern about power does not automatically render one a Machiavelli—that is, manipulative to the extent that one will disregard the rules of fairness and equity, ethical considerations, and allow the ends always to justify the means. (From *Organizational Behavior*, pp. 262–63.)

2. In order to retrieve information from short-term memory, we have to go through all the items being held in it in order until we find the one we want—a process called serial scanning. (From *Psychology*, p. 193.)

3. Maslow believed that the most highly "evolved" motive in the hierarchy is self-actualization. This may be described as a desire to make the best one can out of oneself. (From *Psychology*, p. 379.)

4. Disasters—floods, droughts, epidemics, and war—cause drastic changes in people's lives. (From *Psychology*, p. 457.)

5. If a decision provides help for decisions in other situations, it is said to be a policy decision, because it sets a precedent and provides some guide for decision making in the future. (From *Essentials of Management*, p. 61.)

6. When a person models himself or herself after someone else by assuming the characteristics, values, attitudes or mannerisms of the other person, we refer to the behavior as identification. (From *Organizational Behavior*, p. 77.)

7. When people with legitimacy speak (school principals, police captains, bank presidents, or city building inspectors), teachers, policemen, tellers, and building contractors listen and usually obey. (From *Organizational Behavior*, p. 266.)

8. Although computers were originally designed for mathematical calculation, the twelve business firms which used computers in 1954 used them primarily to process accounting and statistical data and to perform data reduction (summarizing or reducing large volumes of data to a significantly smaller amount). (From *Essentials of Management*, p. 174.)

9. The chief characteristic of management is the integration and application of the knowledge and analytical approaches developed by numerous disciplines. (From *Essentials of Management*, p. 4.)

10. You leave for a weekend trip, suitcase in hand, but you are troubled by the vague feeling that you have forgotten something—and more often than not, you have. (From *Psychology*, p. 195.)

4–9
WRITE

Directions: Write short formal definitions for the following terms from Resource Chapter A. If the terms are not defined in the text in formal fashion, you will have to rearrange elements and/or add words in order to come up with formal definitions. For example, if no class is specifically stated, you must find one— that is, decide whether the term represents a process, a chemical agent, a mechanism, a plant, or a type of motive, for example. Make sure, when you write each definition, that you adequately distinguish the term from other members of its class. (This is particularly important in the case of the first three items on the list.) Read the appropriate sections of the text very carefully before attempting your definitions, and <u>underline</u> the terms in your definitions.

primary drives	the frustration-aggression hypothesis
stimulus motives	manipulation
social motives	glucagon
the power motive	a "sweet tooth"
cognitive dissonance	the thirst satiety center

A Flexible Pattern: The Extended Definition

Given the variety of relationships possible in the act of defining a term, it is natural for a textbook writer to want to expand a short formal definition into a longer type of definition, providing further explanation and a greater variety of detail. This longer kind of definition is called an **extended definition**. There is no one particular pattern to which an extended definition must conform; all depends on the term being defined and the author who is writing the definition. There are, however, certain recurring elements in extended definitions. These include, of course, any of the major thought relationships, even exemplification. Indeed, an extended definition may include *all* of them, and repeat some or all of them at any of the various levels of generality.

Thus, a term could be defined formally, then divided into three types (enumeration), each of which involves a set of steps (process) which, although somewhat similar to the other two processes (comparison), remains fundamentally different from them (contrast) for several reasons (enumeration, causality); moreover, each main type might possibly be further divided into subtypes (enumeration), and this might entail further divisions, causal chains, similarities, differences, and so on.

Moreover, the major thought relationships can be combined with any or all of the following techniques common to many extended definitions:

1. *An analysis of the parts*: After defining a term, an author feels that it is necessary to define certain terms that are part of the main definition
2. *A negative definition*: An author states what a term is by first telling what it *is not*
3. *A stipulated definition*: (a) An author restricts the meaning of a term to a certain field or to certain circumstances; (b) of a number of possible ways of defining the term, the author opts for one rather than for the others; or (c) rejecting all known definitions of the term, the author proceeds to create a personal definition, which is felt to be more appropriate.

The importance of definition in academic writing cannot be overemphasized. Evidence of this importance is the special place given to definition by the writers of most textbooks. On page after page, you will find words in **boldface type**—a signal that the author is in the act of defining a key concept for the reader.

Indeed, an author sometimes feels that understanding a term is so crucial that he or she will devote a short section of a chapter to the term, giving that section a title indicative of definition. Such is the case, for example, in the following selection taken from a chapter called "Personality" in a textbook on organizational behavior. Aside from the causality implicit in the definition, as well as an enumeration of its principal parts, the text depends heavily on the contrasts drawn between various popular definitions of the term *personality* and the one the author feels is more appropriate in this particular context.

What Is Personality?

When we talk of personality, we do not mean that a person has charm, a pleasant attitude toward life, a smiling face, or is a finalist for "Happiest and Friendliest" in this year's Miss America contest. When psychologists talk of personality, they mean a dynamic concept describing the growth and development of a person's whole psychologi-
5 cal system. Rather than looking at parts of the person, personality looks at some aggregate whole that is greater than the sum of the parts.

The most frequently used definition of personality was produced by Gordon Allport over forty years ago. He said personality is "the dynamic organization within the individual of those psycho-physical systems that determine his unique adjustments to his
10 environment."

Personality can be described more specifically as "how a person affects others, how he understands and views himself, and his pattern of inner and outer measurable traits." In this definition, how a person affects others refers to his physical appearance and behavior. Understanding oneself refers to an awareness that each of us is a unique being with a set of
15 attitudes and values, and that we each have a self-concept that is the result of successive interactions with the environment. Finally, the pattern of measurable traits refers to a set of characteristics that the person exhibits. (From *Organizational Behavior*, pp. 62–63.)

Extended definitions are so common, particularly in introductory textbooks in nearly all fields, that chapter sections or subsections—or even *entire chapters*—may constitute long extended definitions, in which terms are discussed from all the points of view and with as much detail as the author feels is pertinent. Resource Chapter A ("Motivation") is, in reality, such a definition; the diagrams and outlines which you have constructed for this chapter are good indications of the variety and the complexity which this kind of pattern can manifest.

4–10
EXEMPLIFY / DISCUSS

Directions: Analyze and discuss all of the extended definitions in each of the six excerpts in terms of the following questions:

A. Which contain *stipulated definitions*?
B. Which contain *formal definitions*?
C. Which contain *negative (inverse) definitions*?
D. Which definitions seem the most effective? Why?

1. What is learning? A psychologist's definition is considerably broader than the laymen's view that "it's what we did when we went to school." In actuality, each of us is

continuously going "to school." Learning is going on all the time. A generally accepted definition of learning is, therefore, *any relatively permanent change in behavior that*
5   *occurs as a result of experience.* Ironically, we can say that changes in behavior indicate learning has taken place, and that learning is a change in behavior.

Obviously, the above definition suggests that we shall never see someone "learning." We can see changes, but not the learning itself. The concept is theoretical and hence not directly observable. (From *Organizational Behavior*, p. 147.)

2. Another recent structural approach toward increasing workers' freedom, satisfaction, and productivity is flex-time. Flex-time is a system whereby employees contract to work a specific number of hours a week, but are free to vary the hours of work within certain limits. Each day consists of a common core, usually six hours, with a flexibility
5   band surrounding the core. For example, the core may be 10:00 A.M. to 4:00 P.M., with the office actually opening at 7:30 A.M. and closing at 6:00 P.M. All employees are required to be at their jobs during the common core period, but they are allowed to accumulate their other two hours before and/or after the core time. Some flex-time programs allow extra hours to be accumulated and turned into a free day off each month.
10 Under flex-time, employees assume responsibility for completing a specific job, and that increases their feeling of self-worth. It is consistent with the view that people are paid for producing work, not for being at their job stations for a set period of hours; hence its motivational aspects.

Flex-time has been implemented in a number of diverse organizations, such as
15 Firestone Tire and Rubber, Gulf Oil of Canada, First National Bank of Boston, and the U.S. Social Security Administration. Response to the concept has generally been favorable. An evaluation of Mutual of New York's flex-time program rated it very successful. There was an increase in employee productivity, fewer errors, improved employee morale, and a significant reduction in lateness and absenteeism. (From
20 *Organizational Behavior*, p. 382.)

3. *Sensitivity Training*

It can go by a variety of names—laboratory training, sensitivity training, encounter groups, or T-groups (training groups)— but all refer to a method of changing behavior through unstructured group interaction. Members are brought together in a free and open
5   environment in which participants discuss themselves and their interactive processes, loosely directed by a professional behavioral scientist. The group is process-oriented, which means that individuals learn through observing and participating rather than being told. The professional creates the opportunity for participants to express their ideas, beliefs, and attitudes. He or she does not accept—in fact, overtly rejects—any leadership
10 role.

The objectives of the T-groups are to provide the subjects with increased awareness of their own behavior and how others perceive them, greater sensitivity to the behavior of others, and increased understanding of group processes. Specific results sought include increased ability to empathize with others, improved listening skills, greater openness,
15 increased tolerance of individual differences, and improved conflict resolution skills. (From *Organizational Behavior*, p. 383.)

4. A second form of popular government is called indirect democracy, representative democracy, or *republic*. Each of these terms refers to the same system. Because the nation's founders used the term *republic* to describe the indirect form of democracy, we

shall also. However, the word *republic* originally did not necessarily refer to a democratic
5 system. It simply meant "government without a king." The Roman Republic, for
example, was governed by the aristocratic class (patricians) through the Senate, but most
of the citizens of Rome (plebeians) could not serve in the Senate. Though it was certainly
not a democracy, this system was a republic simply because it was not ruled by a king.
    British law still uses the traditional definition of republic. There are two kinds of
10 members of its commonwealth. Countries that choose their own head of state, such as
India and Nigeria, are *republican* members of the commonwealth. The nonrepublican
members are those that accept the British monarch as their head of state. They include
Canada, Australia, and New Zealand.
    The term *republic* has taken on a somewhat different meaning in the United States. The
15 word is used in the Constitution and was explained by James Madison in *The Federalist*
(no. 10). Madison made it clear that *republic* referred to a government of elected
representatives who were responsible to the people to some extent. Hence, the term
republic actually means "democratic republic" in American constitutional law, and the
courts have ruled accordingly in the past. A democratic republic is an indirect form of
20 democracy. Instead of the people making the laws themselves, they elect legislators to do
it for them. Thus the people are removed one step from the legislative process, and their
relationship to the policy-making process is less direct than under the pure form of
democracy. (From *Political Ideologies*, pp. 105–106.)

5. *Halo Effect*
    When we draw a general impression about an individual based on a single characteristic
like intelligence, sociability, or appearance, a halo effect is operating. This phenomenon
frequently occurs when students appraise their classroom instructor. Students may isolate
5 a single trait, such as enthusiasm, and allow their entire evaluation to be tainted by how
they judge the instructor on this one trait. Thus, an instructor may be quiet, assured,
knowledgeable and highly qualified, but if his style lacks zeal, he will be rated lower on a
number of other characteristics. (From *Organizational Behavior*, pp. 97–98.)

6. The term *nation* is often used as a synonym for *state* or *country*. This is not
technically correct, but the mistake is commonly made by political leaders as well as by
ordinary people. To be precise, the term *nation* does not have any political implication.
Indeed, the concept of a nation is not political at all but social. A nation can exist even
5 though it is not contained within a particular state or served by a given government. A
nation exists when there is a union of people based on a linguistic pattern, an ethnic
relationship, cultural similarities, or even geographic proximity.
    The American Indians, for instance, were divided into several nations. The people in
these nations were not related to one another. The national grouping was based on
10 linguistic similarities between certain tribes. The Algonquian nation, for example,
extended from North Carolina to Hudson Bay and from the Atlantic coast to the Rocky
Mountains. The people in this Indian nation belonged to any of a number of tribes that
were not necessarily related by blood. People of the Arapaho, Massachusett, Blackfoot,
Micmac, Cheyenne, and Delaware tribes were all members of the Algonquian nation, yet
15 they had no common government.
    Probably the most common feature around which a nation is united is ethnic in nature.
One's *nationality* is often expressed in terms of ethnic background rather than citizenship.
Thus while some people will respond "American" when asked their nationality, it is not

uncommon for loyal U.S. citizens to answer "Dutch" or "Spanish" or "Latvian." These
20 individuals are thinking of nationality as a social or ethnic term, not making a political
comment. The fact that ethnic background can be the basis of a nation does not, however,
mean that people must be related by blood to be members of the same nation, as the
example of the Algonquian nation shows. Switzerland, the United States, and the Soviet
Union all include several ethnic groups. In fact the Soviet Union contains about
25 107 separate and distinct ethnic groups. It is divided into 15 union republics and several
autonomous areas that reflect the territories of its most important ethnic groups. (From
Political Ideologies, pp. 37–38.)

4–11
WRITE

Directions: Write an *extended definition* of a term which is central to the subject matter
in another course you are taking this term. The term you choose to define may require any
or all of the following:

A. *Stipulation*—a definition of the way the term is used in that particular field, as opposed to
   its general meaning
B. *Negation*—defining it by first saying what it does *not* mean
C. *Analysis of the parts*—defining or explaining certain terms within the definition itself

It may also require use of one or two of the *major thought relationships* (for example,
enumeration, causality, comparison, contrast, process, spatial order, chronology, or
exemplification).

PROOFREADING YOUR ACADEMIC PAPERS

The importance of accuracy in language usage in an academic environment cannot be
overstated. When you are speaking, it is difficult for you to monitor each word, phrase,
and sentence you utter. As a result, you may be making a number of usage errors in
speech, but these rarely interfere with the total meaning of your ideas because your
listener has the advantage of being able to pose questions if your meaning becomes
obscured. The reader of your paper, however, has no such advantage, so that you must
make every effort to refine what you have written so as to avoid confusion or
misinterpretation. You should, therefore, take the time to proofread anything you have
written for usage errors *before* you prepare the final version of the paper. The longer the
piece of writing, the greater the possibility that you have made language errors.
    The kinds of usage errors which you could potentially make are endless. As you
become more experienced in writing in English, you will no doubt come to recognize the
special areas which are a problem for you personally. Among the many possibilities, we
will discuss a limited number of the most common types of errors. We will divide them
according to the difficulty you might have in locating them when you are proofreading.

I. Sentence-Level Errors which Are Easily Identified

There are a number of sentence-level usage errors which you should be able to identify and eliminate without great difficulty. These types of errors are generally made through carelessness or haste and concern basic rules of English usage.

A. *NUMBER ERRORS—SINGULAR/PLURAL AGREEMENT*

Examples	*Corrections*
A third important line of research and theoretical development over the last *30 year* combines the work of applied sociologists and psychologists.	*30 years*
Leadership has long been considered one of the most important *factor* influencing organizational performance and achievement of goals.	*factors*

B. *SUBJECT-VERB AGREEMENT*

Examples	*Corrections*
Although a great number of definitions of leadership *has* been proposed over the years, we can say that leadership is the practice of influence.	*have*
For example, is there any optimal combination of traits that *are* most critical in determining one's success as a leader?	*is*

C. *PREPOSITION/VERB FORM*

Examples	*Corrections*
Leadership is thus an important part *to study* in management.	*of study*
It was not until a sociological view of the problem was *combine* with a psychological approach that headway was made.	*combined*
The subordinates were required *filling out* a questionnaire to describe the leader's behavior.	*to fill out*

D. *WORD FORM*

Examples	*Corrections*
The primary emphasis of early research on leadership was *psychologically* and focused on the personality characteristics *typical* found among *success* leaders.	*psychological* *typically, successful*

E. *SPELLING²*

Examples   *Corrections*

Thus, leadership is a process through *wich* the *performance* of   *which, performance*
others is influenced by a person *ocupying* a leadership *roll*.   *occupying, role*

4–12
PROOFREAD

Directions: Proofread the following text for usage errors in each of the five categories
just exemplified. Draw a line through the error and write the correction above it.

In all this entrepreneurial flurry two major questions went unasnwered: 1) How do we
know when a leader is effective?, and 2) What factors determine whether or not a given
style of leadership behavior will be effective? Reliable answers to the first question
remains the subject of continuing research. The problem is that the goals of a leader are
5 many, and each constitute a valid demension of leader effectiveness. At the very least, we
can say that the following are elements of leader effectivenss: a) individual effectiveness
of subordinates to accomplish their tasks, b) the productive or efficiency of groups of
subordinates to accomplish their tasks, c) the morale or satisfaction of subordinates, and
d) the quality of products or services generated by subordinate groups.

10   Fortunately, research on what consitutes the most effective leadership style has become
the topic of serious research efforts during the 1970's. Two such effort deserve our
particular attention: 1) the work of Fred Fiedler, and 2) the path-goal theory of leadership.
Building on the results of the Ohio State studys, Fiedler reasoned that there was probably
no single best leader style to fit all work situations. His research has identify all three
15 major situational factor that determine the appropriate of a given leadership style.

² Most professors consider spelling errors inexcusable on the grounds that it is very easy to check on the
correct spelling of a word if you are uncertain of it.

II. Sentence-Level Errors More Difficult to Identify

As you write longer, more complex sentences, you may begin to make another kind of error, one having to do with whether a group of words does or does not form a sentence. These errors fall into two categories: the sentence fragment and the run-on sentence (or comma splice). It is important for you to learn to look for them and correct them in your writing because they can create serious misunderstanding of your ideas.

A. THE SENTENCE FRAGMENT

A sentence fragment is a group of words that ends with a period but does not form a complete sentence. The fragment does not constitute a complete sentence because a subject, a predicate, or an independent clause is missing.

1. *Subject missing*	*Correction*
Is[3] defined as any group interacting in regard to a common, explicit purpose with formal authority delegated from an appointing executive.	*It is* or *A committee is*
2. *Predicate missing*	*Correction*
Those psychologists who have applied basic knowledge in the subdisciplines of motivation, learning and personality to an understanding of work behavior in organizations.	(long adjective clause) *...are called industrial psychologists.*
3. *Independent clause missing*	*Correction*
Because it maintains world headquarters in one country but performs production, marketing, finance and personnel functions within many nations.	(long adverbial clause) *...a corporation may be termed multinational.*

B. THE RUN-ON SENTENCE/COMMA SPLICE

A run-on sentence is two complete sentences written together without any punctuation to separate them. When a comma is used instead of a period to separate two complete sentences, it is called a comma-splice.

1. *Run-on*	*Correction*
We can see changes, but not learning itself the concept is theoretical and hence not directly observable.	Period (.) or semicolon (;) after "itself"

---

[3] The deletion of "it" in the expression "it is" is common among Romance language speakers. They, in particular, should proofread for this error.

2. ***Comma-splice***   ***Correction***

In fact, the Soviet Union contains about 107 separate and   Delete comma (,)
distinct ethnic groups, it is divided into 15 union republics and   Period (.) or semico-
several autonomous areas.   lon (;) after "groups"

4–13
PROOFREAD

Directions: Proofread the following text for sentence fragments, run-on sentences, and comma-splices. Add the required punctuation.

This model has been labeled a *Path-Goal Theory* of leadership effectiveness. Because it proposes that a leader's choice of these behaviors should be premised upon a goal of increasing personal payoffs to subordinates for work-goal attainment, and on making the path to these payoffs as free of obstacles as possible. The path-goal model, furthermore, is

5   a contingency model, in that it posits that the appropriate mix of such leader behaviors depends on two major sets of factors: (a) the individuals being supervised, and (b) the characteristics of the work environment.

Individual characteristics influencing the impact of leader behavior are the following: (1) Ability—the greater the employee's perceived level of ability to accomplish a task, the

10   less the individual will accept direction or instrumental behavior on the part of the leader. (2) Locus of control—this is the degree to which employees believe they have control over what happens to them. Those who believe that they have a great deal of control over what happens to them are said to react more favorably to a participative leader, others would prefer a more directive leader. (3) Needs and motives—the particular set of needs

15   that are felt strongly by an employee will affect the impact of a particular set of leader behaviors on that person's performance. People with a high need for autonomy will probably react negatively to instrumental kinds of leader behavior.

A number of organizational characteristics, in addition to subordinates, are also proposed by path-goal theory as influences on the effectiveness of leader behavior

20   specifically, three broad groups of work environment properties have been studied: (1) subordinates' tasks—the degree of structure involved in work operations; (2) the work group—informal work group norms and cohesiveness; and (3) organizational factors— stress levels in the work situation, situations involving high uncertainty, and the degree to which rules, procedures and policies govern an employee's work.

25   A full explication of contingency leadership theories is beyond the scope of this chapter. Is important, however, to note that present research on the topic of leadership is just now beginning to yield an understanding of the complexities of leadership phenomena. The practice of leadership involves elements of the leader's own personality and behavior, complex relationships between the leader and subordinates, informal group

30   characteristics and a variety of characteristics of the formal environment within which work activities are carried out, any formula, then, that proposed to make one an effective leader by adopting a single style is hopelessly wrong, and anyone purporting to sell such a formula is no more of a help than were the snake oil salesmen of 70 or more years ago.

5 The Summary

OF ALL THE WRITING SKILLS YOU WILL NEED AS A STUDENT, one of the most useful is the ability to write a summary. A summary is a short version of a text; its purpose is to give the reader a clear idea of the most important information in that text. A summary can be of any length, depending upon the student's goal in writing it. Summaries generally range from one sentence to about one-fourth the length of the original. A final characteristic of summaries is that they are written in *your own words* rather than copied from the original. Thus, to become an effective summary writer, you must polish the skill of *paraphrasing*, which you have been practicing in limited ways up to this point.

WHY LEARN TO SUMMARIZE?

There are several good reasons why a student should want to become proficient at summary writing. In the first place, it is a valuable *study technique*. Students who get into the habit of summarizing on paper what they have read end up with a clearer understanding of the material. Likewise, writing down summaries of what has just been heard in a class lecture helps to show students how well they have understood what has been said, and it forces them to crystallize and organize their thoughts about the lecture.

Summary writing thus becomes an invaluable tool in *studying for examinations*. Since exams usually cover the important points in a subject area, the summarizing of texts and lectures represents a very efficient way to prepare for these exams. Rather than rereading all the material covered—sometimes hundreds of pages—students can refresh their memory on the major points covered, then refer selectively to texts and notes from lectures in those areas where there are still problems.

In addition, many professors require *formal summaries* of articles, sometimes as many as one a week. A student who has a good grasp of what is involved in writing a summary will have less difficulty with this kind of assignment than one who has never had systematic practice in summary writing. (Note: many professors will not teach students how to write summaries—they expect students to know how.) However, even when formal summary assignments are not required in a course, summaries frequently serve as the basis for longer writing assignments—reports, reviews, term papers, and so on.

Thus, a knowledge of the principles of good summary writing makes a student more careful both as a reader and as a writer.

WHAT TO INCLUDE IN A SUMMARY

In order to write a good summary, it is first necessary to thoroughly understand the text to be summarized. Use a dictionary to clarify the meanings of unfamiliar words or phrases. Two or more readings may well be required: the first should be devoted to understanding the author's controlling idea or thesis, as well as the purpose of the text; subsequent readings can then serve to help you gain a better grasp of the details of the text.

Once you have read—and *reread!*—the text and are satisfied that you have understood what the author is trying to say, you should decide how much of this information will go into your summary. This is always a difficult decision to make, of course, and your choice will depend to some extent on the length and purpose of your summary. However, some general guidelines can be given.

A Good Summary Usually Includes:

1. the controlling idea
2. the major thought relationships used by the author to provide support
3. any important definitions of key terms (the use of informal definition techniques* are particularly effective in giving short definitions in a summary)
4. an indication of the author's attitude toward the subject matter—is the author describing, praising, or criticizing? is he certain or uncertain about what is being discussed?

The thought relationship of exemplification deserves special consideration. Ordinarily, minor examples and details are *not* included in a summary; on the other hand, there are situations where certain examples and details *should* be included. The guidelines which follow can help you to determine when examples might be included in a summary and when it might be better to omit them.

- In a very short summary (a one-sentence summary, for example) restate only the controlling idea; mention *no* examples or details.
- As your summary gets longer, you can include more of everything: a lengthier version of the controlling idea and of the primary thought relationships, as well as some examples or details.
- If a text is made up almost entirely of examples, a few should be included in even a moderately short summary so as to accurately reflect the original text; choose only the ones that you consider to be most representative of the author's thought.
- If the concepts in the text are so complex that the summary could not be understood without examples, include a few.

5–1
EXEMPLIFY / DISCUSS

Directions: Study the following text and the summary which appears beside it. Identify the thought relationships in the original text and determine which of these thought relationships are included in the summary. Pay particular attention to the thought relationship of exemplification.

---

* Dashes, commas, parentheses, *i.e., that is,* and *or* (see Chapter 4, pp. 116–17).

Language Development

Of all the changes a child goes through, none is more dramatic than the acquisition of language. Like motor abilities and perception, language depends on both physical maturation (control of the muscles that move the mouth and tongue) and experience.

At about 2 months the infant begins cooing (a rather nondescript word for rather nondescript sounds). In another month or two the infant enters the "babbling" stage and starts to repeat sounds. Gradually the infant's babbling begins to resemble the rhythms of adult speech. Between 8 and 10 months, infants seem to take special pleasure in "talking" aloud to themselves as they work at grabbing hold of things and crawling. Vocalization at this age is still primarily nonsocial. Soon, however, infants begin to imitate sounds and to use their voices to get attention. By 10 or 11 months, they show signs of understanding things said to them. At about 12 months infants utter their first word, usually "mama," "dada" or "papa." During the next 6 to 8 months they build a vocabulary of one-word sentences: (Pick me) "Up!"; (I want to go) "Out!"; (Tickle me) "Again!" They may also use a number of compound words, such as "Awgone" (all gone.) To these they add greetings—"Bye-bye" being a favorite—and a few exclamations such as "Ouch!" Most small children are also interested in possessives: (The shoes are) "Davy's." But perhaps the overwhelming passion of 2-year-olds is naming. At play the child will say the word "block," for example, over and over again looking for parent approval each time.

Soon the child begins to formulate two- and three-word sentences of nouns and attributes. Typical beginner's sentences are "Baby crying," "My ball," "Dog barking." A number of psychologists have recorded mother-child dialogs at this age to see just what children pick up and what they omit. Most noticeably, children at this age omit

Summary

In discussing childhood in Chapter 2 of *Psychology*, Charles G. Morris says that language acquisition is among the most dramatic transformations a child undergoes. It is dependent on bodily development as well as practical knowledge. When a baby is about 2 months old, it starts to make a nondescript cooing sound. A month or so later, it begins to babble, slowly beginning to imitate the cadence of adult speech. In approximately 6 months, babies enjoy "talking" aloud, although these sounds are not truly communicative. Imitation of sound and vocalization follow this stage, during which the child begins to understand what is said. A baby will say its first word, perhaps "mama," about the time it is a year old. Between 18 and 24 months, a child will have added one-word sentences, e.g., (Pick me) "Up!" Formulation of 2- and 3-word sentences follows shortly. Research has shown that at this stage, children omit words not emphasized in their parents' speech.

auxiliary verbs (can) "I have that?" "I (am) eating it" and prepositions and articles—"It (is) time (for) Sara (to) take (a) nap?" Apparently children grab hold of the most important words, probably the words their parents stress.

Notice how certain kinds of information are treated in the previous summary:

1. Most of the examples and details used to clarify or illustrate a point are *left out*.
2. Since there were so many illustrative examples in the original text, and since the writer felt that they might help the reader understand exactly what was being discussed, a few were included (not all!).
3. So that the examples would not overshadow the points which they exemplify, the writer tried to confine them, in large measure, to phrases or parenthetical structures.
   - *such as* (a prepositional phrase): ...one-word sentences *such as* (Pick me) "Up!"
   - *like* (a prepositional phrase): ...one-word sentences *like* (Pick me) "Up!"
   - *parentheses* (punctuation): ...one word sentences (Pick me "Up!")

SPECIAL CONSIDERATIONS

The First Sentence

The first step in writing a formal summary is to acquaint your reader with the exact source of the material. This includes the <u>author</u> and <u>title</u> (if there is one) of the text. This is normally done in the first sentence of a formal summary.

Examples of possible first-sentence openings are given in the following list. They are all effective beginnings for a summary. Notice that the first one refers to an article in a magazine, journal, or newspaper; the second, to a chapter of a book; the third, to a report; the fourth, to an article whose author is unknown.

Summary Beginnings

1. Jeffrey Pfeiffer, in his article "The Ambiguity of Leadership," [states / explains / says / argues / describes]...
2. In the seventh chapter of his book *Psychology*, author Charles G. Morris [states / explains / says / argues / describes]...
3. According to Gilbert Couts in his report entitled "Working Conditions and Their Effects on Employees," (+ Controlling Idea)...
4. The author of "Barriers to Communication" [states / explains / says / argues / describes]...

The rest of the first sentence should be as brief and to the point as possible. It should contain, of course, the <u>controlling idea</u> of the text to be summarized. This is very important, since the purpose of this first sentence is to give the reader a quick overview of the entire text. Even when the development in the original text is inductive, the controlling idea should appear in the first sentence of a summary.

5–2
WRITE

Directions: After reading the following text, write the first sentence of a summary of that text. Be sure the following elements are included:

1. The name of the author
2. The source
3. The controlling idea of the text

Are Firstborns Better?

Freud, Kant, Beethoven, Dante, Einstein and Julius Caesar—what do they have in common? All of these eminent men were firstborn children. Although many later-born children also become famous, certain studies hint that a firstborn child is more likely to excel. For example, more firstborns become National Merit Scholars, earn doctor's degrees and rate mention in *Who's Who*.

Researchers suggest several explanations for the higher achievement of firstborns. Some believe that the reason is simply that firstborns are more likely than other children to attend college. They argue that economic factors alone could account for this difference, although firstborns typically get high grades *before* college as well.

Others suggest that firstborn children have a higher need to achieve (Rosen, 1964). This need to achieve may be an outcome of the special relationship between firstborn children and their parents. Firstborns have their parents' exclusive attention and seem to interact more with parents than other children (Gewirtz & Gewirtz, 1965). Parents of firstborns also seem to expect more of them (Hilton, 1967). As a result, firstborns may seek approval by conforming to adult standards, including standards of achievement.

Whatever the reasons, firstborn children do tend to be more conforming, shyer, more anxious than their siblings—and more likely to outdo them. (From *Psychology*, p. 101.)

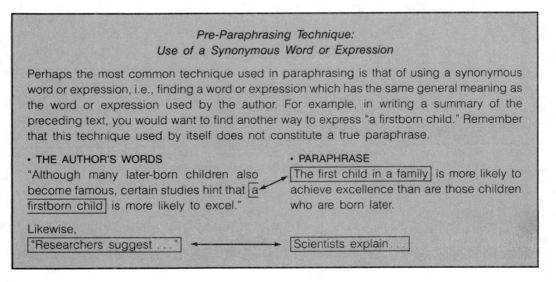

Pre-Paraphrasing Technique:
Use of a Synonymous Word or Expression

Perhaps the most common technique used in paraphrasing is that of using a synonymous word or expression, i.e., finding a word or expression which has the same general meaning as the word or expression used by the author. For example, in writing a summary of the preceding text, you would want to find another way to express "a firstborn child." Remember that this technique used by itself does not constitute a true paraphrase.

• THE AUTHOR'S WORDS
"Although many later-born children also become famous, certain studies hint that a firstborn child is more likely to excel."

• PARAPHRASE
The first child in a family is more likely to achieve excellence than are those children who are born later.

Likewise,
"Researchers suggest . . ." ←——————→ Scientists explain. . .

A Word of Caution!

If you use a synonym dictionary to help you paraphrase, be sure to use a good one (that is, one that contains many *example sentences*). The words listed as synonyms for a particular term do not always have exactly the same meaning in all contexts, but their real differences do not become clear until you try to substitute a wrong synonym into a sentence. A regular thesaurus usually accentuates this problem for an international student because it does not contain any example sentences at all. The following example, taken from a student paper, demonstrates the pitfalls of improper use of a thesaurus.

Original Text	*Faulty Paraphrase*
"A scientist can *submit* his article to a scientific *journal*."	"A scientist can *yield* his article to a scientific *diary*."

Yield is, of course, a possible synonym for *submit*, and *diary* can sometimes be used in place of *journal*, but within this context, both are inappropriate. The student who wrote this faulty paraphrase obviously used only a thesaurus or a very small abridged synonym dictionary—one which gave no examples—and had no way of knowing which words among the many listed would be appropriate. The same was true for another student, who paraphrased *a disease carrier* as "a disease *aircraft*."

The best way to avoid this problem is to use a good dictionary, one which provides usage examples, *in addition to* a synonym dictionary. If you still have doubts about the appropriateness of the synonym you have chosen, consult a native speaker of English. This is particularly true when you are dealing with idiomatic expressions. For instance, the phrase "beneath their dignity" cannot be paraphrased by making word-for-word changes, "under their repute." In cases such as this, your friends or colleagues may not be able to tell you *why* certain terms cannot be used synonymously, but they may be able to tell you *when* a term can be used and when it cannot.

A final word of warning: *Not every word in a sentence can or needs to be replaced by a synonym!* If this technique is overused, it can lead you into writing very unidiomatic sentences. Keep in mind that this technique *must* be used in combination with the other "pre-paraphrase" techniques suggested in this book, in order to form a true paraphrase in natural-sounding English.

5–3
EXEMPLIFY / DISCUSS

Directions: (1) For each of the underlined words in the following sentence, decide which thesaurus category or categories you would choose to look up for each word.

The sociological approach of the human relations school over the past 40 years has been <u>paralleled</u> by the efforts of industrial psychologists to understand the <u>nature</u> and <u>operation</u> of motives in influencing work behavior.

parallel:	*nature:*	*operation:*
relate	essence	functioning
be like	kind	employment
equal to	characteristic	surgical
co-extend	tendency	action
compare	universe	military
	temperament	
	natural state	
	naturalness	

(2) For the underlined words in the sentence below, a thesaurus gives as possible synonyms the words (and their categories) which follow the sentence. Indicate which words might be appropriate. Would you have to consult a dictionary? Would you have to consult a native speaker of English?

Industrial psychologists' efforts originated in an attempt to identify the specific needs that motivate work behavior; in effect, they concentrated on the content of work motivation.

originate (category: BEGIN)

commence
fall into
head into
plunge into
set out
start out
start off

content (category: ESSENTIAL CONTENT)

gist
heart and soul
marrow
matter
pith
sum and substance
substance
stuff

(3) Use a thesaurus to find appropriate synonyms for the underlined words in the sentence that follows. Consult a dictionary or a native speaker of English if necessary. Do *not* rewrite the sentence, replacing the original words with the synonyms that you have chosen (remember that this is not a proper way to paraphrase a sentence).

More recently they have begun to address themselves to process questions, that is, issues regarding the dynamics or mechanics by which motives influence work behavior and performance.

5–4
PRE-PARAPHRASE

Directions: Carefully compare the following summary of "Are Firstborns Better?" with the original. Write the synonymous words and expressions that have been used for the following.

According to Charles G. Morris in his discussion of firstborns on p. 101 of *Psychology*, the first child in a family is more likely to have achieved excellence than are those children who are born later. Scientists explain this in a number of ways. The firstborn has a greater opportunity to receive higher education, if only financial elements are considered. Another suggestion is that these children have a deeper motivation for achievement, possibly resulting from the way they relate to adults, particularly their parents, who have very high expectations for them. Thus, firstborn children try to gain acceptance through conformity and meeting the high standards set for them.

The Author's Words	*Paraphrase*
"suggest several explanations"	_____
"are more likely to attend college"	_____
"economic factors"	_____
"may be an outcome of"	_____
"as a result"	_____
"may seek approval"	_____

5–5
PRE-PARAPHRASE

Directions: In order to practice this pre-paraphrasing technique, turn to Resource Chapter A, p. 233, "Sleep and Dreaming." In the first paragraph replace the words or phrases in the list with synonymous words or phrases. Be sure to read the entire paragraph in order to understand the context in which these terms are used.

lamented	_____
vivid	_____
refers to	_____
all night	_____
In short	_____
to function	_____

Summary Length

How long should a summary be? A summary may vary in length from one sentence to several pages, depending on your purpose in summarizing and the length of the original text. If your purpose in summarizing is to concisely state the main information in the text, it can be done in one sentence. The text "Language Development," summarized earlier in this chapter, could be summarized in one sentence.

In acquiring language, a child begins with meaningless vocalization and imitation, moves on to single word communication and eventually uses simple 2- to 3-word sentences.

One-sentence summaries, however, have obvious limitations. In general, a summary written for any academic purpose should be approximately one-fourth to one-third the length of the original. Within this framework it is possible to establish the controlling idea, point out the logical relationships among the supporting ideas and mention examples, if necessary, to clarify the main points.

5–6
DISCUSS

1. Which information has been included in the one-sentence summary?
2. Which information has been omitted?
3. Does the one-sentence summary give you an accurate indication of what the original text was about?
4. What are the advantages and disadvantages of one-sentence summaries?

5–7
WRITE

Directions: Write one-sentence summaries for the sample texts on page 47 (enumeration), page 51 (chronology), page 54 (process), and pages 33–34 (contrast).

When Not to Paraphrase: Specialized Vocabulary

Each academic discipline has its own special vocabulary or *jargon*. These special terms may be words or symbols which are meaningful only to people involved in that field, such as "*nAch*" (the need for achievement defined in Resource Chapter A); or they may be words which have one general meaning, but take on another special meaning within that particular discipline, such as *manipulation*, which in psychology means more than simply moving with the hands (Resource Chapter A, p. 243). Frequently, such terminology is underlined, *italicized*, or printed in **boldface** type when it is found in a textbook or article. Because such terminology is central to its discipline, it is generally repeated in a summary. You should not attempt to try to paraphrase jargon or other words of an extremely technical nature.

5–8
EXEMPLIFY / DISCUSS

Directions: Study the following text and the summary that appears beside it, and then answer the following questions.

A. How long is the summary in proportion to the original text?

B. Which information from the original text has been included in the summary? Which has been omitted?

C. A number of words in the summary are the same as those in the original. Which are they? Why do you think they have not been paraphrased?

D. Are any details or examples included in the summary?

SAMPLE SUMMARY

The Neuron

Summary

The number of cells, or **neurons**, that make up the nervous system has been estimated at 100 to 200 billion. Although neurons come in many different shapes and sizes, they are specialized to receive and transmit information.

In common with all other cells, a neuron has a nucleus, a cell body where metabolism and respiration take place, and a cell membrane which encloses the whole cell.

What makes a neuron different from other cells are the tiny fibers that extend out from the cell body. These extensions are what enable the neuron to perform its special job—to receive messages from surrounding cells, carry them a certain distance, and then pass them on to other cells. The short fibers branching out around the cell body are called **dendrites**. Their role is to pick up the incoming messages from their surroundings and carry them to the cell body.

The single long fiber extending from the cell body is called an **axon**. The axon fiber is very thin and usually much longer than the dendrites. In adults the axons that run from the brain to the base of the spinal cord can sometimes be as long as 3 feet, but most axons are only an inch or two in length. The axon's job is to carry outgoing messages—either to pass them on to the next neuron in a series or to direct a muscle or gland to take action. When we talk about a **nerve**, we are referring not to a single fiber but to a group of axons bundled together like parallel wires in an electrical cable. (From *Psychology*, p. 32.)

In *Psychology* Charles G. Morris explains that the nervous system consists of cells called neurons whose purpose is to convey information. In addition to the elements the neuron shares with other cells (a nucleus and cell membrane), it also has a group of fibers called dendrites and a long single fiber called an axon. The dendrites receive messages and transmit them to the cell body, while the axon transmits messages, either to the dendrites in the next cell or directly to a muscle or gland which is then activated.

Author's Attitude

Since a summary should reflect the essential elements of an original text in a condensed form, the attitude of the author toward the subject must be considered if it is present in the original. In regular textbook prose, authors usually do not express a personal opinion. They may, however, indicate that the information being discussed is not generally accepted as fact or present alternate positions or approaches on a topic. For instance, in "Are Firstborns Better?" the writer indicates, by his choice of words, that the findings he is reporting have not been proven conclusively. The choice of words tells the reader that there is a degree of uncertainty about the data being reported.

Although many later-born children also become famous, *certain studies hint* that a firstborn child *is more likely* to excel.

Researchers *suggest*...

Some *believe*...

Notice how the summary of this article also reflects that the author is not completely certain that the information being reported is true.

The firstborn child *is more likely*...

Another *suggestion*...

...*possibly* resulting from...

5–9
DISCUSS

Directions: Find other words in the text, "Are Firstborns Better?", which reflect the author's uncertainty about the data he is reporting.

In other instances, particularly in journal articles and books whose purpose is not simply to convey information, a writer gives a personal interpretation of or states his opinion about facts. Read "Point" at the end of Resource Chapter B, pp. 256-258. Notice the writer's direct expressions of opinion. Some are:

I think the basic problem with society today is tremendous disillusionment with power.

I see two faces of power.

I can answer that from *personal experience*.

The fact that a writer is expressing an opinion is commonly noted in the first sentence of a summary. Hence, a summary of this article might begin with any of the following:

David C. McClelland's views on the use of power are expressed in an interview published in *International Management*, July 1975.

According to David C. McClelland, in an interview in *International Management* (July 1975), contemporary views on power are inaccurate.

In clarifying his feelings about power, David C. McClelland criticizes his contemporaries in a recent interview published in *International Management* (July 1975).

REDUCTIONS

EXPANSIONS

Pre-Paraphrasing Technique:
Alternating Clause/Phrase Structures

A further method of paraphrasing is to alter the structures which appear in the original text. It is possible, for instance, to change a complete sentence to a dependent clause, or a clause to a phrase. This reduction technique is particularly helpful in summary writing. Remember that this technique used by itself does not constitute a true paraphrase.

• THE AUTHOR'S WORDS	• PARAPHRASE
(Adverb Clause) *"Although neurons come in many different shapes and sizes, they are all specialized to receive and transmit information."*	(Adverb Phrase) *Despite their different shapes and sizes,* neurons are all specialized to receive and transmit information. ↓ (Noun Phrase) *The different shaped and sized neurons* are all specialized to receive and transmit information.
(Adjective Clause) *". . .the axons that run from the base of the spinal cord. . ."*	(Adjective Phrase) *. . .the axons running from the base of the spinal cord. . .*
(Sentence) *"The axon fiber is very thin."*	(Noun Phrase) The *very thin axon fiber. . .*

In situations other than summarizing, this technique may also be reversed, that is, you may paraphrase by going from simple structures to more complex ones.

• THE AUTHOR'S WORDS	• PARAPHRASE
(Adjective Phrase) *"The short cells branching out around the cell body are called dendrites."*	(Adjective Clause) The short fibers which branch out around the cell body are called dendrites. ↓ (Sentences) *Short fibers branch out around the cell body;* they are called dendrites.
(Noun Phrase) *"In common with all other cells, a neuron has a nucleus."*	(Noun Clause) *What a neuron has in common with all other cells is a nucleus.* ↓ (Sentence) A neuron has something in common with all other cells, and that is a nucleus.

5–10
PRE-PARAPHRASE

Directions: Express each of the following sentences in an alternate manner by using the guide which has been provided. Remember that you will be alternating between phrase and clause structures. Supply as many words as needed.

1. There are two fundamental theories which attempt to explain obesity.

   There are two fundamental theories which attempt to explain why <u>people become obese</u>.
   (noun clause)

2. One view, proposed by Stanley Schachter, stresses the importance of food as a powerful stimulus affecting obesity.

   Schachter's _____
   (possessive phrase)

   stimulus which _____ .
   (adjective clause)

3. In Schachter's opinion, fat people are particularly sensitive to environmental food cues, perhaps because their hypothalamus is not functioning.

   Schachter _____ that _____ ,

   perhaps because of _____ .
   (adverb phrase)

4. An alternative explanation, offered by Donald Thomas and Jean Mayer, presents obesity as an internally controlled physiological phenomenon.

   An alternate explanation, offered by Donald Thomas and Jean Mayer, presents obesity as

   a physiological phenomenon which _____ .
   (adjective clause)

5. In one experiment, subjects were given either a regular vanilla milkshake or a milkshake that had quinine in it.

   In one experiment, subjects were given either a regular vanilla milkshake or _____
   (parallel

   _____ milkshake.
   structure)

6. Obese subjects drank more of the vanilla milkshake than did normal-weight subjects.

   Subjects who _____
   (adjective clause)

   subjects who _____ .
   (adjective clause)

7. In another study, subjects were offered bags of almonds, some of which had shells.

   In another study, subjects were offered bags of almonds, some _____ .
   (-ing phrase)

8. While 19 out of 20 obese subjects ate almonds without shells, only one ate the almonds that had shells.

   While 19 out of 20 subjects who_____ate almonds that
   (adjective clause)

   _____ , _____ almonds
   (adjective clause)

   _____.
   (-ing phrase)

9. Thomas and Mayer feel that Schachter has isolated an important characteristic, not a cause, of obesity.

   Thomas and Mayer's_____ an _____
   (possessive phrase)

   _____ of _____ , but that he_____.
   (noun clause)

   _____

10. They see surplus energy—mainly due to inactivity—as an important cause of weight problems.

    _____that weight problems_____
    _____ largely by _____ , which_____
    (adjective

    _____.
    clause)

Objectivity

The purpose of a summary is to report the essential information in a text in shortened form. Therefore, the summary should be completely *objective*. You should not comment on, express an opinion about, or add data to the text you are summarizing. The reader of a summary expects to find *a condensed form of some other text, not your opinion or addition to it*. The only exception to this general rule would be an assignment in which a professor specifically asks you to summarize and respond to the text you have summarized. Even in this case, the summary itself should be objective, with your personal opinion about it clearly set off. (See Chapter 6 for a more thorough treatment of critical writing.)

5–11
EXEMPLIFY / DISCUSS

Directions: Below are five summaries of a text from p. 231 of Resource Chapter A. Read the text and the summaries of it carefully and then decide which of the summaries are objectively written. Be prepared to explain whether the summary writer added information or expressed an opinion.

1. In "The Fat of the Land," Charles G. Morris reports two hypotheses which have been proposed to explain the reasons for obesity, although neither fully explains the problem. Stanley Schachter's research suggests that obese people become that way largely because of over-response to *external* stimuli—namely food, but he is not certain whether
5   this is caused by improper functioning of the hypothalamus. Schachter feels that obese people are more sensitive to such stimuli as taste, and that they will eat only when food is easily acquired. Jean Mayer and Donald Thomas, on the other hand, offer evidence that obesity is a result of *internal* causes. They claim that an obese person cannot depend on body signals that indicate hunger or fullness. Moreover, their research indicates that being
10   inactive, with resultant unused energy, is a major cause of obesity.

2. In "The Fat of the Land," Charles G. Morris reports on two hypotheses which have been proposed to explain the reasons for obesity. Stanley Schachter's research suggests that obese people become that way largely because of over-response to *external* stimuli— namely food, although this may be caused by improper functioning of the hypothalamus.
5   Schachter feels that these unfortunate obese people are more sensitive to such stimuli as taste and that they are so lazy that they will eat only when food is easily acquired. Jean Mayer and Donald Thomas, on the other hand, offer evidence that obesity is a result of *internal* causes. They claim that an obese person cannot depend on the body to signal if he is hungry or full. Moreover, their research indicates that being inactive, with resultant
10   unused energy, is a major cause of obesity.

3. In "The Fat of the Land," Charles G. Morris reports on two hypotheses which have been proposed to explain the reasons for obesity. Stanley Schachter's research suggests that obese people become that way largely because of over-response to *external* stimuli— namely food, although this may be caused by improper functioning of the hypothalamus.
5   Schachter feels that obese people are more sensitive to such stimuli as taste and that they will eat only when food is easily acquired. Jean Mayer and Donald Thomas, on the other hand, offer evidence that obesity is a result of *internal* causes. They claim that an obese person cannot depend on the body to signal hunger or fullness. Moreover, their research indicates that being inactive, with resultant unused energy, is a major cause of obesity.

4. In "The Fat of the Land," Charles G. Morris reports on two hypotheses which have been proposed to explain the reasons for obesity, but fails to consider the high sugar and fat content of American food. Stanley Schachter's research suggests that obese people become that way largely because of over-response to *external* stimuli—namely food,
5   although this may be caused by improper functioning of the hypothalamus. Schachter feels that obese people are more sensitive to such stimuli as taste and that they will eat only when food is easily acquired. Jean Mayer and Donald Thomas, on the other hand, offer evidence that obesity is a result of *internal* causes. They claim that an obese person cannot depend on the body to signal hunger or fullness. Moreover, their research indicates
10   that being inactive, with resultant unused energy, is a major cause of obesity.

5. In "The Fat of the Land," Charles G. Morris reports on two hypotheses which have been proposed to explain the reasons for obesity. Stanley Schachter's research suggests that obese people become that way largely because of over-response to *external* stimuli— namely food, although this may be caused by improper functioning of the hypothalamus.
5   Schachter feels that obese people are more sensitive to such stimuli as taste and that they will eat only when food is easily acquired. Jean Mayer and Donald Thomas, on the other

hand, offer evidence that obesity is a result of *internal* causes. They claim that an obese person cannot depend on the body to signal hunger or fullness. Moreover, their research indicates that being inactive, with resultant unused energy, is a major cause of obesity.

10   There is probably some truth to both the external and internal explanations.

5–12
PRE-PARAPHRASE (CUMULATIVE)

Directions: Referring back to the third text of the previous exercise, complete the guided paraphrase of that text by filling in the blanks below with as many words as necessary. Remember that you can use any of the "pre-paraphrase" techniques that you have practiced thus far. (Note that the symbol = means that you should supply a synonym; thus, in the first line, you should supply a synonym for the word *hypotheses*.)

Two _____ (= hypotheses) _____ as to why _____

obese _____ the subject _____ Charles G. Morris'

_____ entitled "_____."

_____ opinion of _____ , _____

_____ is due to the fact that _____ too sensitive

_____ external stimuli—that is, _____ (per-

haps because of an _____). Schachter's _____ (= experiments)

_____ suggest that for obese _____ , both the _____

_____ of food and its _____ are important.

According to _____ , however, the _____

obesity are _____ rather than external: (1) an obese person's

_____ (= negative) give _____ food cues, and (2) obesity

_____ often _____ the unused _____

_____ that _____ inactivity.

5–13
WRITE

A. Write a summary of the section of Resource Chapter A entitled "Sleep and Dreaming," p. 233.

B. Write a summary of the insert article "Biological Clocks," in Resource Chapter A, p. 233.

C. Write a summary of the Counterpoint article, "The New Manager: A Game-Player Rather Than a Power-Seeker," Resource Chapter B, pp. 258–59.

D. Write a summary of the "Bases of Power" section of Resource Chapter B, pp. 246–48.

GUIDELINES FOR SUMMARY WRITING

1. Read the original text carefully.
2. Identify the controlling idea and the relationships among the major supporting ideas.
3. Decide which examples are necessary for a clear understanding of the text.
4. Make use of the pre-paraphrasing techniques studied so far.
5. Write a first sentence which includes the source of your summary and the controlling idea.
6. Indicate whether the author is uncertain of the facts or is expressing a personal opinion.
7. Avoid making comments about or adding information to the text.
8. Make the summary approximately one-fourth to one-third the length of the original.

6 The Critical Review

ONE TASK THAT YOU WILL HAVE TO PERFORM at one time or another in your academic career is to write a **critical review** of an article or a book. The critical review is a slightly more complex task than those to which you have been introduced so far, since it demands proficiency in all the skill areas we have been studying: the ability to analyze a text as to the author's purpose, main idea or thesis, and organizational techniques, as well as proficiency at summarizing. The first part of this chapter will concentrate on organizational techniques and terminology useful in writing critical reviews of articles. However, the guidelines which it presents are appropriate to any kind of review (this will become more obvious in the second part of the chapter, which deals with critical reviews of books.) These guidelines will indicate to you: (1) what kinds of information a review usually contains and (2) how this information can be organized into a coherent, readable whole.

REVIEWING AN ARTICLE

Unless you are otherwise instructed by your professor, there is a twofold purpose to any critical review of an article: (1) to let your readers know enough about the *content* of the article so that they can understand your comments without actually having read the article, and (2) to form your own impression as to the *value* of the article and to present that subjective impression to your readers clearly and honestly.[1]

There is no one "correct" way to write a critical review. Your professor might give you a specific format to follow; if he or she does, use it, by all means! If no format is given to you, the one which we suggest here may be used as a basis for any critical review assignment. This format calls for four sections:

    I. Introduction
   II. Summary
  III. Critique
 (IV. Conclusion)

The introduction should be considered obligatory. The summary and critical comments sections, also obligatory, may of course vary in length, depending on the length and

[1] These remarks on critical reviews would not apply, obviously, to class assignments where the professor makes it clear that he or she expects you to read several articles outside of class and simply to summarize them on paper.

complexity of the article being reviewed. A conclusion may or may not be necessary, depending upon what has been said in the review and how those comments have been organized.

The Introduction

Your introduction need not be overly long or elaborate. It should follow the same general format as that proposed for introductions to short papers (see Chapter 3), with the stipulation that the introduction be adapted to the requirements of the critical review. This means that it should include certain essential types of information.

ESTABLISHING THE CONTEXT. Your introduction should mention the *title* of the article, as well as the *author*,[2] if there is one (some articles are anonymous). A very short review can do this in a straightforward, deductive fashion. In most cases, however, it is more elegant to make use of the same kinds of simplified introductory techniques mentioned in reference to the short paper: shared knowledge, a rhetorical question, background information, or a quotation. These are always useful "lead-ins" or "links" to attract the reader's attention to the general area of interest which is to follow.

CLARIFICATION OF THE SUBJECT: FURTHER FOCUS. As is the case with the introduction to the short paper, the next few sentences of the introduction to the critical review should direct the reader to focus more clearly on the subject of the paper. In the critical review this part of the introduction should include, whenever possible, the author's purpose in writing the article. A careful reading should indicate to you what this purpose is. In fact, it is not uncommon for writers to state their purpose explicitly. Among other things, an article might be intended by its author to

- explain some important point in a field
- report the results of an experiment
- present opposing arguments concerning some point, without necessarily choosing sides
- argue a specific (and perhaps controversial) point
- report an interview with a specialist
- respond to another article which takes a different point of view

In addition to indicating the author's purpose, you can further focus the reader's attention on the subject of the review by including one or two more sentences of definition or description. You may wish to mention the following:

- the identity of the author (the person's professional qualifications)
- the reasons why the subject is important or timely
- further information about the historical context of the subject
- examples or details which clarify the subject matter

---

[2] According to academic convention, an author is referred to only once by his full name; thereafter, the last name only is used. For example, in reviewing an article by David C. McClelland, you should refer to the author first as "David C. McClelland," then only as "McClelland."

Study the following texts, which are all examples of context-establishing techniques combined with further focus. They might all be used to introduce critical reviews of the article "McClelland: An Advocate of Power," which follows Resource Chapter B.

Straight Deduction

In a 1975 interview appearing in *International Management*, David C. McClelland discusses his findings concerning the motivating factors characteristic of successful managers.

Shared Knowledge

The cartoon caricature of the office manager as a slave-driver may not be an exaggeration, according to David C. McClelland's view, expressed in a 1975 interview in *International Management*.

A Rhetorical Question

What successful manager has not, at one time or another, been accused of being power hungry? None, says David C. McClelland in a 1975 interview appearing in *International Management*.[3]

Background Information

The democratization of managerial function during the last fifteen years has made the concept of the Machiavellian manager outmoded. However, David C. McClelland, in a 1975 interview in *International Management*, expresses the view that in fact power has always been a motivating characteristic of the successful manager.

A Quotation

"I can see two faces of power. The face which social science has presented has been the Nazi face, the face of Theory X, which says that power is bad; we must do away with it. But there is another face of power. This is the one to be found in the successful manager." So says David C. McClelland in a 1975 interview in *International Management*.

ESTABLISHING YOUR CRITICAL POINT OF VIEW: THESIS. Your introduction should also include your *overall impression* of the article. Do not elaborate on it here, but do give some clue to your professor as to your general attitude toward the article. Put in the simplest terms, your professor should be able to tell from this first paragraph whether your reaction is one of *agreement* or of *disagreement*. In establishing your critical point of view, you are also presenting your *controlling idea* (thesis) for the review; it is therefore expected that the rest of the paper will explain in further detail the critical comment you have made at the beginning.

There are many ways to express approval and disapproval in English. This may be accomplished in a single word, in a phrase, or in a complete statement. The choice of the correct adjective or verb is probably the simplest, most direct means of indicating that you either like or dislike something.

---

[3] Note that in this case the question is answered, the answer constituting a very effective lead-in to the main point of the article.

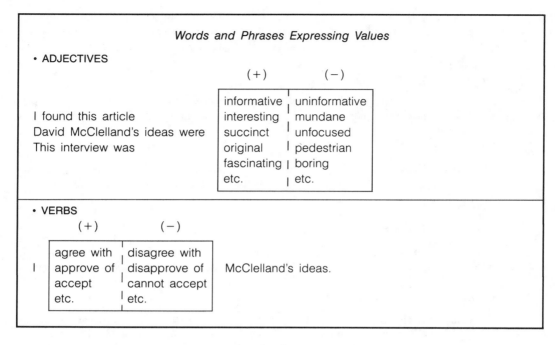

Words and Phrases Expressing Values

• ADJECTIVES

	(+)	(−)
I found this article David McClelland's ideas were This interview was	informative interesting succinct original fascinating etc.	uninformative mundane unfocused pedestrian boring etc.

• VERBS

	(+)	(−)	
I	agree with approve of accept etc.	disagree with disapprove of cannot accept etc.	McClelland's ideas.

TEXTUAL COHERENCE THROUGH CONCESSIVE CONTRAST. In many instances you will not react to an article in a completely negative or completely positive way. Rather, you will find parts of it interesting or worth remembering and other parts unacceptable. In expressing this kind of mixed opinion, you will of course want to mention both positive and negative points. This is commonly done by using a particular kind of contrast known as **concession**. Concession, or concessive contrast, shows two or more differences about the same subject (as opposed to the "pure" or "adversative" kind of contrast presented in Chapter Two, where differences between two separate subjects are pointed out):

"Pure" Contrast

McClelland's views seem reactionary; the views expressed by McGregor, on the other hand, are more in tune with the results of contemporary behavioral research. (*The writer's opinion of* McClelland *is contrasted with his opinion of* McGregor.)

Concessive Contrast

Although some of McClelland's views seem to be reactionary, I found the article thought-provoking and well worth reading. (*The writer has two differing impressions of McClelland.*)

Thus, in expressing this kind of mixed opinion about an article, what you are doing, in effect, is saying, "There is something I *dislike* about it, but there is something I *like* about it, too."

When you use concessive contrast to express both approval and disapproval, you should start out by expressing the weaker (or less dominant) side and *conclude with the stronger (or more dominant) side*. The signals used to this end are mostly the same as those used to express the other type of contrast. They are quite useful words, indicating that your opinions are not one-sided and that you have given some consideration to both sides of a question. They are quite common in English and are found in critical commentary about any subject.

Signals of Concessive Contrast

• **SENTENCE LINKERS**

Coordinate Conjunctions

His views seem reactionary,
$\begin{bmatrix} \text{but} \\ \text{yet} \end{bmatrix}$
I (still) found the article to be thought-provoking and well worth reading.

Conjunctive Adverbs

His views seem reactionary;
$\begin{bmatrix} \text{however} \\ \text{nevertheless} \\ \text{all the same} \\ \text{still} \\ \text{even so} \\ \text{in spite of this} \\ \text{this said} \\ \text{this notwithstanding} \end{bmatrix}$
, I (still) found....

Subordinate Conjunctions

$\begin{bmatrix} \text{Although} \\ \text{Even though} \\ \text{Though} \\ \text{While} \\ \text{In spite of the fact that} \\ \text{Despite the fact that} \\ \text{Notwithstanding the fact that} \\ \text{Albeit that} \end{bmatrix}$
his views seem reactionary, I....

• **PREPOSITIONS**

$\begin{bmatrix} \text{Despite} \\ \text{In spite of} \\ \text{Notwithstanding} \end{bmatrix}$
the reactionary nature of his views, I....

His views,
$\begin{bmatrix} \text{though} \\ \text{although} \\ \text{even though} \\ \text{albeit} \end{bmatrix}$
reactionary, are (still) thought-provoking.

• **INTENSIFIERS**

Even the reactionary nature of some of his views cannot obscure the basic soundness of his reasoning.

Though the article was thought-provoking, I found his views *too* reactionary.

Notice the implications in the way the mixed point of view is expressed:

> Although some of McClelland's views seem to be reactionary, I found the article thought-provoking and well worth reading.

In the first clause, the writer has expressed some reservation about the article. However, the second and main clause partially dismisses this reservation and gives emphasis to his positive impression of it. If the writer's opinion had been just the opposite, his point of view would have been expressed by reversing the clauses and dropping the phrase "well worth reading":

> Although portions of McClelland's article were thought-provoking, I found that many of his opinions were reactionary.

6–1
WRITE

Directions: The statements that follow express mixed reactions to the McClelland article. Complete each of the statements in a logical way. After each statement, indicate whether the *main* reaction is positive or negative. Be sure to punctuate correctly. Do not use the adjective *reactionary*.

1. Although I find his ideas interesting, _____
   Although I find his ideas interesting, <u>I do not think that he presents enough facts to support his conclusions.</u> (–)
2. I found it a/an _____ but challenging article.
3. In spite of McClelland's claims that he is part of a new generation of behavioral scientists who "will eventually come up with well-researched data to show today's widely-held views of motivation are wrong, _____.
4. McClelland's claims, though _____, are _____
   _____.
5. McClelland obviously means well; however, _____.
6. While McClelland's responses to questions seem convincing at first glance, _____
   _____.
7. In this interview, McClelland does not present hard data as evidence for his positions; nevertheless, _____.
8. This interview with McClelland lacks the depth of an academic report, yet _____
   _____.
9. Despite the use of a simplistic interview format, _____.
10. McClelland's clearly stated and _____ ideas add to the understanding of the motivation of managers.
11. McClelland's clearly stated but _____ ideas add _____
    _____ to the understanding of the motivation of managers.

6–2
EXEMPLIFY   /   DISCUSS

Directions: Read the following model introduction to a review of the McClelland article and then answer the questions which follow.

The democratization of managerial function during the last fifteen years has made the concept of the Machiavellian manager outmoded. However, David C. McClelland, in a 1975 interview in *International Management*, expresses the view that, in fact, power has always been a motivating characteristic of the successful manager. A psychology professor at Harvard, McClelland uses this interview as a forum to expound on the results of his research—results which run counter to many popularly held beliefs about effective management. Democratic management, according to McClelland, is so ineffective that companies which use it quickly go out of business. Although some of McClelland's views seem to be reactionary, I found the article thought-provoking and well worth reading.

1. What technique has been used as an initial focus?
2. How is further focus achieved?
3. Will the review be primarily positive or primarily negative? How do you know?

REPORTING VERBS. When you are referring to what someone else has written, whether in a critical review or in any other type of writing assignment, the most commonly used verbs are *write, say, tell*, and *think*. However, there are a number of other verbs which can also be used to restate someone else's ideas, and it is good to make use of these other verbs to provide variety in your writing.

We will divide these "reporting verbs" into four categories, based on the general area of meaning they convey. Although the verbs within each category are very close in meaning—*say* and *tell*, for example, are so close in meaning that they are considered interchangeable—you should be aware that for the most part, the verbs have slightly different meanings. If you are not sure whether the verb you wish to use is appropriate for the context in which you wish to use it, consult a good dictionary to help you decide.

In addition, note that the structures which the various verbs require may differ. These structures fall into three general categories: (1) Verb + Noun Phrase, (2) Verb + Preposition, and (3) Verb + Noun Clause. Furthermore, sometimes an indirect object *must* be present ("He reminds *the reader* that no studies have been done"), sometimes it is optional ("He remarks [to the reader] that the issues are complex"), and sometimes no indirect object is allowed ("He questions the results of earlier research"). Once again, if you are not sure which structure to use, *consult a good dictionary or advanced grammar which gives many examples*!

A. Neutral Verbs of Restatement. This category of verbs may be used when what you wish to report from another source is simply informative and does not necessarily express an opinion or deal with a controversial issue. These verbs include the following[4]:

---

[4] A verb followed by a preposition without parentheses—*speak of*, for example—indicates that the preposition must be used and that no other structure is possible. A preposition in parentheses—*inform (of)*, for example—indicates that although the preposition may be used, other structures are possible.

add	inform (of, about)	remind (of, about)
clarify	present	report (on)
describe	remark	speak of

Note, in the usage examples, the various structures which are possible.

Usage Examples

"McClelland *clarifies*	the goals of his training program."
	the goals of his training program for the reader."

(Indirect Object optional; followed by a Noun)

"McClelland *informs*	the reader of the many issues involved."
	the reader that many issues are involved."

(Indirect Object required; followed by a Preposition and a Noun, or by a Noun Clause)

"McClelland *reports*	the results of that study."
	the results of that study to the reader."
	on the results of that study."
	to the reader on the results of that study."
	that the results of the study are inconclusive."
	to the reader that the results of the study are inconclusive."

(Indirect Object optional; followed by a Noun, by a Preposition and a Noun, or by a Noun Clause)

B. Verbs of Restatement with a + or − Connotation. This second category of reporting verbs is very close to the first category in that they both may be used to report simple factual information. The verbs in this category differ, however, in that they commonly assume a positive or negative connotation based on the information which is reported. These verbs suggest, in a very general way, that what is being reported is an expression of the writer's personal judgment. These verbs include the following:

apprise (of)	explain	indicate
argue (about)	express	observe

Usage Examples

"McClelland *apprises*	us of the success of the program."

(Indirect Object required; followed by a Preposition and a Noun)

"McClelland *explains*	that the affiliative manager is not effective." to the reader that the affiliative manager is not effective." the success of the program." the success of the program to the reader."

(Indirect Object optional; followed by a Noun or by a Noun Clause)

"McClelland *expresses*	his contempt for all such thinking." to the reader his contempt for all such thinking."

(Indirect Object optional;
followed by a Noun)

C. Verbs of Opinion. This category of verbs is used when the content of what is being reported is an expression of another's opinions, conclusions, or suggestions. These verbs include the following (a + by a verb indicates that an author who uses this verb is expressing a *positive* opinion):

affirm +	claim	point out
agree (with) +	concur (with, in) +	praise +
applaud +	determine	support +
assert	expound (on)	think
believe (in)	maintain	

A few verbs in this category are always used to *report a suggested course of action*:

advise	set forth	urge
recommend	suggest	

Usage Examples

"McClelland *affirms*	the importance of the power motive." that the power motive is extremely important."

(followed by a Noun or by a Noun Clause)

"McClelland *believes*	in the importance of the power motive." that the power motive is extremely important." the results of a study done last year."

(followed by Noun, by a Preposition and a Noun,
or by a Noun Clause)

"McClelland *expounds*	on the importance of the power motive."

(followed by a Preposition and a Noun)

| "McClelland *asserts* | that power is a very important motive."
the importance of the power motive." |

(followed by a Noun or by a Noun Clause)

| "McClelland *supports* | the position taken by traditional theorists." |

(followed by a Noun)

| "McClelland *recommends* | a training course for managers."
that a manager be aware of the implications of power." |

*(followed by a Noun, or by a Noun Clause in which
the verb is in the simple form.)*

D. Verbs of Uncertainty. A final category of verbs is used when the writer whose words you are reporting expresses doubt about or disagreement with the subject matter being dealt with. This category includes the following:

challenge	dispute	question
disagree with	doubt	suspect (of)
dismiss	mistrust	wonder (at)

Usage Examples

| "McClelland *challenges* | the conclusions reached in that study." |

(followed by a Noun)

| "McClelland *disagrees* | with the conclusions reached in that study." |

(followed by a Preposition and a Noun)

| "McClelland *questions* | the results of earlier research on power." |

(followed by a Noun)

| "McClelland *wonders* | whether the power motive has been underestimated."
at the suspicion surrounding the power motive." |

(followed by a Noun or by a Noun Clause)

6–3
PRE-PARAPHRASE

Directions: To practice using a variety of reporting verbs, paraphrase the statements which follow. Choose the verb from the group which will convey the appropriate meaning. A change in structure will be required for some of the statements.

1. McClelland <u>has observed</u> that affiliative managers spend too much time on the telephone.   (*present, apprise, argue*)

   McClelland *apprises us of the fact that* affiliative managers spend too much time on the telephone.

2. McClelland <u>describes</u> the rationale for the training program which he conducts for managers.   (*point out, mistrust, present*)

3. McClelland <u>doubts</u> the validity of the conclusions of Chris Argyris.   (*wonder, remind, claim*)

4. McClelland <u>remarks</u> that power has been given a bad image by social scientists.   (*set forth, report, assert*)

5. McClelland <u>maintains</u> that employees respond better to a well-defined authority system.   (*suspect, claim, support*)

6. McClelland <u>argues</u> that managers must understand the positive side of power.   (*point out, dispute, express*)

7. McClelland <u>recommends</u> that managers attend a training course to make them aware of power.   (*describe, challenge, urge*)

8. McClelland <u>dismisses</u> the work of McGregor, Maslow, Argyris, and others.   (*observe, speak, disagree*)

9. McClelland <u>reminds</u> the reader of the evidence that has shown that high morale results from a well-defined authority system.   (*question, determine, speak*)

10. McClelland <u>thinks</u> that democratic management is so ineffective that companies which use it go out of business.   (*assert, present, doubt*)

11. McClelland <u>believes</u> that the institution is more important than the individuals who compose it.   (*support, report, wonder*)

The Summary

In the second paragraph of your article review, you should simply summarize the contents of the article—the thesis or controlling idea, all important thought relationships, and any examples which seem particularly important to you. Use the guidelines from Chapter 5 for writing your summary. For a short article, you will probably want to restrict the length of this summary to one paragraph; a longer article might require two or three paragraphs.

The Critique

This section of your review, which may vary in length, is the most important part of the review. The instructor's purpose in assigning a critical review is to elicit personal comments on a topic from the student. In order to make these personal comments, you are forced to analyze and evaluate the contents of the article. Unlike a "pure summary," the critical review, by its very nature, is *subjective*. You must make judgments on and comments about the article you are reviewing.

Thus, after introducing the review and summarizing the contents of the text, you must now elaborate on the critical reaction expressed in your introductory paragraph.

Depending on the nature of that reaction and on the length and complexity of the article being reviewed, this section of your review will most probably consist of from one to three paragraphs. Study these guidelines:

If your introduction suggests:	*Your critique should probably contain:*
A positive opinion	2–3 paragraphs which elaborate on the *positive aspects* of the text (possibly more in the case of longer, more complex articles)
A negative opinion	2–3 paragraphs which elaborate on the *negative aspects* of the texts (possibly more in the case of longer, more complex articles)
A mixed opinion:	
1. positive/*negative*	3 paragraphs, arranged in the following manner: • the weaker (positive) opinion first; 1 paragraph • the *stronger* (negative) opinion last; 2 paragraphs (both of the above may, of course, be longer in the case of longer, more complex articles)
2. negative/*positive*	3 paragraphs, with the above order exactly reversed

THE CRITERIA FOR CRITICAL COMMENTARY. Paragraphs of critical commentary are focused on the personal judgments the writer has made about the article. These judgments have been expressed in very general terms in the introduction to the paper. This section of your review will elaborate on and specifically support your judgments.

The question of making these judgments is commonly the most difficult part of writing such a paper. Students who are new to a discipline frequently feel that they do not have enough knowledge about the subject matter to make clear-cut and convincing arguments about an article or book. Although this is, to a certain extent, true, there are some general criteria which are applied to articles and books when they are discussed in academic circles, and which even an inexperienced student may use. These include:

1. *The importance of the subject matter*: Is the subject under discussion one which is central to the field, or is it one which is peripheral?
2. *The timeliness of the article*: Is the subject of current interest, or is it an issue which has already been thoroughly discussed?
3. *The length of the article*: Does the writer adequately cover the subject within the limits of the article? Should the ideas be developed more completely? Is it too long or too short? Is too much information included?
4. *The objectivity of the writer*: If the writer intends to present the results of research (objective data), does he or she do so? Are personal opinions added? If so, are they clearly identified as such?
5. *The interpretation of data*: Does the writer's interpretation of data seem to be valid, or does it seem that data are manipulated to support preconceived opinions? Are the conclusions logical, based on the evidence presented?

6. *The thoroughness of treatment of the subject matter*: Has the writer reported all of the pertinent data about the subject, or has important information been overlooked or deliberately omitted? (Notice that this criterion is related to that of length but can be dealt with separately.)

7. *The practicality of the suggestions*: Do the writer's conclusions seem realistic, or do they seem too theoretical to have any "real-life" application?

8. *Other expert opinion*: Do the ideas proposed contradict other information you may have read about the subject, or are they supported by most leaders in the field?

9. *Personal interest in the subject*: Is the subject of the article of particular interest to you, or do you find it completely uninteresting or not applicable to your purposes in reading the article? Give specific reasons why it is or is not.

In a short review, of course, you would not apply all of these criteria. You should choose two or three as your main focus and then develop them thoroughly. One or two more criteria might be mentioned, but only in a cursory way. Notice how some of the criteria have been applied in the following sample critique.

Sample Critique (Positive)

Support of the Controlling Idea

expert opinion

Contemporary research in the social sciences, much of it well documented, does not seem to have influenced McClelland's thinking. He dismisses the work of McGregor, Maslow, Argyris and others, and he claims that in actual practice, good managers are "high in the need for power" and are "not interested in people." Is he, in fact, suggesting a return to the 19th century autocratic manager? I think not. Although control and authority are stressed in this interview, McClelland presents a number of interesting and practical corollaries which soften the reactionary premise.

the first clause

("...some of McClelland's views seem to be reactionary....")

interpretation of data; practicality

In the first place, he tells us that over the years power has been seen only as a negative force. In contrast to this popular view, McClelland presents evidence that power, or more specifically, a well-defined authority system created by managers who understand the positive side of power, creates high morale within an organization. Further, he says that these managers "believe in justice above everything else" and see that their employees are treated fairly. I see this as a very reasonable approach to managerial function.

interpretation of data

the second (dominant) clause

("...I found the article thought-provoking and well worth reading.")

Another interesting aspect of the interview was the concept of training people to be more effective managers. McClelland speaks of using certain behavioral techniques to focus a manager's attention on specific areas in which the power-authority approach is more advantageous than the affiliative approach. As a potential manager, I find this concept quite intriguing. In short, this article has stimulated me to read more about and by McClelland.

practicality

USE OF EVALUATIVE LANGUAGE. Since the purpose of this section of your review is to express your own judgments, you may use personal pronouns. Phrases such as "I feel that...", "In my opinion...", and "It seems to me that..." are commonly used in critical writing. It is also possible to indicate personal opinion by selective use of words or by making a simple statement which says something good or bad about the article. Notice how evaluative language has been used in the previous model critique.

"Is he, in fact, suggesting a return to the 19th century autocratic manager? *I think not."* (*personal pronoun; negative statement*)

"...McClelland presents a number of *interesting* and *practical* corollaries which *soften* his reactionary premise." (*word choice*)

"*I* see this as a very *reasonable* approach to the managerial function." (*personal pronoun; word choice*)

"Another *interesting* aspect..." (*word choice*)

"*I* find this concept quite *intriguing.*" (*personal pronoun; word choice*)

6–4
EXEMPLIFY / DISCUSS

Directions: There follows another critique taken from a review of the McClelland article. The writer of this review has taken a generally *negative* approach. After reading the review carefully, identify:

1. the point where the commentary shifts from positive to negative; any contrast signals which are used
2. the evaluative language used to indicate the writer's opinions
3. the *critical criteria* used to evaluate McClelland's thoughts on his subject
   - importance of the subject matter
   - timeliness of the article
   - length of the article
   - objectivity of the writer
   - interpretation of data
   - thoroughness of treatment
   - practicality of the suggestions
   - other expert opinion

Model Critique (Negative)

Among a number of wide-ranging topics dealt with in this interview, perhaps the most interesting is the distinction which McClelland makes between what he calls the "Nazi face of power" and the sort of power motivation which is found in a good manager. Indeed, it seems to me that a successful manager must know how to deal with power and
5   must create an authority system within his organization. In addition to making this important distinction, McClelland goes on to recommend special training methods which can help managers in adapting their motivations to the jobs they are doing.

However, McClelland's views on other aspects of the subject seem, at best, to be based on rather tenuous evidence. For instance, his claim that "...a second generation of
10   behavioral scientists, following in the spirit of his own beliefs, will eventually come up with well-researched data to show today's widely held views on motivation are wrong" is,

to this reader, somewhat premature. McClelland also suggests that the reason why no studies have been done on businesses with a democratic management is that these organizations were so unsuccessful that they didn't stay operational long enough to be
15 studied. Without further documentation, this concept is hard to accept. Moreover, he calls upon personal experience in a firm he founded on democratic principles, stating that these same principles caused the firm to go into debt. Again, I think more details need to be made available. Was the implementation of democratic procedures the only factor which contributed to the debt?
20   Perhaps the most serious fault in McClelland's reasoning is his claim that the successful manager "...believes...that the institution is more important than the individuals in it." It seems highly unlikely to me that in the twentieth century—the age of specialists and organized labor—this approach is really a practical one. I wonder how McClelland would suggest that a manager whose only concern is with the institution deal at labor
25 negotiations with the AFL-CIO? It seems to me that, in general, his recommendations are more appropriate for a nineteenth-century sweatshop manager than for a manager who has to deal with contemporary problems.

THE USE OF TENSE. Throughout the critical review, you will frequently refer to what has been written in the article or book you are reviewing. Although the article (or book) was obviously written prior to the review you are writing of it, you are not required to use past tense when restating information from it. In fact, academic convention allows for the use of present tense or present perfect tense in restating information in a review. Perhaps the most commonly used among the three which are acceptable is present tense.

It is important, however, that you choose one—past, present perfect or present tense—at the very beginning of your review and then use the same tense throughout. Although any of the three is acceptable, you must choose one and use it consistently. Notice that in the sample critical review present tense is used in the introduction ("He *dismisses* the work of...") and is then used each time the text is referred to throughout the paper.

THE USE OF QUOTATION. A well-chosen quote adds to the effectiveness of critical commentary. When you quote an author in a review, it is not necessary to follow the conventions for footnoting introduced in Chapter 3 since it is obvious that you are quoting directly from the article under discussion. Notice how the use of direct quote contributes to the criticism made by the writer of the positive review on page 165.

He claims that in actual practice, good managers are "high in the need for power" and "are not interested in people."

In the model critique, McClelland's own words are immediately followed by a critical statement from the writer—a statement which dismisses a negative interpretation of the quoted information. To support the overall positive impression, the writer of the review again quotes the author of the article:

...he says these managers "believe in justice above everything else" and see that their employees are fairly treated.

The Conclusion

If you feel that your review needs a conclusion—not all short reviews do, particularly when the critical paragraphs are very specific and do, in effect, conclude the writer's thoughts on the subject—use the same guidelines as those presented in Chapter 3 for writing conclusions.

6-5
WRITE

Directions: Read "The New Manager: A Game-Player Rather Than a Power-Seeker," Counter-Point Section, Resource Chapter B, pp. 258–59. Write a critical review of this article.

REVIEWING A NON-FICTION BOOK[5]

The format and techniques used in writing a book review correspond, to a large extent, to those used in writing an article review. The major difference, of course, is that certain sections of the book review will be longer because of the book's greater length and complexity. We will go over the format suggested for an article review and point out how it can be expanded to meet the requirements of a full book review.

The Introduction

The introductory techniques remain the same. However, the introduction may be expanded to two or three paragraphs if the subject matter or your critical point of view warrant a detailed exposition. It is frequently useful to look for a direct statement of the author's purpose in writing in the preface or introduction to the book.

The Summary

The purpose of the summary section of a book review is to give the reader a general idea of the contents of the book. It is not possible to summarize the entire book in this section. Your summary should include the following:

1. The controlling idea or thesis of the book
2. The main concepts dealt with
3. The kind of development used (if there is a controlling idea) or the evidence presented (if there is a thesis)

---

[5] Although the format for reviewing fiction is generally the same as that for reviewing non-fiction, the techniques and approaches to evaluation of literature are significantly different. Furthermore, very few non-native speakers of English are enrolled in courses which require this type of review. Therefore, we are dealing with only non-fiction reviews in this text.

4. Whether the author is uncertain about the information or is expressing a personal opinion
5. The theoretical framework for the writer's thesis
6. Examples of the subjects dealt with in the book

In other words, the summary section should provide enough information about the book so that the reader will be able to understand the critical commentary to follow.

The Critique

The criteria we will suggest for reviewing a book can be divided into two main groups: those which can be applied to the book as a whole, and those which are best applied only to specific sections of the book.

CRITIQUING THE WHOLE BOOK. There are basically four criteria which you can apply to the book as a whole. Two of them have already been mentioned in connection with reviews of articles:

1. *The length of the book:* Does the writer adequately cover the subject within the limits of the book? Should the ideas have been developed more completely? Is the book too long or too short, given the purpose of the author? Is there too much or too little information included? (Is it all relevant and to the point?)
2. *The thoroughness of treatment of the subject matter:* Has the writer reported all of the pertinent data about the subject, or has important information been overlooked or deliberately omitted?

These two criteria are related, but they can be dealt with separately. If you decide to apply either of them, you should avoid vague generalizations *by supporting your opinion, positive or negative, with specific references to the book.*

The criteria not previously mentioned, but which may also be applied to the book as a whole are the following:

3. *The effectiveness of the organization:* Are the ideas in the book presented in a logical, orderly way, or are they presented in a haphazard, confusing way?
4. *The effectiveness of the language:* Is the vocabulary or sentence structure too complex or too technical (or too simple), or does the writer's use of words add to the interest level and your personal enjoyment of the book?

CRITIQUING PARTS OF THE BOOK. The following criteria, all mentioned in reference to reviewing an article, are most useful when applied to specific sections or specific ideas within the book.

1. *The importance of the subject matter:* Is the subject or subjects under discussion critical to the particular area of study, or are they areas with which few people are concerned?
2. *The timeliness of the book:* Is the subject(s) of the book of current interest to the general public or to scholars in that field, or is it one which has been exhaustively written about?

Are any new ideas, theories or interpretation of evidence presented which make it interesting?

3. *The objectivity of the writer:* Are the writer's intentions to be objective or subjective made clear? Does he or she consistently distinguish between personal opinions and those of others?

4. *The interpretation of data:* Is the writer's thesis substantiated by convincing, logical evidence, or do parts of the evidence seem to be presented in such a way as to "appear" to support the thesis?

5. *The practicality of the suggestions:* How realistic is the author in making suggestions based on the thesis proposed? Do one or more of the suggestions seem too impractical for use in the foreseeable future?

6. *Other expert opinion:* Is the thesis or supporting evidence contradictory to what most other experts in the field think about the subject? Have a number of other writers taken a different approach to the subject?

7. *Personal interest in a subject:* Are one or more of the subjects discussed of particular interest to you? Do you wish to agree or disagree with any of the topics based on your own interpretations or beliefs?

In most cases it would be difficult to apply these criteria to the book as a whole. For instance, if you wish to comment on the *validity of the author's conclusions*, you might not, within the limits of a book review, be able to discuss every conclusion in the book. Rather, you would refer to one or two specific conclusions, perhaps by quoting the author. Likewise, you may wish to apply the criterion of *practicality*. Again, choose one or two suggestions made by the author and then say why they are or are not practical.

Keep in mind that the critique is the most important part of any book review assignment. It may be as long as necessary to substantiate your opinions about those aspects of the book which you have chosen to discuss. In selecting which criteria you wish to apply, you should consider which parts of the book seem to you to be most important, most interesting or most deserving of comment. Although a particularly long or complex book may require an appropriately lengthy commentary section, if you have sufficiently limited the focus of your criticism, this section should probably be between five and ten paragraphs in length.

The sample book review of *The Dragons of Eden*[6] which follows was written by a student who has made use of the techniques suggested in this chapter. Read it carefully, noticing which introductory, summary, and critical techniques were chosen to review this rather long and complex book. Pay particular attention to the fact that the student writer *does not* try to summarize all of the information in the book, nor does she try to apply all of the criteria.

---

[6] This paper and the one in Ex. 6–6 were written by students enrolled in Reading and Composition courses at The American University during the Fall, 1981 semester. The students themselves edited the papers for usage errors, and the authors of this book edited them slightly, primarily for nonidiomatic usage. The content and structure of each review, however, are the work of the students whose names are cited.

Sample Book Review

The subject of evolution has been a matter of controversy among scientists for a long time. It is not surprising, therefore, that a great scientist like Carl Sagan deals with this subject in his book, *The Dragons of Eden*. In this book, he seeks the source of human intelligence in order to find out more about the future evolution of the human brain. This matter is of great importance to us because we depend on our human intelligence to help us solve future problems. Sagan seems to have most of the qualifications which are necessary to deal with this subject. He is an astronomer, astrophysicist, geneticist, exobiologist, teacher, writer, and humanist. In spite of all his qualifications, Sagan presents his ideas with some uncertainty because he considers most of them to be speculations which have yet to be proven. Although I had difficulty in reading the book, I found it to be a very fascinating one.

In the introduction to his book, Sagan talks about evolution and the biological principle of "natural selection." His main premise concerning the brain is that brain structure has a lot to do with its workings. He provides data to support the idea of the relationship between intelligence and brain size and distinguishes genetic and extra-genetic information, comparing the human brain with a modern computer. The concept of the "triune brain," which was developed by MacLean, is discussed at length, and a description of the structure and function of each of the three parts as evolutionary additions is given. The R-complex, which we seem to share with other mammals and with reptiles, controls aggressive behavior and the establishment of social hierarchies and rituals. The limbic system's function seems to be that of generating strong emotions, and we share this system with other mammals. The neocortex controls the most unique human characteristics—the ability to reason and associate abstractly.

Sagan is also concerned with the functions of the left and right hemispheres of the brain and how the corpus callosum coordinates these functions. According to Sagan, "legal and ethical systems, art and music, science and technology were made possible only through collaborative work of the left and right cerebral hemispheres." He claims that our only hope for solving future problems lies in the corpus callosum.

The only aspect of this book which kept me from enjoying it to the fullest is that it is filled with many confusing technical terms. Although Sagan states that he has written the book for the layman and has provided a glossary, I didn't find the book to be "smooth-sailing." The second chapter, for example, is

---

ANALYSIS

I. Introduction
  A. Background information (Use of present tense)
  B. Title/Author
  C. Author's purpose

  D. Importance of subject

  E. Qualifications of author

  F. Author's certainty about subject
  G. Thesis of this review

II. Summary
  A. Thesis of book
  B. Examples of subject matter

  C. Theoretical basis for thesis of book

  D. Detailed example of subject matter

  (Use of direct quote)

III. Critique (Negative)
  A. Effectiveness of language use

difficult to read because of so much scientific terminology. An example of this is the paragraph that discusses mutations. "The raw material of evolution are mutations; inheritable changes in the particular nucleotide sequences that make up hereditary instructions in the DNA molecule." I don't think the ordinary layman could grasp these technical terms easily, and this would surely affect his understanding of the main ideas in the book.

B. Specific example to support criticism

(Use of direct quote)

Sagan's choice of subject for the book seems to be very appropriate. The theory of evolution has raised many questions in the last few years, and laymen are in need of a book like *The Dragons of Eden* to give them a better understanding of themselves and of the treasure they hold in their brain. Sagan believes that the human brain is capable of almost anything and that the "rapid evolution of human intelligence is not only the cause of, but also the only conceivable solution to the many serious problems that beset us." By comparing memory storage of a modern computer to the memory storage of the brain, he makes us realize the actual capacity of our brains.

C. Reemphasis of the importance of the subject matter

(Use of direct quote)

Another positive aspect of Sagan is that he is scientifically objective. In his opinion, such things as the Bermuda Triangle mystery, astrology, spiritualism, and modern prophecy are "mystical and occult doctrines" which are "impervious to rational discussion." I see his approach to these topics to be very reasonable.

D. Author's interpretation of data

E. Personal commentary

Such a scientific approach does not make the book dry and uninteresting, however. For example, the experiments which have been done on chimpanzees and their language acquisition are very interesting to me. The thought of an animal being able to communicate with a human seems strange, but then these experiments actually lead us to think that this might be possible.

F. Interest level

Thus, in spite of the fact that the book's language was rather confusing, I have to say that it was still worth reading. In my opinion, *The Dragons of Eden* is a stimulating book on an extremely important topic.

IV. Conclusion
  A. Restatement of thesis of review
  B. Reemphasis of book's importance

Lamia Saleh
(United Arab Emirates)

6–6
EXEMPLIFY / DISCUSS

Directions: Read the following book review carefully. Then, to the right of the text, label the following parts:

I. Introduction
Initial focus
Further focus
Thesis of review

II. Summary
Writer's thesis
Theoretical basis for thesis
Examples of subject matter

III. Critique
Specific criteria applied
Personal comments
Method of supporting criticism

IV. Conclusion (method used)

Sample Book Review

Do our spirits still exist even after we are dead?
According to Carl Sagan in his book, *The Dragons of
Eden*, there is no spirit in life or after death. In the book,
Sagan uses the myth from the Garden of Eden as a
5   metaphor to explain the evolutionary development of
human intelligence. Sagan feels that we are living in a
rapidly advancing world, and it is possible for us to have a
better understanding about where we are coming from and
where we are heading to. After reading this book, I can
10   say that I find Sagan's ideas and arguments interesting and
convincing.

Sagan's purpose in writing this book is to prove that
mind-body dualism does not exist in man. He believes
that the so-called "mind" or "spirit" is in the human
15   brain, specifically in the neocortex. If a man is dead, his
brain is no longer functioning, and the mind or spirit no
longer exists. Based on the evolutionary development of
the human brain, Sagan explains why the human being is
the most intelligent animal on earth. Also, based on
20   scientific evidence, Sagan provides reasons why women
have such pain during childbirth and why there is mutual
hostility between humans and reptiles. He also expresses
his opinions about the issue of abortion, the future use of
computers and the possibility of creatures living on other
25   planets.

To explain the evolution of the brain, Sagan goes into
great detail by describing the brain based on Paul
MacLean's model. Sagan tells us that this model consists
of three parts—The Reptilian Complex (R-complex), the
30   limbic system, and the neocortex. The reptilian complex

is the first evolutionary stage, which we share with both
cold- and warm-blooded animals. This part of the brain
dominates our aggressive behavior, territoriality, ritual,
and the establishment of social hierarchies. The second
35   stage of our brain development is the limbic system,
which surrounds the R-complex. Both humans and warm-
blooded animals have this part of the brain. The third
development of the brain is the neocortex, which is the
highest and most intelligent part. So far, the human is the
40   only animal that has a fully developed neocortex, a fact
which has helped humans to learn and reason. I find that
Sagan's detailed explanation of the brain model gives
effective support to his later assumptions.

Sagan is a very effective writer. He uses the inductive
45   method of writing to present his thesis. I am fascinated by
his reasoning on the abortion issue because I always
viewed abortion from a philosophical perspective, not a
biological one. I used to think that, if a baby is not
welcomed by the world, it is better for that baby not to be
50   born than to be born and later be abused. But Sagan uses
the biological development of the neocortex as a logical
premise to debate on this subject. He says, "But perhaps
we might set the time when (neocortical) activity begins,
as determined by electroencephlograms of the fetus." I
55   think that what he means is that as long as the neocortex
has not yet developed in the brain of an infant, then the
infant is not yet a human. Therefore, an abortion before
the development of the infant's neocortex would not be
considered murder. I feel this is a strong argument.

60   I also find it interesting the way that Sagan uses the tale
of the Garden of Eden as a metaphor for the evolutionary
stages of human intelligence. Sagan writes, "Nevertheless, I cannot resist...the Genesis myth of the exile
from Eden because it is a reptile, of course, that offers the
65   fruit of the knowledge of good and evil—abstract and
normal neocortical activities—to Adam and Eve." What
Sagan means is that the story of the Garden of Eden is
parallel with the evolution of the human brain. The myth
somewhat explains human brain evolution. However,
70   Sagan does not believe in Genesis because it is figurative
and only symbolically represents the evolution of the
brain.

As a business major, I was unfamiliar with much of the
biological vocabulary and technical terminology in the
75   book. However, a glossary of vocabulary is supplied,
which helped me to have less difficulty in understanding
The Dragons of Eden. Overall, I find this book interesting

to read, and the assumptions that Sagan makes are convincing and fascinating.

80

Keny K. Wu
(Republic of China)

6–7
WRITE

Directions: Your teacher will assign a nonfiction book which must be read by a specified date. After a class discussion of the ideas in the book, you will write a critical review of it. Follow the suggestions given in this chapter.

GUIDELINES FOR WRITING
THE CRITICAL REVIEW

1. Establish a context for your discussion of the article (book) in the introduction.
2. Include your overall opinion about the article (book) in the introduction in the form of a thesis.
3. Summarize the article (book) briefly so that the reader will be able to interpret the comments you will make about it in the review.
4. Make specific judgments about the article (book or parts of the book) based on the suggested criteria.
5. Use direct quotes and specific examples from the article (book) to substantiate your judgments.
6. Remember that your critique is the most important part of the review and should therefore be the longest part.
7. Use the same tense to report information from the article (book) throughout your review.
8. Conclude a book review by reinterpreting your thesis in terms of the criticism you have made.

7 The Essay Examination

LIKE IT OR NOT, EXAMINATIONS ARE A CENTRAL FACT OF EVERY STUDENT'S ACADEMIC LIFE. Though disliked by many students, exams actually serve a worthwhile purpose. They allow your professors to assess how well you have mastered a certain segment of the material they have been teaching. In doing so, they permit you to *measure your own progress*. This is quite valuable, since a high grade on an exam can show you that your studying has been effective, a lower grade, that there are still areas which need improvement.

There are two basic types of exams: the "objective" type (multiple-choice questions, for instance) and the "subjective," or "essay" type. In this chapter we will concentrate on the latter type. The tasks involved in preparing for an essay exam will be broken down into three areas: anticipating questions, understanding the exam, and writing the exam.

ANTICIPATING THE QUESTIONS

A systematic approach of analytical reading and outlining throughout the semester is the best way to prepare for any type of exam. When the time comes to study for the exam itself, however, there are certain steps you can take to assist you in preparing for it effectively. In an exam, a professor is trying to find out, within a limited amount of time, how well the students have mastered the subject matter of the course. Therefore, the first factor influencing the questions to be included on the test is *selectivity*.

Selectivity

Because time is limited, most professors will choose to include questions which touch on the most fundamental principles of the course.[1] In preparing for an exam, then, you can make use of your classnotes and textbook to determine which part of the subject matter is generally considered most basic, important, or fundamental.

CLASSNOTES. Classnotes provide good clues for anticipating (or "psyching out") the material which will be on an exam. When reviewing your notes, you should ask yourself what points have been emphasized in class discussions, which principles the professor has explained in greatest detail, and even which aspects of the subject seem to be his or her

---

[1] According to academic folklore, at every institution there is at least one professor who bases exams only on footnotes and obscure supplementary readings. Although you may hear about such exams, they are the exceptions to the rule.

favorites. All of these are clues for the student preparing for an exam. It is common for a professor to have a review class prior to a major examination. If this is done, pay special attention to the topics stressed during the session. A professor will rarely say exactly which questions will be asked, but will frequently indicate the precise subject matter which will be included.

CHAPTER OUTLINING. Chapter outlining provides additional help in anticipating which questions will be on an exam. If you turn your major divisions from your chapter outline into a question, you can be relatively sure that the answer to such a question will cover information basic to the subject matter. For example, in reference to the outline which you constructed for Resource Chapter A (p. 113), changing "I. The Process of Motivation" into "What is the process of motivation?" forces you to focus on the five stages of motivation, and this certainly constitutes essential information from the chapter.

Preparation for an exam which is based on material emphasized in class lectures and which is implied by major divisions and subdivisions of textbooks involves selecting that information which is most likely to appear on the exam. At the same time, a student is "selecting out" that material which is supplementary or extraneous and therefore not something which is likely to appear.

7–1
WRITE / DISCUSS

Directions: Turn to Resource Chapter A, p. 235, "Stimulus Motives," and analyze the text to the end of the chapter to decide what questions a professor might ask on an essay exam on this material. Write eight possible questions and be prepared to discuss with your classmates why you think those questions would be asked.

UNDERSTANDING THE EXAM

Assessing the Task

One of the important factors that contributes to writing good essay examinations is a thorough understanding of the exam itself. Before you write anything, you should read through the directions and the *entire* exam to make sure that you understand precisely how much time will be allowed, what the point value is for each question, and what each question is really asking.

TIME. In a typical essay exam a student is given a list of questions which must be answered *within a specified time*. It therefore becomes important to read over the questions to compare their level of difficulty in terms of the amount of time available. You will find it helpful to mentally allocate approximately how much time you will allow yourself for writing each answer. If you do this and make a serious attempt to work within these limits, you will avoid the shock of discovering that you have only ten minutes left to answer four questions.

CHOICE. Related to the question of time is the fact that frequently *the student is given a choice* among the questions to be answered. For instance, there may be a total of fifteen questions with instructions to choose the eight you feel most competent in answering. If a student has not carefully read the instructions, he or she might make the fatal mistake of attempting to answer all the questions, thereby lowering the quality of all the answers.

POINT VALUE. Another consideration in surveying the exam is the *point value for each question.* If the first question is worth twenty (20) points and the second one is worth only ten (10), you immediately know that you should spend more time on developing your answer to the first question.

DIFFICULTY. After you have determined the questions you will answer and the amount of time you want to spend on each, it will be helpful to plan the order in which you intend to answer the questions. There are two approaches to ordering questions based on difficulty. Some students prefer to answer the longer or more difficult questions first while the information is still fresh in their minds. Others prefer to answer the shorter, more general questions first and save the more difficult ones until the end. You must decide for yourself which approach seems to be the most effective in a test situation.

7–2
DISCUSS

Directions: Below is an essay exam based on previous chapters of this book. Plan the way you would write this exam in terms of the following: (1) time, (2) choice, (3) point value, and (4) difficulty.

74.200
READING & COMPOSITION I
Midterm Exam

Directions: All of the following questions can be answered in one paragraph, with the exception of number 2, where the terms may be defined in one complete sentence. You have 1½ hours to complete the exam. There are a total of 100 points. Answers will be judged on relevance and on clarity of presentation.

1. Discuss the importance of summary writing in an academic environment. (15 points)
2. Define five of the following terms. (3 points each)

induction	listing structures
paraphrasing	chronology
coherence	chain-reaction
analogy	intensive analytical reading
deduction	objectivity

3. Explain the difference between simple comparison and analogy. (10 points)
4. Why are the relationships of comparison and contrast often found together? (10 points)
5. When can enumeration be called "classification"? When can it be called "partition"? (5 points)

6. List and give a brief example of the three types of causality. (15 points)
7. Under what conditions should examples be included in a summary? (15 points)
8. Discuss the qualities of a good summary. (15 points)

Examination Terminology

There are a number of common terms used in questions to elicit specific answers. These terms, along with the wording of the question itself, frequently require one or another of the major thought relationships to be used in writing the answer. These terms, however, do not always mean the same thing each time they are used and may be confusing to students who are not completely familiar with the full implications of examination terminology. For example, in the question, "Discuss the importance of summary writing in an academic environment," the term *discuss*, coupled in this context with the word *importance*, is not asking for a long general discussion, but rather is signaling a causal relationship. It is really asking, "Why is summary writing important in an academic environment?" Because of this type of ambiguity, it is important to read the entire question carefully as well as to understand all of the possible interpretations of question terminology.

Our discussion of question terminology will be divided into three categories: terms eliciting a specific thought relationship, terms eliciting personal interpretation, and the special term *define*.

TERMS ELICITING SPECIFIC THOUGHT RELATIONSHIPS. Terms which require the student to respond to a question by arranging information according to specific thought relationships are generally asking for a repetition of data from a textbook, readings, or classnotes. Because of the time limitation, of course, this information will usually be expressed in a shortened form (a summary, in effect). Let us now look at the terms commonly used in essay exams and explore the possible relationships they might indicate.

1. *Enumerate*
   • Simple listing, classification, partition:
   Enumerate the three kinds of managerial skills Katz considers capable of development.
   • Causality, process, chain-reaction:
   Enumerate the barriers to effective communication within a business organization.
   Enumerate the stages of the hunger mechanism.

   As these examples show, almost anything can be implied by the word *enumerate*. It is imperative that you carefully read the question for other words which indicate the kinds of items to be enumerated.
2. *Compare*
   • Similarities *and/or* differences:
   Compare Skinner's behaviorist theory to that of Watson.
   Compare the field of economics with that of business management.

   As can be seen from these examples, the verb *compare* is most often used to mean showing both similarities and differences—or even *only* similarities or *only* differences, whichever the subject matter seems to dictate.

3. *Contrast*
   - Differences:

     Contrast Skinner's behaviorist theory with that of Watson.

     The verb *contrast* asks only for differences. Any similarities which exist should be mentioned only in passing—if at all—and the essay answer should definitely focus on *differences*.

4. *Outline / Trace*
   - Chronology:

     Briefly trace (outline) the development of the computer.

   - Process, causality:

     Trace (outline) the functions of the parasympathetic nervous system.

     Note that this term does not specifically call for a formal outline. It asks, rather, for *major points*.

5. *Describe / Explain / Discuss*[2]
   - Spatial order:

     Describe (explain, discuss) the physical structure of the neuron.

   - Process

     Explain (describe, discuss) the stages of language acquisition in an infant.

   - Chronology:

     Briefly discuss (describe, explain) the background of the field of management from the Middle Ages to the eighteenth century.

   - Enumeration:

     Describe the three skills which are considered fundamental in a good manager.

   - Causality / Process:

     Discuss the hunger mechanism.

   - Comparison and/or Contrast:

     Describe the differences (and/or similarities) between the fields of economics and business management.

7–3
EXEMPLIFY   /   DISCUSS

Directions: The following questions are taken from an essay exam in a comparative anatomy course. Even though you are probably unfamiliar with the subject matter, you should be able to understand what is being asked for. Analyze the questions in terms of the main "signal words" in the question, as well as the relationship(s) which are being signaled.

1. Compare the *dermal armor* of ostracoderms and placoderms with the *scale* of reptiles. (6 points)

---

[2] Notice that these three terms are sometimes used interchangeably, and that they may signal almost any thought relationship. The term *outline* may also be used in this group.

2. Describe the structure of a vaned or contour feather. You may incorporate a labeled diagram to which your answer refers if you wish. (12 points)

3. Discuss some (3) of the selective forces that led to changes in the vertebral column when vertebrates moved from water to land. (9 points)

4. Using your knowledge of basic evolutionary principles, enumerate, in evolutionary terms, how these changes in the vertebral column might have occurred. Include in your discussion the following concepts: *variation, selection, fitness,* and *preadaptation.* (8 points)

TERMS ELICITING INTERPRETATION OF DATA, RESTRUCTURING, OR SPECIAL EMPHASIS. Some terms that appear in examination questions are doing more than asking for a simple repetition of data. You must pay particular attention to the kinds of questions in which these terms appear.

1. *Prove* may signal a causal relationship, but it may just as frequently require any other type of relationship. This word asks you to provide strong evidence—possibly including examples—for something, a skill which goes beyond simple summary writing and paraphrasing. You may have to rearrange or put a different emphasis on the data from your text or notes or possibly synthesize information from several sources in order to give sufficient evidence.

Prove that the total demand for an industry is an important factor in forecasting.

Prove that even with proper routing of communication, barriers to effective communication exist in business organizations.

Prove that the interpretations of behaviorism held by Watson and Skinner are similar.

Notice that the first question, based on the text on p. 21, requires that the reader disregard the complex combination of thought relationships in the full text and focus on only one aspect of the general process of forecasting economic conditions. It requires that you take information from the second paragraph—the idea that large firms usually keep track of all factors affecting the industry because it is very important for them to do so and that smaller firms then make use of these findings. You could also draw the conclusion (from the last paragraph) that large firms would play an important role in planning for an estimated share of the market. In other words, the response which the question is eliciting is not an explanation of the process of economic forecasting, but rather a synthesis of the information pertaining to one aspect of it: *the role of large firms.*

7-4
EXEMPLIFY / DISCUSS

A. The second of the above questions ("Prove that even with proper routing of communica-tion....") is based on the text on p. 57:

1. From which sentences in the text would data be taken to answer this question?

2. Would the thought relationship in the answer be the same type as that in the original text?

3. Would the information be the same?

B. The third question ("Prove that the interpretations....") is based on the text on p. 37:

1. Would the thought relationship in the answer be the same as that in the text?
2. Would the information be the same?
3. Which, if any, data would *not* be included?

2. *Illustrate* may indicate any number of relationships (or combinations thereof). The term implies, moreover, that appropriate examples be given for the concept which is being illustrated. It may require personal interpretation of data.

Illustrate the manner in which a child acquires language.

Illustrate the importance of forecasting the conditions of the business environment.

Illustrate the importance of glucose in the hunger drive.

Notice that the first question is asking about the manner (or process) by which a child acquires language. Thus, the organization of this answer will be very similar to the original text. The answer will, however, go beyond a simple summary of the language acquisition process because the question asks for illustration, thereby requiring the inclusion of examples. This question is based on the text on p. 131.

7–5
EXEMPLIFY / DISCUSS

A. The second of the above questions ("Illustrate the importance of forecasting. . . .") is based on the text on p. 21.
   1. Would the thought relationship in the answer be the same as that in the original text?
   2. Which information would it be necessary to include in order to *illustrate*?
   3. Which information would *not* be included?
B. The third question ("Illustrate the importance of glucose. . .") is based on the text on p. 61:
   1. Would the thought relationship in the answer be the same as that in the original text?
   2. Would all of the information in the text be included?

3. *Evaluate/Analyze*: Both of these terms may signal any of the thought relationships. They imply that the student must carefully examine the nature, function, parts, importance, or interrelationship of the subject of the question. Once again, these terms may require more than a simple repetition of factual information. They may force the student to make a personal judgment about the information.

Analyze the relationship between economics and business management.

Analyze the coding method used in long-term memory.

Evaluate the importance of conceptual skills in good management.

Notice that in order to answer the first question, the student must make a general statement about what the relationship between the two fields is and then give more information and perhaps examples of how these two fields function together. The thought relationship in the answer will not follow that of the original text—comparison/contrast—but will explain the two terms using a process thought relationship. This question is based on the text on p. 25.

7–6
EXEMPLIFY / DISCUSS

A. The second of the above questions ("Analyze the coding method. . . .") is based on the text on p. 40.

   1. Would the thought relationship in the answer be the same as that in the original text? If not, what would it be?

   2. What part of the text would be included in the answer?

   3. The text contains an *analogy*. Would the analogy be included in the answer?

B. The third question ("Evaluate the importance. . . .") is based on the text on p. 47:

   1. Of the three skills mentioned in the text, which would be included in the answer?

   2. Does the question require the student to make a personal judgment? (That is, does the *author* make a judgment?)

   4. *Comment/Respond*: These terms may also signal any of the thought relationships, but they often require a personal interpretation or choice when dealing with the information contained in the text. In addition, they frequently require that students *contradict* the statement to which they are responding or on which they are commenting. Thus, they constitute potentially the most difficult type of essay question.

   A child's position in a family has little or no influence upon his or her achievement later in life. Respond.

   Comment on the importance of Parliament in the parliamentary-cabinet system.

   According to Piaget, during the preoperational stage, a child's mental work consists in establishing relationships between experience and action. Comment on this theory in terms of a child's acquisition of language.

   Notice that the statement in the first question is a direct contradiction of what the student will have learned from the textbook. The student is thus required to respond by indicating that it is *not true* and then to go on to provide evidence as to *why* it is false. The general thought relationships in the answer would then be contrast and causality. A good answer to this question would, in other words, draw a contrast between the statement and the textbook and provide reasons why that contrast is true. This question is based on the text on p. 133.

7–7
EXEMPLIFY / DISCUSS

A. The second of the above questions ("Comment on. . . .") is based on the text on p. 33:

   1. In order to answer the question, what general statement would have to be made first?

   2. Would the thought relationship in the answer be the same as that in the original text? If not, what would it be?

B. The third question ("According to Piaget. . . .") is based on the text on p. 131:

   1. Does Piaget's theory contradict the information in the original text (that is, the information concerning a child's language acquisition)?

2. In order to answer the question, would the student have to explain the entire process of language acquisition in children?

3. Does the question require the student to interpret the information differently from the way it is presented in the text? Does it require that a *personal judgment* be made?

THE SPECIAL TERM "DEFINE." Because the purpose of an essay examination is to enable the professor to determine whether or not you understand the basic concepts of the subject matter, the term *define* or its alternate forms (*Give the meaning of . . .* or *Explain what is meant by . . .*, for example) occur with high frequency on this type of exam. Even the term *identify* may be used to elicit a definition, as in the instruction "Identify B. F. Skinner," which asks the student to indicate who he was and why he was important.

Remember that a *formal definition* is a brief method of defining terms. It includes the term to be defined, the class (or category) to which the term belongs, and the features which distinguish it from the other members of that class. If a question specifically says, "Briefly define . . . ," or if the point value of the definition is relatively low (2 to 5 points, for instance, out of 100 points), then you should probably limit yourself to writing a short formal definition, unless other information is specifically asked for. Examples of such questions are:

Briefly define acoustic coding.
Give a short definition of glucose.
Define the term *pons*. (2 points)
Give a brief definition of motivation.

Notice that in writing a formal definition for the term in the first question, the student would do the following:

1. Name the term: Acoustic coding is . . .
2. Classify the term: . . . a method of storing and recalling information in long-term memory . . .
3. Mention distinguishing features: . . . which is based on sound.

7–8
EXEMPLIFY / DISCUSS

A. To write a formal definition of *glucose* (refer to the text on p. 61):
   1. How would you classify the term?
   2. How would you distinguish it from other members of that class?
B. To write a formal definition of *pons* (refer to the text on p. 20):
   1. How would you classify the term?
   2. How would you distinguish it from other members of that class?

C. To define *motivation* (refer to the text on pp. 229–30, Resource Chapter A):
   1. How would you classify the term?
   2. How would you distinguish it from other members of that class?

   Certain kinds of definition questions, however, ask not for short formal definitions but rather for longer *extended* ones. Besides classification and comparison/contrast, a longer or more heavily weighted definition often implies other thought relationships, since terms sometimes imply a process, or the fact that members of a class are distinguished from each other by causes, effects, relative order in time, size, etc. (refer back to pp. 119–20 if you need to refresh your memory of what can be implied by the term "extended definition"). In a longer, more thorough definition, you may have to include a combination of these relationships as well as some examples of the term being defined. Look at the following examples:

   What is meant by the term *sympathetic nervous system*? (10 points)
   Thoroughly define the term *medulla*. (10 points)
   Define the term *managerial economics*. (10 points)

   Notice that the first question is worth ten (10) points and therefore requires a somewhat extended definition. To answer it, you would begin by naming, classifying (". . . a part of the central nervous system. . ."), and distinguishing (". . . which prepares the body to respond to an emergency."). To *extend* the definition, you would explain the process by which the sympathetic nervous system accomplishes this preparation (that is, it increases heart beat and breathing, stops digestion, and activates the adrenal glands). You might also mention that these nerve fibers connect to every internal organ, causing the body's reaction to be quite widespread (causality).

7–9
EXEMPLIFY / DISCUSS

A. In defining the term *managerial economics* (refer to the text on p. 25):
   1. How is the term to be classified?
   2. How could it be distinguished from other items in that category?
   3. What information from the original text could be included to *extend* the definition? What possible relationships would there be in the definition?
B. In defining the term *medulla* (refer to the text on p. 20):
   1. How can the term be classified?
   2. How could it be distinguished from other members of that class?
   3. How could it be extended? What possible thought relationships would be present in the extended definition?

WRITING THE EXAM

The techniques used in answering essay-type examinations differ somewhat from those which you have learned for analyzing long and short texts. They contrast most notably with the techniques used to introduce chapters and chapter parts, where an author takes time to interest the reader in the subject in a general—and often *roundabout*—way, then gradually focuses the reader's attention on the point in question. Authors, particularly those who write introductory texts, need to do this since most of their readers are relatively unfamiliar with the subject matter. When writing an exam, however, you will not have to focus your professor's attention with a lengthy introduction to a short essay-type answer. Professors generally intend for their questions to provide sufficient focus.

Moreover, there are sometimes a hundred or more students in an introductory course. In an exam composed of, say, six essay-type answers, this means that the professor might have to grade as many as 600 short essays! He or she will therefore appreciate your being *concise* and *to the point*.

The remainder of this chapter will give you suggestions as to how you can best do this when taking an exam.

The First Sentence

Just as in the first sentence of a summary you must briefly acquaint your reader with the controlling idea of the text in question, so in an essay exam you must immediately indicate to your professor the controlling idea of your answer. By doing this, you are indicating the direction which your answer will take. Your first sentence should provide this information in two ways: (1) by repeating or restating the question, and (2) by providing a brief but pointed summary of your answer to the question.

REPEATING OR RESTATING THE QUESTION. You should begin an essay question answer by *repeating the essential information of the question*. When this has been done, your professor realizes that you have understood what is being asked for and that you are addressing yourself to the question rather than "writing *around* it" (sometimes called "beating around the bush"—a common technique which is, unfortunately, certain to earn an "F" from many professors).

What information should be repeated? This varies, depending on the nature of the question itself. In those questions which elicit a primary thought relationship, the first sentence of the answer (1) should identify the subject of the discussion with *words and phrases* from the question or with synonymous or related expressions, and (2) should indicate, by using *key words and phrases*, which *thought relationships* will be used in the rest of the answer. Study the following sample answer:

Question: Although the theories of Skinner and Watson differ slightly, their general approach to psychology is similar. Discuss.

Answer:

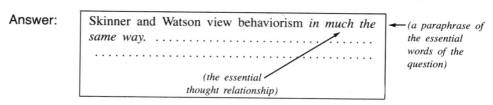

Skinner and Watson view behaviorism *in much the same way.* .... ←—(a paraphrase of the essential words of the question)

(the essential thought relationship)

Question #2: Enumerate the three kinds of managerial skills which Katz suggests can be developed.

Answer:

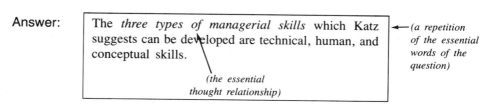

The *three types of managerial skills* which Katz suggests can be developed are technical, human, and conceptual skills. ←—(a repetition of the essential words of the question)

(the essential thought relationship)

Those questions which elicit an interpretation of information may sometimes begin by repeating the question; frequently, however, they require that a *generalization* be made in response to the question instead of a mere repetition or restatement. If it is possible, the thought relationship(s) involved in the answer should also be indicated in your first-sentence generalization. Consider the following two examples:

Question #3: Illustrate the importance of glucose in the hunger drive.

Answer:

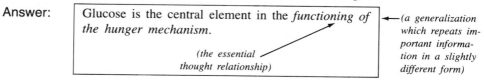

Glucose is the central element in the *functioning of the hunger mechanism.* ←—(a generalization which repeats important information in a slightly different form)

(the essential thought relationship)

Question #4: A child's position in a family has little or no influence upon his or her achievement in later life. Respond.

Answer:

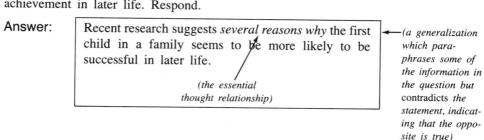

Recent research suggests *several reasons why* the first child in a family seems to be more likely to be successful in later life. ←—(a generalization which paraphrases some of the information in the question but contradicts *the statement, indicating that the opposite is true)*

(the essential thought relationship)

PROVIDING A ONE-SENTENCE SUMMARY. Notice, in each of the four preceding examples, that the question has actually been answered in the first sentence, although in a very simplistic way. These first sentences thus constitute *controlling ideas*, or *topic sentences* of the paragraphs which are to follow. They are all one-sentence summaries. In the first example, the student has not only restated the idea that Skinner's and Watson's approaches are similar (comparison), but has stated what that approach is: behaviorism. In the second, the student has indicated a division of skills (enumeration) and has actually named the three skills involved. In the third, glucose has been shown to be *very* important (it is called "a central element"); thus, the discussion will revolve around its crucial role in the hunger mechanism (process). In the last example, the generalization constitutes a *contradiction* of the statement in the question. The student's answer will argue the opposite point of view by listing reasons (enumeration, causality) and by citing recent research that backs up the general statement.

In each of these examples, the way the first sentences are phrased suggests to the professor that the student understands the question and knows the answer to it. It "sets the stage" for what will follow—actual causes, types, comparisons, examples, and so on. The body of the answer will, of course, let the professor know this first impression of competency is justified.

7–10
WRITE

Directions: Identify the thought relationships indicated in the following questions. Then write the first sentence of the answer to each question, as though you were actually taking an essay exam. All of the questions are based on the "Physiological Motives" section of Resource Chapter A (pp. 230–35).

1. *Question*: Physiological motives are called *primary drives*. Explain.

   Relationship: ⸺⸺⸺⸺⸺⸺⸺⸺⸺⸺⸺⸺⸺

   First sentence: ⸺⸺⸺⸺⸺⸺⸺⸺⸺⸺⸺⸺⸺⸺⸺⸺⸺⸺⸺⸺⸺⸺⸺⸺⸺⸺⸺⸺⸺⸺⸺⸺⸺⸺⸺⸺

2. *Question*: Discuss the relationship between the blood-sugar level and hunger.
3. *Question*: Compare the physiology of thirst with that of hunger.
4. *Question*: How does pain differ from the other primary drives (hunger, thirst, sleep)?
5. *Question*: Enumerate the physiological and learned factors which contribute to the maternal drive in higher animals.
6. *Question*: Comment on the fact that the sex drive in humans cannot be described in physiological terms alone.

Completing the Answer

Writing the rest of the answer to the essay question is dependent on what you remember about the subject matter and on what thought relationship is stated or implied in the question. If you have understood the question and have written a first sentence in which you have repeated the essential information of the question, indicated the thought relationship to be developed, and, in effect, summarized your answer, then you have predicted what will appear in the rest of your answer.

   The following question and complete answer correspond to the second example from the preceding section. They are based on the sample enumerative text in Chapter 2 (p. 47); assume that this is the only information which you have been given concerning Katz's classification of managerial skills.

Question #2: Enumerate the three kinds of managerial skills which Katz suggests can be developed.

Answer: According to Katz, the three kinds of skills which can be developed in a manager are technical, human, and conceptual skills. <u>Technical skills</u> are those which concern proficient performance through use of the proper techniques, and they are especially important at the lower levels of management. Accounting, selling, and production are examples of technical skills. As a manager moves up to higher levels, <u>human skills</u> become more important. These skills involve cooperation and the ability to get along with people without seeming to manipulate them. The most important set of skills, but the most difficult to analyze, are those involving <u>conceptual ability</u>. These kinds of skills enable a manager to view each factor in relationship to the whole, to create and carry out new ideas, and to discard those things which are unimportant.

   This answer represents a condensation (summary) from memory of the original text, and it includes examples to clarify what is being talked about. Notice that the first sentence determines the organization of the entire answer. The three kinds of skills are briefly enumerated and then described more fully in the sentences that follow.

   Notice that the answer does not include all of the information from the original text, but only those things which will indicate to the professor that the student understands and is able to define the three skills being asked about. Nor is the answer expressed in exactly the same words used by the author of the text. The student has instead expressed the information by way of a paraphrase.

   A final remark about the student's answer is in order. You will note that after listing each of the items in the first sentence, the student then <u>underlined</u> each of them as it was presented for discussion. This kind of visual technique is extremely useful in that it allows the professor who is grading the exam to immediately locate the important divisions of the paragraph. Because it does this, it constitutes an extremely valuable kind of device to use in answering a question. However, even more visually striking than simple underlining is the following arrangement:

   According to Katz, the three kinds of skills which can be developed in a manager are technical, human, and conceptual skills:

1. <u>Technical skills</u> are those which concern proficient performance through use of the proper techniques, and they are especially important at the lower levels of management.
2. <u>Human skills</u> become more important as a manager moves up to higher levels. These skills involve cooperation and the ability to get along with people without seeming to manipulate them.
3. The most important set of skills, but the most difficult to analyze, are those involving <u>conceptual ability</u>. These kinds of skills enable a manager to view each factor in

relationship to the whole, to create and carry out new ideas, and to discard those things which are unimportant.

Both of these techniques—underlining within a paragraph and separation into smaller indented paragraphs with numerals—are "visual tricks" that you should learn to use when writing an essay-type answer that divides something into distinct parts, whether these parts correspond to members of a class, reasons, causes, results, steps, stages, or any other series of items. (Note: The other information in the answer, of course, must be precise and accurate; these techniques will not, in themselves, guarantee success in an essay examination.)

7-11
WRITE

Directions: Referring back to Exercise 7–10, complete the answers to the six essay questions. Use the first sentences which you have written. Be sure to use correct paragraph form (i.e., indent the first word). Remember to do the following:

1. Make use of paraphrasing techniques—i.e., try to express the information in your own words.
2. Include in your answer only that information which is related to the question.
3. Use such visual aids as underlining and numerals wherever appropriate (distinguishing two or more main terms, enumerating items, etc.).

7-12
WRITE

Directions: Prepare to take an essay exam on Resource Chapter A, beginning with the section "Stimulus Motives" (pp. 235–37) and continuing to the end of the chapter. During a future class meeting—the date will be announced by your teacher—you will have an essay exam based on this portion of the chapter. Carefully analyze and study the text, just as if you were preparing to take an exam in a psychology course. You will not be able to refer to the chapter or to your notes when you take this exam.

7-13
WRITE (Supplemental)

Directions: Prepare to take an essay exam on Resource Chapter B, pp. 245–59. If your teacher feels you need additional practice in taking essay exams, one based on this chapter will be given during a future class meeting. Follow the directions for Exercise 7–12 in preparing for this exam.

GUIDELINES FOR TAKING
ESSAY EXAMS

1. Keep up with regularly assigned reading throughout the term.
2. Try to anticipate the types of questions which will be asked based on reading assignments and class notes.
3. Study specialized vocabulary.
4. Read through and assess the entire exam before beginning to write.
5. Determine the thought relationship suggested by each question.
6. Repeat the question and essentially answer it in the first sentence of your response.
7. Include in your answer only that information which supports and contributes to the controlling idea as stated in your first sentence.

8 The Research Paper

ONE OF THE MOST COMMONLY ASSIGNED TYPES OF ACADEMIC WRITING IS THE RESEARCH PAPER.[1] It is a formal, relatively long paper (anywhere from 1,500 to 5,000 words) in which a student proposes a thesis and supports that thesis with pertinent data from a number of outside sources. The purpose of such an assignment is to familiarize the student with a particular subject through library research to the extent that the student will have sufficient expertise to draw specific conclusions based on the information which has been gathered. The approach to writing such a paper will thus be *inductive*. However, the paper itself will be presented in *deductive* fashion: the thesis, proposed by the student on the basis of the information which has been gathered, is stated at the beginning of the paper.

In this chapter we will discuss the stages in the preparation of such a paper, as well as the conventions which must be followed in writing it. These include:

• Choosing and limiting a topic
• Proposing a working thesis
• Compiling a working bibliography
• Taking notes
• Developing a working outline
• Assembling the rough draft
• Writing the final draft

At the end of this chapter, you will prepare a "mini" research paper which makes use of the resource material in this text.

CHOOSING AND LIMITING A TOPIC

The subject of a research paper can be virtually anything. The variety in topic is limited only by the imagination of the professor who assigns it. Sometimes a professor will be very specific in describing the topic to be researched, even to the extent of providing a thesis for the student; at other times, the student is free to choose anything which has been discussed in the course as a subject for investigation. In either case, the first thing you must do is to familiarize yourself in a general way with the subject matter. This means that you must do enough reading so that you will be able to decide which subject or approach

---

[1] A research paper may also be called a *term paper*, a *library paper*, or an *investigative paper*. No matter what name a professor gives it, the procedures and conventions are the same.

to the subject you will eventually take. If, for instance, your management professor assigns a research paper on the general topic of "leadership," you may wish to review the sections of your textbook(s) or other assigned readings having to do with this subject. In addition, you might consult a general reference book, such as an encyclopedia or handbook. This kind of reading is called *preliminary research*. Its purpose is to provide you with enough familiarity with the subject so that you can decide on the specific aspect of leadership you wish to investigate in the preparation of your paper. In doing this preliminary reading, you may wish to take notes, and it is always wise to keep a record of the reading you have done in case you wish to refer, later in the research process, to some of these early sources.

Research Tip

- Even at this early stage, make out a separate *index card* for every book you consult.
- Include all necessary *bibliographical information* on each card.
- Keep your cards filed in alphabetical order, according to the *authors' last names*.

Topics to Avoid

Although you may be particularly interested in the most current theories of leadership, it would not be wise to select one of these theories as your topic: If an issue is too current, it will not be possible to find enough information on it to do a thorough job of researching it. For example, if you read an article in a current issue of *Business Week* which reports new research findings on corporate leadership, it is unlikely that you will be able to find sufficient information on these new findings to do a complete research project on them.

Other topics which should be avoided in doing academic research are those which are too controversial. Depending on the topic, you may well be able to find sufficient information; however, because the topic is controversial, you might have great difficulty separating fact from opinion and drawing a conclusion based on what you have read.

Interest Level

You should also keep in mind that, whenever possible, it is best to choose an aspect of the subject in which you have some real interest. You will be spending a great deal of time reading and writing about this aspect of the subject, and it will certainly help your motivation if you find the subject interesting.

Narrowing the Topic

Once you have decided on a general aspect of the assigned subject which is both interesting and likely to produce a sufficient number of objective sources, you must decide, given the assigned length of the paper, what portion of that topic can be adequately treated within the length limitations of the paper. Obviously, the whole subject of "leadership" could not be fully developed, nor could the subject of "leadership in the business community." You must therefore *restrict* the scope of your topic to a *very specific aspect* of the overall topic, one which can be fully researched and developed within the word or page limitation imposed by the assignment.

Although there are a number of ways in which this can be accomplished, there are several general kinds of restrictions which can be applied systematically to a subject in order to limit it to something specific enough to write about. These restrictions are (1) *place*, (2) *type*, (3) *time*, and (4) *aspect*. For example, the general subject of leadership might be restricted in the manner shown in the diagram. (Note, as you study the branching diagram, that this is only one of many different ways in which the subject can be restricted to research-worthy proportions.)

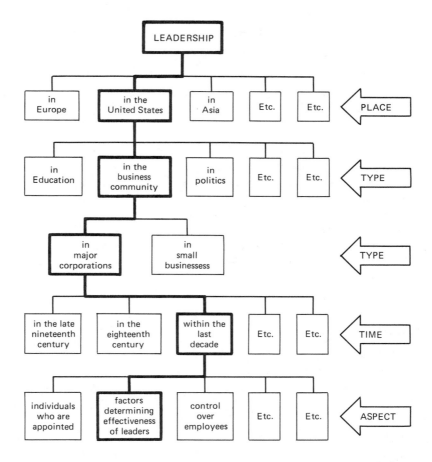

By thus limiting the topic, we have arrived at a *more specific subject* which is related to the general topic of "leadership" and which could be researched in greater depth:

<u>factors determining the effectiveness of leaders</u> <u>in major</u> <u>U.S. corporations</u>
(Aspect)   *(Type)*   *(Place)*
<u>within the last decade</u>
(Time)

Many other subjects are, of course, possible on the general subject of "leadership":

individuals who are appointed to leadership positions in international organizations which promote welfare programs
or
the control of U.S. educational leaders over their employees during the early twentieth century

8-1
EXEMPLIFY / WRITE

Directions: Apply the restrictions of place, type, time, and aspect to two of the five general topics listed here in order to limit them to subjects which are appropriate for a research paper.

1. the need for power
2. work motivation
3. expert power
4. the need for achievement
5. leadership (*in another way*)

PROPOSING A WORKING THESIS

The second step in preparing a research paper is to propose a "working thesis"—that is, to make a statement about the limited topic which you will either prove or disprove in the course of your research. Your preliminary reading should have provided you with enough data about that subject to enable you to propose a thesis. It is important to do so since by having such a thesis, you have established a control and limit for the reading you will do. Keep in mind, however, that *this thesis is tentative!* At the time you propose it, you will know very little about the subject. Thus, as you do your research and gain more expertise in the subject, *you may have to revise your thesis one or more times.*

When you propose a working thesis, you do so by making a statement about your subject which further limits it. In other words, you say something about your already limited subject, or *predicate* it. Such a statement is usually expressed in one simple or complex sentence and will, of course, involve a personal judgment or evaluation of the subject matter. Since the judgment is expressed objectively, however, you should avoid such expressions as "In my opinion. . ." or "I think. . .".

For instance, if the limited topic which you have finally decided on is the one suggested in the preceding diagram ("factors determining the effectiveness of leaders in major U.S. corporations within the last decade"), there are any number of predications that could be made. Your choice of predication depends entirely on the amount of information you have about the subject matter. If the only information you had about this subject initially was the "Path-Goal Theory,"[2] you might predicate your subject in one of the following ways:

The most effective leaders in major U.S. corporations within the last decade <u>have been those who have set clear goals for their employees and provided a smooth means for the accomplishment of those goals.</u>

Predication

or

The most effective leaders in major U.S. corporations within the last decade <u>have been those who have exhibited achievement-oriented behavior.</u>

Predication

The importance of establishing such a premise is that as you continue your research, you will be looking specifically for *evidence which can support the statement you have made.* If your reading later included the interview with David C. McClelland,[3] and if you were convinced of his arguments, you might then revise your working thesis accordingly:

The most effective leaders in major U.S. corporations within the last decade <u>have been those who have known how to make positive use of power.</u>

Predication

Further reading might influence your thinking to again revise your thesis. Thus, it will not be until you have completed your research that you will make your final decision as to what your thesis will be. In the meantime, though, you are directing your research to the extent that you are searching for a specific answer or explanation to a specific problem.

Research Tip

Don't throw anything away; you may need it later. This includes

- preliminary versions of your thesis statement
- important ideas that have occurred to you already in the course of your reading
- interesting quotations which you have come across

File all these things in a convenient way so that you can retrieve them easily. But *KEEP THEM!*

---

[2] A description of this theory can be found on pp. 270–71 of Resource Chapter C.
[3] Resource Chapter B, pp. 256–58.

8–2
WRITE

Directions: Taking the topics which you have limited in Exercise 8–1, propose a *working thesis* for each of them. (Note: You are not expected to do any research for this exercise; simply show, in the type of predication which you choose, that you have understood the nature of this second kind of limiting technique.)

COMPILING A WORKING BIBLIOGRAPHY

The initial reading that you have done on your subject will have been very general. However, after you have proposed a working thesis, you will then direct your subsequent reading to those specific areas that will give you the data to prove your thesis. Your next step, therefore, is to locate the kind of texts which will help you in your analysis of the problem you have selected.

The material you will be reading will probably be an even balance between books, journal articles (and perhaps newspaper articles), documents, and interviews—although this may vary considerably, depending on the nature of your research. In locating this information, you will make use of two valuable research tools in the library: the **card catalog** and an **index to periodical literature** in the field you are investigating. Because you do not have time to read everything which is available on your particular subject, you must be selective. Both the card catalog and the index can help you in your selection of appropriate reading material.

The Card Catalog

For every book in every library, there are at least three card entries in the card catalog:

1. a *title* card
2. an *author* card (there may be more than one if there is more than one author)
3. a *subject* card (there may be more than one subject card if the book deals with more than one subject)

Generally speaking, a researcher concentrates on the *subject card entries* when looking for books on a particular subject. Of course, he or she may have occasion to look for a particular book by a particular author and would therefore make use of the other two types of entries; our concern here, however, is to analyze the kind of information found on a subject card entry that is of help to a student who is doing research. Study the following sample subject card for *Essentials of Management*, the book from which Resource Chapter C has been taken.

```
HD31
.M335        Massie, Joseph L
1979              Essentials of management / Joseph L. Massie. — 3d ed. —
             Englewood Cliffs, N.J.: Prentice-Hall, c1979.
                  x, 262 p.: ill.; 24 cm. — (Prentice-Hall essentials of management series)
                  Includes bibliographies and index.
                  ISBN 0-13-286351-0.   ISBN 0-13-286344-8 pbk.




                  1. Industrial management.   2. Management.   I. Title.
             HD31.M335   1979              658                78-23326
                                                              MARC

             Library of Congress             78
```

In addition to the Library of Congress identification number,[4] which provides information as to the book's *location in the library*, this card gives the student researcher a number of valuable clues. (1) Of importance to the student looking for *current books* on this subject is the fact that the book was published in 1979. Since this is the case, it is likely that it might contain timely information about leadership. On the other hand, if you were to find a book about leadership published in 1955, it is unlikely that the information in it would be current enough to use in researching your topic. (2) Moreover, the card tells you that this book includes a *bibliography*, where you might find other books that would be helpful to you. (3) The fact that it has an *index* also tells you that it will be easy for you to locate those sections dealing specifically with your subject. (4) A further piece of information to be found on the card is the section at the very bottom, where *other subject entries* for this book are listed. In this case, you know that if you can find this book under the general heading "Industrial management," you are also likely to find other books on the same topic under that heading. No matter what your subject is, the card catalog entry will give you this information about the book so that you can decide—in very general terms, of course—whether it will be helpful to you before you even see it. Any other subject headings under which the book is listed may also guide you to other pertinent books.

[4] We have used the Library of Congress card catalog system because it is the one most used by university libraries. The Dewey Decimal System, used by many public libraries, employs a different subject classification system and a different numbering system, but the cards will still contain the same information.

Research Tip

If you are having trouble finding your subject in the subject card catalog, consult *Library of Congress Subject Headings* to find out how this subject is expressed in the Library of Congress system. You will find, for example, that "achievement" does not appear, but "motivation" and a cross-reference to "achievement motivation" do.

Your first step in doing research, then, will be to use the card catalog in the library to compile a list of books on your subject which will be useful to you in your investigation. When you are working with the card catalog, make sure that you copy down the title, author, all of the numbers and the letters in the call number, and other facts of publication for the books that you intend to use. You may need this information later when you are compiling your final bibliography. This bibliography will be a list of all the books which have affected your thinking on the subject you are investigating, whether or not you refer to them directly in your paper; the only sources you will not include are those which you discard immediately as not being relevant.

Research Tip

- Continue to make out a separate *index card* for each book you consult.
- Keep all your cards filed together in alphabetical order, according to the *authors' last names*.

8–3
EXEMPLIFY   /   WRITE DOWN

Directions: Go to the card catalog in the library. In the subject-card section, find three books you feel would be helpful in researching one of the thesis statements which you wrote in Exercise 8–2. Copy down all the information for these books. Be prepared to explain which information in the card catalog entry convinced you that each particular book might be helpful. *Do not get the books.* Base your decision on the card catalog entry.

Periodical Indexes

A second valuable way of finding information on your subject is to make use of the periodical indexes in your field of investigation. Since a periodical index lists current magazine and journal articles according to subject matter, use of such indexes is extremely helpful to the researcher. If you are looking for current articles on the subject of leadership, for instance, it is much easier to go to the *Business Periodicals Index* and look under the heading of "leadership" than it would be to search through the periodicals section of the library at random for articles on your subject. Periodical guides are issued cumulatively for each year and at various times (monthly or quarterly, depending on the index) for the current year.

KINDS OF INDEXES. Each area of academic study has its own periodical index. These include, but are not limited to, such items as the following:

1. *Business Periodicals Index*
2. *Social Science Index*
3. *Humanities Index*
4. *Applied Science and Technology Index*
5. *PAIS Bulletin (Public Affairs Information Service Index)*

In some cases, you would not limit yourself to using only one index. For example, the subject of leadership is cross-disciplinary, and you would therefore be able to make use of articles in the *Business Periodicals Index* and the *Social Science Index*, because both disciplines are concerned with this subject.

In addition to the indexes for each academic field, there is a more general index—*The Reader's Guide to Periodical Literature*—which includes articles found in the general press. However, because articles from popular magazines such as *Newsweek* or *Psychology Today* are generally not academic in nature, a researcher would not make use of this index unless articles from the academic indexes could not be found.

Another type of index is the newspaper index. If you wish to find *very* current articles on a subject, you might consult a newspaper index, which lists articles according to subject matter. For example, if your library receives *The New York Times*, it might also have *The New York Times Index*, which will tell you exactly where and in which issue you can find articles on your subject matter. Once again, however, newspaper articles are not academic in nature and therefore are not used frequently by the researcher unless (1) the topic happens to be of a very current nature, (2) historical documentation is necessary, or (3) a current example related to your subject would add a great deal to the support of your thesis. Another drawback to using newspaper articles is that a library generally microfilms its newspaper collection, making it more difficult to read.

INTERPRETING THE ENTRIES. Although the articles listed in each of the academic periodical guides differ according to the discipline, the way in which they are listed is the same. You should be aware of several conventions involved in this format. In order to save space, many *abbreviations* are used in the article entries, a fact which can make them difficult to understand. At the front of a periodical index, you will find a list of abbreviations, both for journal titles and other kinds of information. Until you are familiar with these abbreviations, you can expect to be referring to this list constantly. You should be aware, too, that *an entry is not written in conventional academic form.* Entry format in an index violates the punctuation and capitalization rules for both formal footnoting and bibliography, so that you cannot use an entry as it is for a footnote or a bibliographic entry. The purpose of the index entry is only to tell you what the article is about and where you can find it in the periodicals section of the library.

Notice how abbreviations, punctuation, and capitalization are used in the following sample subject entry:

Sample Subject Entry

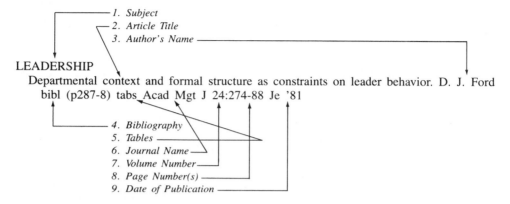

8–4
EXEMPLIFY / DISCUSS

A. Which appears first after the subject—author or title? How would this be done in a formal footnote?

B. What mark of punctuation separates the title and the author's name? What seems to be the only capitalization rule which is followed in writing the title? How would the title have been written in a formal footnote?

C. How does capitalization and/or punctuation help the eye to locate the journal title? How would this be done in a formal footnote?

D. What mark of punctuation separates the volume and the page number(s)? How would this be done in a formal footnote?

E. Is the bibliography in this sample entry found at the beginning or the end of the article?

Note that the *Business Periodicals Index*, as well as most other indexes of academic articles, do *not* include author entries. When you find a person's name listed, it is an indication that the entry is *about* that person.

Sample Entry

LAUTENBERG, Frank
  ADP trades up. Forbes 128:148+ Jl 6 '81

8–5
EXEMPLIFY / DISCUSS

A. What is the title of the article? How do you know where the title ends?

B. What is the name of the journal?

C. How do you know that the article is more than one page long?

8-6
EXEMPLIFY / DISCUSS

Directions: After studying the sample page and the two guides to abbreviations used in the *Business Periodicals Index,** show that you understand how to read the index by answering the questions which follow.

Subject heading → LATIN AMERICA
  See also subhead Latin America under the following subjects
  Banks and banking
  Forests and forestry
  Investments, Foreign
  Oil and gas leases
  Railroads
  Terrorism

Subject subheading ——————— Commerce
  United States
  Latin markets. B. J. Dooley. Am Import/Export Mgt 96:20 Ja '82
  US apparel exporters go south, explore growing Latin markets. R. S. Edwards. Bus Am 5: 12-13 Ja 11 '82

Foreign relations
United States
Latin America: outcasts no more. Economist 281:40 N 7 '81
LATIN AMERICANS in the United States. See Hispanics in the United States
LATIN square design. See Experimental design
LAUNCH vehicles (astronautics)
  Ariane 4 proposed to ESA. Interavia 36:1077 N '81
  ESA evaluating new Ariane 4 launcher. J. M. Lenorovitz. Aviation W 115:87-9 O 12 '81
  RL10 cryogenic engine life extended. E. H. Kolcum. il Aviation W 115:61+ O 5 '81
  Soviet booster advance believed to exceed Saturn 5 capability. Aviation W 115:48-9 N 2 '81
LAURE, Maurice
  Alchemist at Société Générale [interview] P. Fallon and A. Sington. por Euromoney p 174-6+ O '81
LAW
Other subject entries where articles might be found
  See also
  Children—Law
  Evidence (law)
  Jurisdiction
  Last words on governing law. J. S. Carroll. Euromoney p 129+ D '81
LAWYERS
  See also
  Black lawyers
  Legal clinics
  Claim jumpers in three-piece suits [Hyatt Regency Hotel disaster] J. Blyskal. Forbes 128: 40-1 D 7 '81
  Discharge rights of attorneys in the excepted service. W. B. Morgan. Labor L J 33:46-56 Ja '82
  Lawyer by day, cartoonist by night. L. Williamson. Ed & Pub 114:46 N 14 '81
  Why corporations need an annual legal review. R. M. Shafton. tabs Mgt Acct 63:66-9 N '81
  Working with attorneys in commercial and investment real estate. S. Petersen and K. Ross. Real Estate Today 14:32-5 N/D '81

Advertising
Attorney advertising. M. A. Humphreys and J. J. Kasulis. bibl tabs J Adv Res 21:31-7 D '81
High court hears arguments on lawyer ad rules. Ed & Pub 114:12-13 N 14 '81

Client relationship
Fiduciary audits and the attorney-client privilege. P. S. Hirzel and J. D. Mamorsky. Pension World 17:41-4 N '81

Great Britain
Making the best use of your company lawyer. C. K. Cash. Director 34:56-7 O '81
Should institutes act as both judge and jury? H. Rowan. CA Mag 114:89-91 O '81

LEAD
  Lead helps solve critical nuclear waste disposal problem [advertisement] Elect World 195:60 O '81
  Lead oxide prices decrease; producers cite low metal price. Chem Mkt Rept 221:25 Ja 18 '82
  Sherwin-Williams' finish accords OSHA ruling. tab Beverage Ind 71:76A-76B D 18 '81
LEAD industry
  Evaluating the economics of lead smelting. D. B. C. King and G. M. Meisel. il tabs World Min 34:48-52 N '81
LEAD mines and mining
Sardinia
Mechanized Masua. J. R. Chadwick. il World Min 35:36-9 Ja '82
LEAD poisoning
  Inner-city black children at high risk to lead. Chem & Eng N 60:9 Ja 18 '82
  Lead-poisoned children win structured award. R. L. Rundle. Bus Insur 15:2+ N 9 '81
LEADERSHIP
  Causal attributions and perceptions of leadership. J. S. Phillips and R. G. Lord. bibl tabs Org Behav & Hum Perform 28:143-63 O '81
  Critique of leader match and its implication for leadership research. B. Kabanoff. bibl(p762-4) Pers Psychol 34:749-64 Wint '81
  Is there a problem with the LPC score in leader match? S. Shiflett. Pers Psychol 34:765-9 Wint '81
  Leaders of the future will they be individuals or a committee. Mgt R 76:46 D '81
  Leadership and development. W. Bennis. Train & Devel J 35:7+ O '81
  Leadership: some principles and concepts. R. I. Lester. Pers J 60:868-70 N '81
  Life at the top: the struggle for power. R. M. Kanter. Can Banker & ICB R 88:51-5 O '81
  Manager behavior in a social context: the impact of impression management on attributions and disciplinary actions. R. E. Wood and T. R. Mitchell. bibl(p376-8) tabs Org Behav & Hum Perform 28:356-78 D '81
  Reappraisal of leadership theory and training. J. Owens. Pers Adm 26:75-6+ N '81
  Substitutes for leadership: test of a construct. J. P. Howell and P. W. Dorfman. bibl tabs Acad Mgt J 24:714-28 D '81
  What's it all about. Alpha? M. Stearns. Data Mgt 19:50 O '81
LEAK detection
  API ponders tank leak strike forces [annual meeting, Chicago] NPN 74:51 Ja '82
LEAKING of information. See Official secrets
LEAR Siegler, Inc.
  Lear Siegler prunes its diverse garden and comes up green. C. T. Post. Iron Age 224:63+ N 2 '81
  Lear Siegler takes action in terminal price war. F. Catalano. Mini-Micro Syst 14:19 S '81
LEARNING, Psychology of
  Audio-workbook—an interactive approach to learning. H. Komras. Train & Devel J 35: 20-2 D '81
  Memory aids in the learning of probabilistic inference tasks. J. Kuylenstierna and B. Brehmer. Org Behav & Hum Perform 28:415-24 D '81
LEARNING curves
  Model for life cycle cost analysis with a learning drive. D. S. Remer and others. bibl tabs Eng Econ 27:29-58 Fall '81
LEASE and rental services
  See also
  United States Leasing International, Inc.
  Leasing business revolution. A. Hershman. Duns Bus M 118:60-1+ O '81
Political activities
Tax leases bug the leasing business. il Bus W p90+ Ja 18 '82

* *Business Periodicals Index* Copyright © 1982 by The H. W. Wilson Company. Material reproduced by permission of the publisher.

Abbreviations

+	continued on later pages of the issue	m	monthly
AB	Aktiebolaget	Mr	March
abr	abridged	My	May
AG	Aktiengesellschaft	N	November
Ag	August	no	number
Ap	April	O	October
Aut	Autumn	p	page
Ave	Avenue	Pl	Place
bibl	bibliography	por	portrait
bi-m	bi-monthly	pt	part
bi-w	bi-weekly	q	quarterly
Blvd	Boulevard	Rd	Road
Bp	Bishop	rev	revised
Co	Company	S	September
comp	compiled, compiler	SA	Sociedad Anónima
cond	condensed	sec	section
cont	continued	semi-ann	semi-annual
Corp	Corporation	semi-m	semi-monthly
D	December	Spr	Spring
ed	edited, edition, editor	Sq	Square
F	February	St	Street
GmbH	Gesellschaft mit beschränkter Haftung	Summ	Summer
		supp	supplement
il	illustrated	surv	survey
Inc	Incorporated	tab, -s	table, -s
Ja	January	tr	translated, translation, translator
Je	June		
Jl	July	v	volume
jr	junior	w	weekly
Ltd	Limited	Wint	Winter
		yr	year

Selected Abbreviations of Periodicals Indexed

Acad Mgt J—Academy of Management Journal
Acad Mgt R—Academy of Management Review
Adm Sci Q—Administrative Science Quarterly
Arbitration J—Arbitration Journal
Beverage World—Beverage World
Bus Q—Business Quarterly (London, Canada)
Cornell Hotel & Restau Adm Q—Cornell Hotel & Restaurant Administration Quarterly
Director—The Director
Fortune—Fortune
Ind W—Industry Week
MSU Bus Topics—MSU Business Topics
Mgt Int R—Management International Review
Mgt R—Management Review
Mgt World—Management World

Nations Bus—Nation's Business
Omega—Omega: International Journal of Management Science
Org Behav & Hum Perform—Organizational Behavior & Human Performance
Org Dyn—Organizational Dynamics
Pers Adm—Personnel Administrator
Pers J—Personnel Journal
Pers Psychol—Personnel Psychology
Super Mgt—Supervisory Management
Supervision—Supervision
Train & Devel J—Training and Development Journal
U Mich Bus R—University of Michigan Business Review

A. Referring to the sample page reprinted on p. 198, identify other examples of the following:
   1. an entry with subheadings
   2. an entry which lists other possible subjects under which you might find articles related to a topic
   3. the subject heading you would use to find an article on businesses which lease equipment
   4. an entry which appears to be an author entry but which is, in reality, a *subject* entry
B. How many headings do you find under the subject of "Lawyers"? Are any further subdivided?
C. How many headings indicate articles on the subject of "Lead"? Are any further subdivided? For how many can you find authors?

When you are using a periodical guide to find articles, you should first read the title of the article and decide whether or not it indicates that the article might be related to your topic of research. Of course, you will not be interested in many of the articles you find since, although they are about the same general subject, the titles will tell you that they approach the subject in many different ways. For those articles which you decide to pursue, you should copy down all of the information given in an entry and, using the abbreviation guides at the beginning of the index, *write out in full* those parts which have been abbreviated. This will help you in finding the articles in the periodicals section of the library. Do not throw away the information yet, however; transfer it to index cards which you can then file alphabetically, according to the authors' last names, along with your other sources. This information will be needed later when writing your footnotes and compiling your bibliography.

8–7
EXEMPLIFY / DISCUSS

A. Decide which of the articles listed under the subject heading of "leadership" might be helpful in doing research on the subject of "subordinate response to leader behavior." For one of these articles only, write the information necessary to locate it in the library:

BUSINESS PERIODICALS INDEX

LEADERSHIP

Business Periodicals Index Copyright © 1980, 1981, 1982 by The H. W. Wilson Company. Material reproduced by permission of the publisher.

1. name of journal
2. volume number/date of publication
3. title/author
4. page number(s)
5. supplemental elements which appear with the article (bibliography or tables, for example)

B. Take one of the article entries and write it in *formal footnote form* and in *formal bibliographic form.*

TAKING NOTES / DEVELOPING A WORKING OUTLINE

The next stage in your research is to begin reading the books and articles that you have located. Because you have proposed a working thesis, your reading will be directed toward finding proof for the statement you have made. It will further help in directing your reading if you have a *working outline.* Depending on the extent of your preliminary reading and your familiarity with the subject matter, you may be able to develop a full working outline at this stage. Even if you know very little about the subject, however, you can develop an outline that will at least guide you in your preliminary reading and note-taking.

Reading / Note-Taking: The Introduction

Academic convention requires that the first part of a research paper consist of a review of the research which has already been done on the subject. Therefore, you will be able to direct your early reading to this end. To illustrate this process, we will propose the following working thesis and working outline for the first part of a research paper on the subject of "leadership," making use of the resource chapters in this book as our bibliography:

Working Thesis: The most effective leaders in U.S. corporations during the past decade have been those who have exhibited achievement-oriented behavior.

I. Introduction
   A. Focus on subject and thesis[5]
   B. Review of research
      1. —————————   *(The number of subdivisions*
      2. —————————   *depends on the extent of the*
      3. —————————   *research done on the subject*
      4. —————————   *in question.)*

---

[5] The first paragraph of a research paper can follow the same techniques suggested for the introduction to a short paper (Chapter 3). In a research paper, however, you have the option of stating your thesis as a separate paragraph after your review of the research—that is, placing it *at the end of the entire introduction.*

Our first task, then, is to search through our sources for reports of the work which has been done in this field. For our purposes, Resource Chapter C is a good place to start, and we can later look at Resource Chapter B for further information on this subject.

Because the purpose of this section of our paper is to give an overview of the research, the notes we take, though they must be extremely accurate, do not have to be very detailed. The most practical approach here is to *summarize* the information you feel you will later include.[6]

Research Tip

Use *index cards* to take notes. Label each note card with the following information:

- subject
- author
- title

- page number
- heading number from
  the working outline

A summary note card dealing with problems in early research techniques might look like this:

Summary Note Card

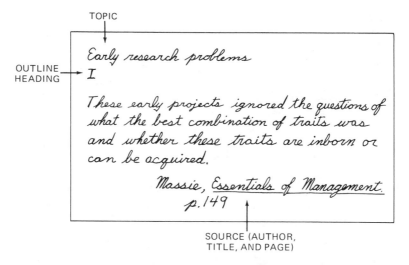

TOPIC

OUTLINE HEADING

Early research problems

I

These early projects ignored the questions of what the best combination of traits was and whether these traits are inborn or can be acquired.

Massie, Essentials of Management. p.149

SOURCE (AUTHOR, TITLE, AND PAGE)

The notes you take are, of course, for your own purposes in writing the paper later. You can therefore include any information which will be helpful to you personally. When you have read all that you can find about research on your subject, you know that your preparation for the introduction has been completed.

---

[6] If necessary, refer again to Chapter 5 to reacquaint yourself with the principles of summarizing, including the characteristics of a one-sentence summary.

Reading / Note-Taking: Evidence

You will next search your sources for data to support your thesis.

Research Tip

If you cannot find supporting data for your thesis, you can do one of the following:

• look for *more sources*[7]
• search in your sources for a better solution to the problem posed by your thesis—that is, *revise your thesis*

In the case of the thesis we are working with, there does not seem to be very much support in our sources. A reading of the McClelland article, however, provided us with a basis for revising our thesis. McClelland's claim that an effective leader is high in the need for power will thus replace our original predication—that an effective leader is achievement-oriented:

The most effective leaders in major U.S. corporations within the past decade *have been those who have demonstrated a high need for power.*

Revised predication

The McClelland article provides specific support for the revised thesis, so we will certainly want to take notes to be used in the paper as documentation. A quote from an expert in the field is a very effective means of supporting your thesis. There are two types of note cards which you can use to record quotes from an expert: a *direct quote* note card and a *paraphrase* note card. Study the following note card, which illustrates the first type:

A Direct Quote Note Card

nPwr, managers
II

"The best managers are high in the need for power and low in the need for affiliation."

McClelland, "An Advocate of Power",
p. 280

---

[7] Although this sometimes works, it can be quite time-consuming. If you have been thorough in preparing your bibliography, the second option—revising your thesis—is more likely to work.

When writing this kind of note card, always make sure to include *quotation marks around the exact words of the author*, so that you won't inadvertently plagiarize later on.

In its final version, however, no more than 10% of your paper should consist of direct quotes. Therefore, it is important to choose your quotations very carefully for their effectiveness in supporting your thesis. You can avoid overuse of direct quotation and at the same time provide expert support for your thesis by making use of paraphrase. The following model note card illustrates this second type of reference to someone else's words:

A Paraphrase Note Card

> managers / characteristics
> II
>
> The 4ᵗʰ power-oriented characteristic of a successful manager is his emphasis on justice in dealing with his own employees.
>
> McClelland, "An Advocate of Power,"
> pp. 280–281

8–8
WRITE

Directions: Choose one of the working thesis statements which you wrote in Exercise 8–2, and find supporting information for the thesis in one of the resource chapters. Write one *direct quotation note card* and one *paraphrase note card* to directly support your thesis. If you find contradictory information, revise your thesis.

In reading and taking notes, then, you are performing the central task in preparing a research paper. Your reading and choice of information to record will eventually form the major part of your paper: the proof of the validity of your thesis. This process is an investigation, and the results will therefore be unknown until the investigation has been completed.

Research Tip

Take notes on *anything* you suspect you might make use of in writing your paper. It can always be discarded later. However, if you don't write it down when you discover it, *you may not be able to find it later.*

The working thesis may be revised once or many times, depending on where your investigation leads you. Similarly, each revision of the thesis will require a new working outline. Take, for example, the paper on leadership which we have been preparing. After having decided on a revised predication based on the McClelland article—that is, one which emphasizes the need for power—we might discover other information which convinces us that the need for affiliation is also important. Moreover, after reading through Fiedler's research on "situational factors" in an organization (Resource Chapter C), we might want to give consideration to this as well. Thus, our final choice of thesis might look something like this:

The most effective leaders in major U.S. corporations within the past decade *have been those whose behavior has demonstrated both the need for power and the need for affiliation, and who have worked in organizations which have made it possible for these needs to be realized.*

Final revised predication

A rough working outline based on this new thesis statement might well resemble the following:

Working Thesis: The most effective leaders in major U.S. corporations within the past decade have been those whose behavior has demonstrated both the need for power and the need for affiliation, and who have worked for organizations which have made it possible for these needs to be realized.

I. Introduction
   A. Focus on subject and thesis
   B. Review of research
      1. Psychological approach
      2. Sociological perspective
      3. Fiedler's research
      4. Path-Goal theory
II. The need for power
III. The need for affiliation
IV. Situational factors

ASSEMBLING THE ROUGH DRAFT

At this point, three important things have been accomplished: (1) you have decided on the exact thesis of your paper, (2) you are quite familiar with the content of all your note cards, and (3) you have a good working outline which indicates how all the information will be organized. This means that you are now ready to write a "rough draft"—that is, the first version of your paper.

As the term suggests, this preliminary version will not be perfect in terms of grammar or style, but it will be *complete*. It should thus include all essential parts of the paper:

- the entire text of the paper, in which information from all sources has been combined with *your* ideas
- all footnotes
- a complete bibliography
- illustrations, tables, or diagrams which you wish to include

There is no one "correct" way to accomplish this process. We will suggest, however, that if you do not know where to begin or how to proceed, the following sequence of steps may prove helpful to you.

Coordinate Note Cards and Outline

Since your working outline represents your best idea—at this point, anyhow—of how the text of the paper is supposed to be organized, use your outline as your guide. Starting with Roman numeral *I*, divide all note cards into groups which correspond to the major divisions (Roman numerals) of the outline. When you have done this, subdivide the note cards into groups which correspond to the next divisions—the capital letters. Continue in this fashion until the outline has been exhausted and you have a number of piles of cards in front of you, each pile representing pieces of information closely related to each other in the outline. The benefit you might derive from doing this, other than having all your information arranged in a logical order, is that you may discover (1) a logical imperfection in your working outline that has escaped notice up to this point, and that you can correct, or (2) a part of the outline for which you have forgotten to gather sufficient information.

Research Tip

- *Label* each pile with a "title card" which shows its place in the outline:

I-B-3 Fiedler's research

- Make sure that each card in the pile is marked accordingly.
- Put a *rubber band* around each pile of cards.
- Stack the piles in their *proper order*, according to your outline.

Write the Paper

If you have worked on yout outline very carefully, all that now remains is to put all your information together into the rough draft of the paper. This will simply be a process of "linking together" the various pieces of information on all your cards in a smooth, flowing manner so that the text moves logically and gracefully from one idea to the next.

SHOWING CLEAR THOUGHT RELATIONSHIPS. Even if you have worked carefully and have been able to collect a very good set of note cards which contain all the necessary information needed to prove your thesis, it is still your responsibility to arrange this information clearly. This means that all important thought relationships must be evident to the reader. Whatever these relationships may be—exemplification, causality, contrast, process, and so on—it is *you* who must make the reader aware of what is going on in the progression of ideas within the paper.

In the case of the research paper on leadership which we are in the process of putting together, we may notice, for example, that there is a seeming contradiction between two of the note cards dealing with McClelland's ideas on the need for power. More specifically, the card on page 204 seems to deny the need for affiliation in a successful manager, yet the one on page 205 seems to be suggesting that power-oriented managers indulge in a kind of affiliative behavior. It is certain that if the information contained in these two cards were simply juxtaposed, it might create some confusion for the reader. Since the need for affiliation and the need for power both figure prominently in the thesis statement, an absolute denial of the former from a recognized expert in the field might require us to revise our thesis. However, on further examination of our notes from the McClelland article, we discover several interesting things. First, the notion of "power" is not meant in a bad sense that would absolutely exclude all affiliative behavior. Secondly, a successful manager, in spite of a high need for power, is "altruistic in that he will sacrifice his own self-interest for the welfare of the company...." Furthermore, this type of manager believes in *equal* justice for all his own employees. Thus, what McClelland seems to be really objecting to in an "affiliative manager" is that he does *not* really believe in being even-handed: he "is always making exceptions in terms of personal needs. For example, he gives somebody a raise because they really need the money. He forgets that there are maybe six other people who feel that they have been unjustly treated as a result."

Nonetheless, McClelland never admits a real need for affiliation on the part of a successful manager. On the other hand, Maccoby—another prominent expert in the field—comes much closer to this when he talks of the typical modern corporate executive being "concerned about being liked." What we will probably decide to do, then, is (1) emphasize the ideas of McClelland insofar as the need for power is concerned, (2) shift to Maccoby on the subject of affiliation, and, through the use of concessive contrast, (3) show that even McClelland's ideas do not totally exclude the possibility of some kind of need for affiliation. We might do this in the following way, using the signal *although*:

Although McClelland claims that "the best managers are high in the need for power and low in the need for affiliation," *even he believes that this same manager is just in dealing with his own employees, a quality which implies at least a modicum of true affiliative behavior.* Indeed, it is only when affiliation is	*The basis for a possible conflict* *The conflict resolved*

pushed to the extreme that even-handed justice suffers through the actions of the affiliative—that is, the *overly* affiliative—manager:

The resolution emphasized

> We find an affiliative manager is always making exceptions in terms of personal needs. For example, he gives somebody a raise because they really need the money. He forgets that there are maybe six other people who feel they have been unjustly treated as a result.

CARRYING IDEAS FORWARD: "STRONG" COHERENCE DEVICES. Do not forget that certain coherence devices—we will call them *"strong* coherence devices*"*—are capable of linking not only sentences but also entire paragraphs together in certain thought relationships. The substitute forms *this, these,* and *such* are good examples of words so powerful in their reference potential that they can represent a phrase, several phrases, a sentence, several sentences, a paragraph, or even longer sections of text. A good example of the power of these reference words occurs in the sample short paper (pp. 90–92) which we recopy in part here:

One of the most obvious traits found in those people who have a high *nPwr* is their tendency to seek positions in which they are able to exert control over others—that is, positions of leadership (Robbins, 1979). **These** positions may be in any domain (business, education, government, and so on), but in all **these** areas, in order to successfully maintain a position of leadership, a person must also have certain other personal characteristics. To get the position in the first place, the individual must be competitive. In order to assume a role of leadership within an organization, one must be able to "learn the ropes" quickly, and to persevere in carrying out long-range plans. To accomplish this, a person must have a high level of energy and a sense of responsibility. Moreover, since the individual is in a leadership position, success rests largely on the internal standards which have been set, as well as on some ability to resist outside pressure. Interestingly enough, **these** traits—competitiveness, the ability to learn quickly, perseverance, a high energy level, a sense of responsibility, the ability to resist outside pressure, and high self-imposed standards—are among those most commonly found in those persons who have a high *nAch* (Morris, 1979, p. 371).

8–9
EXEMPLIFY / DISCUSS

Directions: Determine the precise referent for the word *these* each time it is used in the excerpted material.

The use of the word *moreover* in the preceding text represents yet another type of "strong" coherence device, this time in the area of "relationship signals." Conjunctive adverbs such as *moreover* can be used as signals to express most important thought relationships—including the relationship of conclusion, which was not treated in Chapter 2. Here are some examples:

Exemplification: for example, for instance
"Pure" contrast: in contrast, on the other hand

Concessive contrast: however, nevertheless
Comparison: similarly, in like manner
Enumeration: moreover, finally
Causality: consequently, for that reason
Chronology: afterwards, in the meantime
Conclusion: thus, then

These conjunctive adverbs can link one sentence to another:

_____(Sentence)_____ ; | however moreover etc. | , _____(Sentence)_____

or one sentence to two or three:

_____(Sentence)_____ . | However, Moreover etc. | , _____(Sentence)_____ .
_____(Sentence)_____ .

or even one entire paragraph to another:

_____
_____
_____
_____

| However Moreover etc. | , _____

_____
_____

8–10
EXEMPLIFY / DISCUSS

Directions: Determine the size of the portions of text related by the following conjunctive adverbs in the model short paper (Chapter 3):

• *further,* in the paragraph beginning, "Further, research tends...," p. 91
• *in addition*, in the paragraph beginning, "Politics, one of the fields...," p. 91
• *thus*, in the paragraph beginning, "Thus, although...," p. 92

A CASE OF TOO MUCH TEXTUAL COHERENCE: WORDINESS AND REDUNDANCY. While it is true that ideas should be "carried forward," this can become exaggerated. Sometimes students have the false impression that the more words they write, the better their paper will be. Thus, they "pad" or inflate their writing by using unnecessary words. Errors of this type fall into two categories:

<u>wordiness</u>: using more words than are necessary to convey an idea, and

<u>redundancy</u>: using two or more words which mean the same thing.

Notice the unnecessary use of words in the following sentence:

Further, <u>and in addition to this,</u> <u>research, experiments, and studies</u> have shown that those
　　　　(redundant)　　　　　　　　　　　　*(wordy)*
<u>individual</u> persons who appear, <u>to others who are observing them,</u> to have a high need for
(redundant)　　　　　　　　　　*(redundant)*
power, <u>also</u> have an <u>additional</u> need to dominate group discussions.
　　　　(redundant)

Compare the above sentence with the direct, clear prose of the following one:

Further, research has demonstrated that persons who appear to have a high need for power also
have a need to dominate group discussions.

8–11
PROOFREAD

Directions: Proofread the following paragraphs for wordiness and redundancy. Cross out
unnecessary words, phrases, and sentences.

    A third significant and important line of research and theoretical development, primarily
concerning theory, over the past 30 years or so combines the work of applied sociologists and
psychologists: the study of leadership. These theories are rather recent, since not much work
was done on this subject before the early 1950s. Leadership, or the ability to lead others, has
long been thought of and considered one of the most important factors influencing
organizational performance and activity as well as achievement of goals within a company or
corporation.
    Although a variety of different definitions of leadership have been proposed and suggested
over the years, we can say that leadership is the practice of influence. Thus, as a result,
leadership is a process through which the performance of others is influenced or affected by a
person who is in charge or is occupying a leadership role. Leadership is thus an important part
of study in management, though it is by no means synonymous or refers to the same thing as
management.

    CREDITING SOURCES AS YOU GO. Whichever system you decide to use—formal
footnoting or citation within a text—be sure to take care of all details as you write.
Citations within parentheses are easy enough to integrate immediately into your text, and
they require a minimum of effort to remove if you should change those particular sections
of the paper. Footnotes, however, are another matter entirely. Write them out completely,
paying attention to the conventions of formal footnoting.

Research Tip

Write out your footnotes completely *on a separate sheet of paper.* Thus, if you should happen to decide to change certain sections of your paper, you will still have the appropriate footnotes already written out, and you can simply *renumber* them, waiting until the final draft to insert each one at the bottom of the appropriate page. This saves a lot of time; retyping the same footnote five times is no fun.

Be sure to check a handbook—one is usually suggested by each university, sometimes by each department—about setting up footnotes for any material that does not fit the usual categories. The list that follows gives the most common types of footnotes.

A Book—One Author

[1] Charles G. Morris, Psychology, 3rd ed. (Englewood Cliffs, N.J.: Prentice-Hall, Inc., 1979), p. 354.

A Book—More Than One Author

[2] Martin L. Arnaudet and Mary Ellen Barrett, Paragraph Development (Englewood Cliffs, N.J.: Prentice-Hall, Inc., 1981), p. 68.

One Author Mentioned in a Book by Another Author (Double Reference)

[3] D. G. Winter as mentioned in Charles G. Morris, Psychology, 4th ed. (Englewood Cliffs, N.J.: Prentice-Hall, Inc.), p. 289.

An Article—One Author

[4] David C. McClelland, "The Two Faces of Power," Journal of International Affairs, Vol. 24, No. 1 (1970), p. 29.

An Article—More Than One Author

[5] D. Kipnis and J. Cosentino, "Use of Leadership Styles in Industry," Journal of Applied Psychology, Vol. 53 (1969), p. 462.

An Article by One Author Reprinted in a Book by Another Author

[6] Michael Maccoby, "The New Manager: A Game Player Rather Than a Power Seeker." In Stephen P. Robbins, Organizational Behavior (Englewood Cliffs, N.J.: Prentice-Hall, Inc., 1979), p. 282.

The preceding forms refer, of course, to *initial references*—that is, the first time a writer mentions a source. Subsequent references are much simpler. If you mention the same source again on *the same page* or *on the following page* of your paper, simply repeat the author's family name and the page number:

   [7] Morris, p. 290.

If you have mentioned *two authors with the same family name*, the reader will be confused if you mention only a family name in a subsequent reference. Thus, be sure to mention the first name as well:

   [8] Charles G. Morris, p. 290.

If the subsequent reference occurs *two or more pages after* the original reference, or if you have mentioned *two sources by the same author*, give the title of the one you are now referring to (if the title is long, shorten it):

   [9] Morris, Psychology, p. 290.
   [10] Arnaudet and Barrett, Approaches, p. 25.
        (This is an acceptable short form of Approaches to Academic Reading and Writing.)

8–12
WRITE

Directions: Write the initial and subsequent references for the following sources as indicated.

1. the first reference to the book *Basic Sociology* by Alvin L. Bertrand (the second edition of the book), published in 1973 by Appleton-Century-Crofts in New York; the part you are referring to is on the tenth page
2. the second reference to the same book; this time, you are referring to the thirty-fifth page; this footnote will appear on the same page of your paper as the previous reference
3. the third reference to the same book, this time to page 88; cited in your paper ten pages after footnote 2
4. the first reference to the article "Fear of Success in Males and Females" by L. W. Hoffman; the article appeared in the forty-second volume (1974) of *Journal of Consulting and Clinical Psychology*; you are referring to page 355 of that volume
5. the first reference to the article "Changes in Family Roles, Socialization, and Sex Differences," also by L. W. Hoffman; the article appeared in volume 32 (number 8, 1977) of *American Psychologist*; your text refers to page 651; this footnote appears on the same page as footnote 4
6. the first reference to M. L. Hoffman's article, "Personality and Social Development" in the twenty-eighth volume (1977) of *Annual Review of Psychology*; your text refers to page 297; this footnote appears on the same page of your paper as footnotes 4 and 5
7. the second reference to the article in 4; reference to page 356; this footnote appears 5 pages after footnotes 4–6

8. the second reference to the article in 5; reference to page 650; this footnote appears on the same page of your paper as footnote 7

9. the second reference to the article in 6; reference to page 299; this footnote appears on the same page of your paper as footnotes 7 and 8

PROBLEMS IN FOOTNOTING. Since a large portion of a research paper consists of well-documented support for the thesis, it becomes important to carefully select and evenly apportion the kinds of footnoted material you will include. That is, your research paper should contain a fairly even distribution of summary, paraphrase, and direct quote documentation offered in support of the thesis—all footnoted, of course. Your own explication of the relevancy and importance of what you have taken from other sources should make up a far greater percentage of your paper than do the paraphrases, summaries, and quotes themselves. In other words, you should be sure that your paper does not end up being a long series of data from other sources which you have loosely strung together.

A related problem is that of deciding what information it is *not* necessary to footnote. Any information which is general knowledge (even though you may have read about it in doing your research) does not have to be footnoted. For example, the fact that unemployment is commonly associated with recessionary periods is known by the average person. If you include this information in your research paper, you do not have to write a footnote to inform your reader where you found it. If, on the other hand, supporting data reflect the judgment, original thinking, or research of an individual or a group, you *must* credit the source with a footnote. Thus, if you use statistics which show unemployment during a recessionary period, you would have to write a footnote to say where you found those particular figures.

8–13
DISCUSS

Directions: Decide which of the following supporting information would require a footnote to identify the source in which it is found.

1. Blake and Mouton have developed a managerial grid which cross-classifies managerial styles according to the degree to which managers exhibit concern for subordinates.

2. One of the most critical elements in the management of a firm is the supervisor.

3. A program is an explicit statement of the steps to be taken in order to achieve an objective, and the programmer must anticipate the methods of achieving these objectives prior to the program's actual use.

4. A realistic description of the relationships among systems, the manager's job, and change comes from the work of Leonard Sayles.

5. The popular Murphy's Law—i.e., if anything can go wrong, it will go wrong—has an interesting impact on planning because it is possible to plan for the possibility that things may not work out as planned.

6. One such theory of organizing, called System 4, is built on three concepts: the Principle of Supportive Relationships; the Linking Pins; and Performance Goals.

7. According to Professor Charles Summer, in order for managers to become true professionals, they must learn to use and modify the knowledge of others.

8. Contemporary social pressures have forced managers to increase the numbers of previously under-represented groups on the management team, namely women and minorities.

FINALIZING THE BIBLIOGRAPHY. When you have finished putting the text of the paper together, it is time to turn your attention to the bibliography. Write each reference out completely, paying attention to all the conventions. If you have not already done so, arrange all your note cards alphabetically, according to the authors' family names. Be sure to include all books and articles you have used, even if you have not quoted from some of them.

The bibliography should be given a separate page (or pages) at the end of the paper. The most common bibliographic forms are the following:

A Book—One Author

Morris, Charles G. Psychology. 3rd ed. Englewood Cliffs, N.J.: Prentice-Hall, Inc., 1979.

A Book—More Than One Author

Arnaudet, Martin L., and Mary Ellen Barrett. Approaches to Academic Reading and Writing. Englewood Cliffs, N.J.: Prentice-Hall, Inc., 1984.

An Article—One Author

McClelland, David C. "The Two Faces of Power." Journal of International Affairs, Vol. 24, No. 1 (1970), pp. 28–31.

An Article—More Than One Author

Kipnis, D., and J. Cosentino. "Use of Leadership Styles in Industry." Journal of Applied Psychology, Vol. 53 (1969), pp. 460–466.

An Article by One Author Reprinted in a Book by Another Author

Maccoby, Michael. "The New Manager: A Game Player Rather Than a Power Seeker." In Stephen P. Robbins. Organizational Behavior. Englewood Cliffs, N.J.: Prentice-Hall, Inc., 1979.

A Chapter by One Author Reprinted in a Book by Another Author

Robbins, Stephen P. "Power." In Arnaudet, Martin L., and Mary Ellen Barrett. Approaches to Academic Reading and Writing. Englewood Cliffs, N.J.: Prentice-Hall, Inc., 1984.

WRITING THE FINAL DRAFT

The final version of your paper must be typed on standard size (8½″ by 11″) unlined white paper. Students commonly bind the pages of the finished paper together in a folder for protection. The completed paper should include the following elements:

1. *A Blank Sheet of Paper*
2. *A Title Page.* The title serves to identify the area of research you have undertaken. Therefore, the title should suggest, in abbreviated form, your thesis. The following are examples of possible titles for the model research paper:
   - Personal- and Corporate-Related Factors Which Influence Managers in U.S. Corporations
   - The Realization of the Need for Power and the Need for Affiliation Among Successful Corporate Managers
   - An Investigation into Factors Which Contribute to the Success of Managers in U.S. Corporations

   Notice that the suggested titles are not written as complete sentences, yet they all reflect the topic which has been researched.

   The information on the title page should be single-spaced. The title is centered in the middle of the page. Your name, the course title or number, and the date should appear on the lower right side of the paper, allowing a separate line for each. You should leave 2-inch margins on all sides of the title page.
3. *An Outline.* If your professor requires that an outline be submitted with your paper, it should appear immediately after the title page. The thesis statement appears first and is single-spaced. The outline follows it. Each section and subsection should be double-spaced.
4. *The Text of the Paper.* You should leave 1½-inch margins on all sides of the page, including a margin between the footnotes at the bottom. Double-space the text. Follow normal rules for paragraphing. Do not include headings or the numbers which correspond to your outline.
5. *An Appendix.* Although most undergraduate research papers will not include an appendix, it is possible that you may wish to include tables, graphs, or charts to further document or clarify some point. If so, this supplemental information should appear immediately after the text of your paper. For more specific instructions as to the precise format of such elements, consult a handbook.
6. *The Bibliography.* Your final bibliography is the last typed page (or pages) of your paper. The entries should be single-spaced, and you should double-space between them.
7. *A Blank Sheet of Paper*

The title page is counted as the first page, but the number does *not* appear on the page. The rest of the pages are numbered sequentially, except for the blank page at the end. Notice how this has been done in the model research paper which follows.

Research Tip

- If you do not know how to type and are therefore going to hire someone else to type your paper, be sure to make arrangements with a typist *well in advance of the due date.*
- Be sure that your hand-written version of the paper is *legible* so as to avoid typist's errors.

8–14
WRITE

Directions: Using the sample "mini" research paper as your text, discuss the questions which follow it. (Note that this "mini" research paper is about one-half the length of an ordinary research paper.)

MODEL RESEARCH PAPER

(blank page)

**Personal- and Corporate-Related Factors Which
Influence Managers in U. S. Corporations**

M. Luiz Barnetti
Organizational Behavior 101
March 3, 1982

Personal- and Corporate-Related Factors Which
Influence Managers in U. S. Corporations

THESIS STATEMENT: The successful manager in U. S. corporations is the one whose behavior demonstrates both the need for power and the need for affiliation and who works in an organization which makes it possible for these needs to be realized.

I. Review of research
  A. Psychological approach
    1. Personality traits
    2. Simplistic approach
  B. Sociological approach
    1. Leader-subordinate relations
    2. Leadership style
    3. Power base
  C. Situational approach
    1. Fiedler's research
    2. Path-goal theory
II. The need for power
  A. Need for power demonstrated in job choice
  B. Conscious seeking of executive role
III. The need for affiliation
  A. Efficient employee performance/high morale
    1. Supportive behavior
    2. Concern for employees
  B. Executive's behavior toward others
    1. Ruthlessness in dealings with outsiders
    2. Concern about being liked by employees
    3. Fair treatment of employees
IV. Situational factors
  A. Well-defined power base
    1. Legitimate power base
    2. Reward-coercive power base
  B. Corporate structure
    1. Means to demonstrate concern
    2. Means to consult with and encourage employees

V. The successful manager—a description
- A. "The gamesman"
  1. Risk-taker
  2. Motivator
  3. Energizer
- B. Requisite factors
  1. Power
  2. Affiliation
  3. Corporate structure

In recent years much attention has been given to corporate leaders and their effectiveness in terms of worker morale and, ultimately, in terms of increased productivity. As Maccoby says, "Still, the logic of corporations is to optimize profit and power, and the corporate manager must serve it."[1] The question which then emerges is
5　the following: What exactly are the qualities which the corporate executive must possess in order to best achieve the goals of power and profit?

Because of the importance of goal leadership in carrying out corporate goals, social scientists have been trying to identify precisely what constitutes a "good leader" since the 1950s. Early work in this field attempted to describe leaders from a strictly
10　psychological point of view. It focused solely on personality traits. These initial studies, however, were too simplistic in approach, and they did not answer such questions as what the best combination of personality traits might be, nor whether these characteristics are inborn or are something which can be acquired.[2]

Later research took into account the sociological as well as the psychological factors
15　which contribute to good leadership. In other words, the relationships between leaders and their subordinates were considered along with the personal characteristics of leaders. Emerging from this work is the concept of leadership style—that is, the methods leaders use to control their subordinates. These methods are largely dependent on the leader's position of power within the corporate structure.[3] According to French and Raven, a
20　leader's power could be based on coercion, reward, expertise, legitimacy, or reference.[4]

From the research which was done in the 1970s, important new theories of leadership have been proposed, among them, Fiedler's situational theory and the path-goal theory. Fiedler proposed that there is no one leadership style for every situation, but rather that successful management was dependent on leaders' relationships with their employees,
25　the way the work was structured, and the amount of formal authority vested in the leader. According to the path-goal theory, which is related to the employees and the work environment itself, the leader's role is to make the "path" to the achievement of corporate goals smooth and to encourage workers to see personal benefits in such achievement.[5]
30　By carefully selecting from among the research which has been done, then, we can describe successful business leaders according to their personal qualities, their dealings with those under their control, and the corporate structure of the organization to which they belong. More specifically, in this analysis it will be suggested that the successful modern manager in U.S. corporations is the one whose behavior demonstrates both the
35　need for power and the need for affiliation, and who works in an organization which makes it possible for these needs to be realized.

---

[1] Michael Maccoby, "The New Manager: A Game Player Rather Than a Power Seeker." In Stephen P. Robbins, Organizational Behavior (Englewood Cliffs, N.J.: Prentice-Hall, Inc., 1979), p. 283.

[2] Joseph L. Massie, Essentials of Management, 3rd ed. (Englewood Cliffs, N.J.: Prentice-Hall, Inc., 1979), p. 149.

[3] Massie, pp. 149–50.

[4] John R. P. French, Jr., and Bertram Raven, as mentioned in Stephen P. Robbins, Organizational Behavior (Englewood Cliffs, N.J.: Prentice-Hall, Inc., 1979), pp. 263–67.

[5] Massie, pp. 150–52.

First of all, a good leader has a high need for power. "Those people who have a high need for power (*nPwr*) are attracted to jobs that provide latitude for defining their roles; selecting their actions; and advising, evaluating, and controlling the behavior of
40 others."[6] Thus, the executive has consciously chosen the role of leader because of a strong power motivation.

The need for power alone, however, is not enough to assure success. In order to adequately provide a working environment which promotes high worker morale, a leader must also display supportive behavior. He or she must consider employees'
45 concerns and well-being so that they, in turn, will be willing to perform efficiently in the goals set for them by the executive. This kind of support requires that the leader demonstrate, to some extent, affiliative behavior.

In discussing whether good corporate managers showed concern for their employees, Maccoby says that even some high power-seekers combine ". . .ruthlessness to outsiders
50 with benevolent justice for their own people," and that ". . .on the whole, the modern corporate executive. . .is more concerned about being liked than the empire builder of the past."[7] Although McClelland claims that "the best managers are high in the need for power and low in the need for affiliation," even he believes that good managers are *just* in dealing with their own employees, a quality which implies at least a modicum of true
55 affiliative behavior. Indeed, it is only when affiliation is pushed to the extreme that even-handed justice suffers through the actions of the affiliative—that is, the *overly* affiliative—manager:

> We find an affiliative manager is always making exceptions in terms of personal needs. For example, he gives somebody a raise because they really need the money.
60 He forgets that there are maybe six other people who feel they have been unjustly treated as a result.[8]

Thus emerges a more detailed picture of a leader who is personally concerned with power *and* with the well-being of his or her subordinates.

How, then, does an executive who possesses both the need for power and the need for
65 affiliation fulfill these needs? To begin with, the power base from which the executive operates should be one which is sanctioned and defined by the organization itself. It should, in effect, be a legitimate power base with corollary reward and coercive bases. That is, executives who have formal rights as a result of their positions within a company also have the power to give rewards and to punish. Fiedler calls this situational factor
70 *position power*—"the amount of formal authority vested in the leader's formal position, including the degree of control over rewards and the degree to which upper management supports the leader in the use of authority."[9] If an individual is to function effectively, the organization must provide the structure by which the power drive can be implemented.

Further, the organizational structure must provide a well-defined means for demon-

[6] Stephen P. Robbins, Organizational Behavior (Englewood Cliffs, N.J.: Prentice-Hall, Inc., 1979), p. 268.
[7] Maccoby, "The New Manager," p. 283.
[8] David C. McClelland, "McClelland: An Advocate of Power." In Stephen P. Robbins, Organizational Behavior (Englewood Cliffs, N.J.: Prentice-Hall, Inc., 1979), pp. 280–81.
[9] Fred Fiedler, as mentioned in Massie, Essentials, p. 151.

75 strating concern for subordinates, which, in turn, produces affiliative behavior on the part of the employees toward their superior and finally toward the company itself. This can be accomplished by some formal implementation of what House calls *participative behavior*—leaders must be able to consult with their employees as well as encourage them to improve in their performance of pre-set tasks.[10] If the structure of the

80 organization does not formally encourage these behaviors, leaders will not be effective in terms of affiliation, nor will they easily win the support of subordinates for their programs. In short, leaders in such organizations will fail to create an "esprit de corps," which is certainly an important form of affiliative behavior, one which "...makes an effort to make people feel that they are working for a common goal or against a common

85 enemy."[11]

Perhaps this power-conscious/affiliative leader is best described by Maccoby, who calls this individual a "gamesman":

His main interest is in challenge, competitive activity where he can prove himself a winner. Impatient with others who are slower and more cautious, he likes to take risks

90 and to motivate others to push themselves beyond their normal pace. He responds to work and life as a game. The contest hypes him up and he communicates his enthusiasm, thus energizing others.[12]

It is this sense of competition (power motive) and this ability to instill enthusiasm in others (affiliation motive) which characterize the successful executive.

95 The conclusion may be drawn, then, that in order to be a successful manager, a person must have, among possible others, two major motivations—the need for power and the need for affiliation. Moreover, the structure of the organization in which that person is working must enable him or her to fulfill these motives in some systematic way, namely, a well-defined authority structure and a built-in communications channel though which

100 the executive has contact with those being supervised.

Indeed, Maccoby's analogy may be taken one step further. We might say that in order to play "the game" properly, the corporate executive must first be motivated to play (*nPwr*) so that others are also stimulated to play (*nAffil*) and, second, be provided with the necessary "pieces" (organizational structure) to successfully participate in the play.

---

[10] Robert J. House, as mentioned in Massie, p. 152.
[11] Charles G. Morris, Psychology, 3rd ed. (Englewood Cliffs, N.J.: Prentice-Hall, Inc., 1979), p. 290.
[12] Maccoby, "The New Manager," pp. 282–83.

BIBLIOGRAPHY

Maccoby, Michael. "The New Manager: A Game Player Rather Than a Power Seeker." In Stephen P. Robbins. Organizational Behavior. Englewood Cliffs, N.J.: Prentice-Hall, Inc., 1979, pp. 282–83.

Massie, Joseph L. Essentials of Management. 3rd ed. Englewood Cliffs, N.J.: Prentice-Hall, Inc., 1979.

McClelland, David C. "McClelland: An Advocate of Power." In Stephen P. Robbins. Organizational Behavior. Englewood Cliffs, N.J.: Prentice-Hall, Inc., 1979, pp. 280–81.

Morris, Charles G. Psychology. 3rd ed. Englewood Cliffs, N.J.: Prentice-Hall, Inc., 1979.

Robbins, Stephen P. Organizational Behavior. Englewood Cliffs, N.J.: Prentice-Hall, Inc., 1979.

Winter, D. G. The Power Motive. New York: Free Press, 1973.

(blank page)

Questions for Discussion:

A. The Introduction
1. How many paragraphs make up the introduction?
2. What technique has been used as an initial focus?
3. How has further focus been achieved?
4. Is the thesis stated before or after the survey of research in the field?
5. In terms of coherence, could the thesis be placed elsewhere?

B. The Body
1. Where does the writer begin to offer proof for the thesis?
2. How does the writer organize the documentation of the thesis?
3. Where does the documentation of the second element in the thesis begin? What language is used to indicate that this element will be discussed?
4. In what way does the longer quote in footnote 12 add to the support of the thesis?

C. The Conclusion
1. What concluding techniques does the writer use?
2. How many paragraphs does the conclusion consist of?

D. Language
1. Identify two examples of the use of tentative language.
2. What portions of the text are related by the following "strong" coherence devices:
   - *then* in the paragraph beginning, "From the research...," p. 4
   - *this* in the paragraph beginning, "The need for power alone...," p. 5
   - *further* in the paragraph beginning, "Further...," p. 5

E. Footnotes and Bibliography
1. Explain footnotes 9 and 12.
2. Justify the inclusion of the last item in the bibliography.

8–15
WRITE

Directions: Using the work you have already done in Exercises 8–1, 8–2, and 8–3, write a "mini" research paper. In writing your paper, make use of the resource chapters in this book. In addition, you may find two additional articles in an appropriate periodical index to further document your thesis. Be sure that you do the following:

- Start with a working outline and thesis
- Revise both as much and as often as is necessary
- Use index cards to take notes
- Follow the format suggestions exactly when typing the final version of your paper

Your teacher may want to schedule individual appointments with you to check your working bibliography, working outline, note cards, and rough draft.

8–16
WRITE

Directions: Expand the short paper you wrote in Exercise 3–13 into a "mini" research paper.

GUIDELINES FOR WRITING
THE RESEARCH PAPER

1. Choose your subject carefully.
2. *Narrow the subject* so that you can fully research it.
3. Establish a *working thesis*, but be flexible in revising it as your research progresses.
4. Make use of the card catalog and periodicals indexes to form your *working bibliography*.
5. Develop a *working outline*.
6. Take *accurate* notes on cards and correlate them to your working outline.
7. Prepare a complete *first draft* in which you indicate the placement of footnotes.
8. *Edit* your first draft for technical and usage problems.
9. Carefully assemble the entire paper for typing the final version according to *research paper conventions*.

RESOURCE CHAPTER A
Motivation

Outline

To watch motivation manipulated at a very sophisticated level, we might turn to a detective story. All we know at the beginning is that an act has been committed: After eating dinner with her family, sweet little old Miss Jones collapsed and died of strychnine poisoning. "Now, why would anyone do a thing like that?" everybody asks. The police are asking the same question, in different terms: "Who had a *motive* for doing Miss Jones in?" In a really good murder mystery, the answer is, "Practically everybody."

The younger sister (now 75 years old) still bristles when she thinks of the tragic day 50 years

Source: Charles G. Morris, *Psychology*, 3rd Edition (Englewood Cliffs, N.J.: Prentice-Hall, Inc., 1979), pp. 352-80. Reprinted by permission of Prentice-Hall, Inc.

ago when Miss Jones stole her sweetheart. The next-door neighbor, a frequent dinner guest, has been heard to say that if Miss Jones's poodle tramples his peonies one more time, he'll. . . . The nephew, a major heir, is deeply in debt. The parlormaid has a guilty secret that Miss Jones knew. All four people were in the house on the night that Miss Jones was poisoned. And all four had easy access to strychnine, which was used to kill rats in Miss Jones's basement.

These are the first things that come to mind when we think of motivation in a murder mystery. But look at some of the ordinary things that are happening in the same story. Motivated by hunger, the family gets together for meals. The next-door neighbor is lonely and visits because he wants company. The parlormaid's guilty secret involves her sex drive. The poodle's presence in the peonies may spring from the physiological need to eliminate wastes or from sheer curiosity. When Miss Jones dies, the tragedy draws the family together; their need for affiliation makes them seek each other out. Yet, quickly they become fearful; the drive for self-preservation makes each wonder if the other is actually the murderer. In all these less spectacular forms of behavior, motivation is also present. In this chapter, we discuss all these motives, from the most basic to the most complex.

Why do certain motives lead to certain acts? The network of motives that governs our behavior is not a simple one. A motive may be as basic as hunger or as complex as the set of factors that leads to the choice of one career over another. Motives may be internally or externally triggered. One motive may reinforce another, or be in conflict with it. Motivated by the same thing—ambition, say—one person may go to law school and another might become apprenticed to the local crime ring. On the other hand, the same behavior may spring from different motives—you may buy

Figure 11-1

The stages of motivation. First a stimulus (a bodily need, a cue in the environment) triggers a motive. The motive leads to behavior. When the behavior results in goal attainment, the organism achieves a state of rest, or freedom from tension, until the next stimulus.

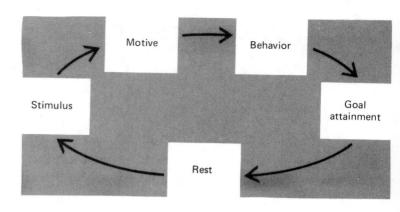

liver because you like it, because it's cheap, or because your body "knows" that you need iron.

We might best think of motivation as a series of stages that we are continually going through. Each series begins with a *stimulus* (perhaps a bodily need or a cue in the environment). The stimulus triggers a *motive*—a sort of arousal to action of one kind or another. The motive, in turn, activates *behavior*. When this behavior leads to *goal attainment*, the motive is satisfied and the chain of motivation is complete. It should be noted, however, that this process takes place whether we are aware of it or not. We do not have to know we are feeling hungry to go to the refrigerator, or be conscious of a need for achievement to study for an exam.

PHYSIOLOGICAL MOTIVES

For sheer survival, the body must have a certain amount of food, water, and sleep. Other basic physiological motives include the need to maintain proper body temperature, to eliminate wastes, and to avoid pain. We call these physiological motives **primary drives**. A primary drive is unlearned and common to every animal, including humans. It expresses the need to sustain life. A certain physiological state—brought on by lack of food or sleep, cold, the presence of pain—activates these primary drives. How we behave once they have been triggered may be simply a reflex, like shivering when we are cold, or it may be the result of learning. Babies do not have to be taught to be hungry or sleepy, but they can learn to eat certain foods and to sleep at certain times. All such behavior is aimed at reducing the state of arousal,

but the patterns of that behavior may vary according to learning and experience.

Hunger

When you are hungry, you eat. If you cannot do so, your need for food will increase the longer you are deprived of it. You may skip lunch if you are busy with something else, but it is likely that by dinnertime no concern will seem as pressing as getting something into your stomach. When we talk of hunger, we do not mean a need for food. The obvious signs of **hunger**—a growling stomach or hunger pangs—may make you remember you skipped lunch, but they are not the same as the need for food. For example, if the body is deprived of food, it continually needs food, but the hunger pangs that we feel are only intermittent.

Physiological Mechanisms of Hunger. Laboratory experiments demonstrate that the hunger drive is set in motion by a chemical imbalance in the blood. A simple sugar called *glucose*, which forms the basis of carbohydrates, can be stored in the liver only in small quantities and for a short time. When the amount of glucose in the blood (the blood-sugar level) falls below a certain point, an area in the hypothalamus is activated, signaling you to eat and replenish your glucose supply. After eating, when the blood-sugar level has risen, the hypothalamus seems to turn off the hunger drive. When the blood of an animal that has eaten is transferred to an animal that has been deprived of food, the animal will refuse to eat, even though it still needs food (Davis, Gallagher, & Ladove,

The Fat of the Land

There are two fundamental theories as to why people become fat. One view, proposed by Stanley Schachter and his colleagues (1971a, 1971b), stresses the importance of food as a powerful stimulus affecting obesity. In Schachter's opinion, fat people are particularly sensitive to environmental food cues, perhaps because their hypothalamus is not working properly. An alternate explanation, offered by Donald Thomas and Jean Mayer (1973), presents obesity as an internally controlled, physiological phenomenon. Thomas and Mayer see the obese person as being unable to rely on normal internal signals of hunger and satiety.

Schachter's theory is supported by a number of important studies. In one such effort, subjects were given either a vanilla milkshake or a milkshake that had quinine in it. Obese subjects drank more of the vanilla milkshakes than did normal-weight subjects, but they drank less than normal subjects when the milkshakes were filled with quinine. This supported Schachter's view that obese people are more sensitive to external stimuli (such as the taste of food). In another study, subjects were offered almonds in bags. Some of the almonds had shells, while others did not. Normal subjects ate nuts more or less equally from both batches. But while 19 of the 20 obese subjects ate almonds without shells, only 1 ate the almonds that had shells. This suggests that obese people do not like to work very hard for food and will only eat when food is easily available.

Thomas and Mayer feel that Schachter has isolated an important characteristic, not a cause, of obesity. They see surplus energy—mainly due to inactivity—as an important cause of weight problems. One of their studies found that overweight girls ate several hundred calories *less* per day than girls of normal weight. The cause of their obesity seemed to be a lack of exercise; the overweight girls engaged in only one-third as much physical activity as the normal-weight girls. Thomas and Mayer (1973) feel that opportunities to be inactive are built into our automobile- and convenience-oriented culture. Their advice? "Walk, don't ride. Take the stairs, not the elevator" (p. 79).

1967). Similarly, when hungry people are injected with glucagon, a hormone that raises the blood-sugar level, they cease to eat, even though they still need food (Schulman et al., 1957).

This hunger mechanism regulates our day-to-day intake of food. But there appears also to be a second hunger regulator, one that operates on a long-term basis to regulate the body's weight. With the exception of humans and some of the animals we have domesticated, very few animals ever become grossly overweight. The body seems to have a way of monitoring its own fat stores and regulating the intake of food to provide just enough energy to maintain normal activities without storing up excessive fat deposits (Kennedy, 1953).

For years, researchers believed that two particular areas of the hypothalamus worked together to monitor the level of blood sugar and the amount of body fat. Recent studies, however, have cast doubt on these traditional beliefs. In carefully conducted animal experiments, researchers made cuts along

some nerve fibers that travel close to the hypothalamus but did not damage the hypothalamus itself. Depending on the location of the cuts, animals either increased or reduced their intake of food and water. This suggests that nerves near the hypothalamus—not the hypothalamus itself—may control food intake (Gold, 1973; Ziegler & Karten, 1974).

Recent research has also suggested that other brain structures, such as the limbic system and the temporal lobe, may also play a role in controlling food intake (Balagura, 1973), although their exact role has not been precisely defined.

Specific Hungers. If you have let yourself get so hungry that you begin to feel faint, you have probably grabbed at a chocolate bar or other sweet without even thinking about your choice. Without "knowing" why, you chose the most efficient food for restoring glucose to your blood. Specific hungers of this kind seem to indicate that, to some extent, the body itself knows what food it needs to maintain itself. In one study (Davis, 1939), infants were given free choice from among nutritional foods. Over a long period of time, the foods they selected in their meals satisfied their bodies' nutritional needs. In another experiment (Richter, Holt, & Barelare, 1938), rats fed a diet deficient in vitamin B were given a choice of bottles, one of which was a very strong vitamin B solution. They showed an unvarying preference for this bottle.

All of our hungers, however, do not stem from our bodies' nutritional needs. An excessive craving for sweets, for example—commonly called a "sweet tooth"—seems to be a learned preference rather than an unlearned drive. Culture can also influence the way in which specific hungers are satisfied. Americans, for example, love milk, but the Chinese have a strong aversion to it (Balagura, 1973).

Learning and Hunger. Even though certain cravings for food may be unlearned, much of the way we eat is influenced by learning. For example, while most people eat three meals a day at more or less regular intervals, external cues like the smell of a cake baking in the oven can trigger the hunger drive at any hour of the day. One explanation of why people become overweight suggests that the fat person may be more easily aroused by the sight or smell of food than the person whose weight is normal (Schachter, Goldman, & Gordon, 1968).

To a large extent, what we choose to eat is governed by learning and habit—a cola drink may provide the sweetness of orange juice and the stimulation of coffee, but it is unlikely that you would have it with bacon and eggs for breakfast. Emotional factors can also affect hunger—you may sit down to the table starving, but have an argument that "turns off" your desire to eat. Social factors can make a meal a ceremony, and elaborate rituals have grown up around offering and accepting food.

Thirst

The physiology of **thirst** is very similar to that of hunger. When you are hungry, your stomach growls. Similarly, when you are thirsty, your mouth is dry and your throat is scratchy. However, as we have seen with hunger, the thirst drive goes much deeper than that. It is controlled by delicate biochemical balances within the body, and has been linked to the level of salt (sodium chloride) in the bloodstream. Salt causes water to leave the body's cells, and a high level of salt in the blood would therefore cause the cells to become dehydrated. When the level of sodium chloride in the blood reaches a certain point, indicating that the tissues need more water, a *thirst center* in the hypothalamus is stimulated, thus activating the thirst drive. After a drink has been found, the chemical balance returns to normal, and a *thirst satiety center*, also in the hypothalamus, is activated.

Scientists believe that there is a second thirst regulator. Although this mechanism is not yet fully understood, a reduction of the amount of fluid *outside* the body's cells appears to be involved. When the level of extracellular fluid drops, less blood flows to the kidneys. The kidneys react by emitting a substance—thought to be a protein called *renin*—that in turn releases another chemical, *angiotensin*, into the bloodstream. The bloodstream carries angiotensin to certain areas of the brain, which then activate the thirst drive (Epstein, Fitzsimmons, & Simons, 1969). The control mechanisms for this second system also seem to be located in the hypothalamus. To some extent, the two thirst controls are independent—one can be damaged without affecting the other. But gross interference with the hypothalamus will inactivate both mechanisms. Under normal conditions, the two regulators appear to interact and to strengthen one another.

Learned, individual, and cultural factors can also affect how we respond to the thirst drive. Some people avoid coffee, having been brought up to believe that stimulants are harmful; for others, a cup of coffee symbolizes a welcome 10-minute break from work. As flipping through magazine advertisements indicates, our self-image may be linked to what we choose to drink—one beer may be said to appeal to a "man's man," another to someone who wants to "stay on the light side." In many cases, these preferences involve other, more subtle motives, which we will touch upon later.

Sleep and Dreaming

People have often lamented the fact that we spend a third of our lives asleep. Think what we must be missing! What we are actually missing by being able to sleep are the following: visual, auditory, and tactile sensory disorders; vivid hallucinations; inability to concentrate; withdrawal; disorientation of self, time, and place; lapses of attention; increased heart rate and stress hormones in the blood; and the onset of psychosis. This alarming list, of course, refers to extreme instances— people who have stayed up, on a bet or for a television marathon, for over 200 hours. But if you have been up all night, you may be slower in taking notes or answering questions on an exam the next day, or you may even fall asleep in class. In short, the human body needs **sleep** to function, just as it needs food and water.

The **need to dream** appears to be less crucial than the need to sleep. People dream about 2 hours a night on the average, whether or not these dreams are remembered. In studies of the effects of dream deprivation, Dement (1965) originally concluded that subjects who slept but did not dream experienced such symptoms as anxiety, irritability, hunger, difficulty in concentrating, and even hallucinations in their waking hours. However, these conclusions were not substantiated by Dement's later experiments. He found no evidence of these harmful changes in humans kept from dreaming for 16 days nor in cats deprived of dreaming for 70 days (Dement, 1974).

This does not mean that prohibiting a person from dreaming has no effect at all. Rather, studies suggest that dream deprivation affects our ability to recall emotion-laden material and to adjust to anxiety-producing events (Carlson, 1977). In addition, there seems to be a strong need to compensate for dreaming time that has been lost (Dement, 1960). Many people who take drugs or alcohol, or who lose dreamtime because of illness or worry, say that when these inhibiting factors are removed they compensate by dreaming more intensely, often having nightmares.

Biological Clocks

What does the birthrate have to do with crime? Not much—except that both are linked to inner body cycles that scientists are just beginning to understand.

One such cycle we all share is the 24-hour circadian cycle of body activity (from the Latin *circa dies*, "about a day"). The cycle seems to be inherited and to relate to hormones and body chemistry. At the high point of the cycle, functions like white cell formation, pulse, and the production of glycogen and other substances are greatest. People feel best at this high point, sometime during the day. For human beings, the low point comes at night, during sleep. Scientists have found that postsurgical deaths and ability to withstand stress and illness are lowest at the low point of the cycle. In addition, body temperature varies between the high and the low points of the cycle. Studies have shown that body temperature is highest around 5 p.m. and lowest between 4:00 and 5:00 a.m. (McFarland, 1975).

If our personal daily rhythm is upset, we may feel tired and irritable or even become ill. Pilots, flight attendants, and frequent international travelers know that crossing time zones can cause physical problems, but people can adapt to these disruptions up to a point. (Night-shift workers, for example, can get used to sleeping during the day.)

Scientists are certain that other cycles also affect our behavior, though they have not yet fully identified and classified all of them. The menstrual cycle clearly can affect mood, but there may be "mood cycles" of varying lengths in all people. Depression or elation, accident proneness, and efficiency have all been shown to vary in cycles.

Pain

Hunger, thirst, and sleepiness are drives that cause a person to seek food, drink, or sleep. **Pain**, on the other hand, leads not to seeking but to escape or avoidance. Escape from or avoidance of pain is as necessary to survival as are eating, drinking, and sleeping. When we feel pain, we know we are in some sort of danger and we seek to escape from it. If you have a headache and your throat and legs are sore, you may be coming down with the flu. Therefore you take measures (going to bed, taking aspirin, calling the doctor) to fight the illness.

To what extent are the experience of pain, and the behaviors of escaping or avoiding pain, learned? Some experiments by Melzack and Scott (1957) provide partial answers. One set of puppies was brought up under normal circumstances; a second set grew up in isolated cages that made the usual sensory stimuli, experience, and learning— especially the normal bumps and scrapes from puppy play—impossible. Upon maturity, both groups were exposed to pain—shock, a match held under the nose, being pricked with a needle. The dogs that had been raised normally showed awareness of pain by yelping or wincing, and they took measures to avoid its source. The isolated group, on the other hand, did not seem to know how to avoid the pain and in many cases did not even seem to experience it. When a needle was jabbed into the leg of one of these dogs, a localized twitch was the only sign of pain.

In humans, also, responses to pain are conditioned by learning and experience. Some people are more sensitive to pain than others, as dentists surely know. And responses to pain can be culturally conditioned as well. The physiological process of childbirth is presumably the same everywhere, but in some societies a pregnant woman will work until the last minute, have her baby without apparent discomfort, and return to work immediately afterward.

Sex

Sexual motivation is many things, in humans especially, but first and foremost it is a physiological drive, just as hunger, thirst, and pain are. But while those drives are vital for the survival of the individual, the sex drive is important for the survival of the species.

In animals, hormones (principally *testosterone* for males and *estrogen* for females) are undeniably essential to the sex drive. Both hormones are present in both the male and the female, but in greatly differing quantities. In most species, the female is receptive to sex only during certain times—when she is *in heat* or, in more technical language, during the **estrus cycle**. At this time, her ovaries are secreting a greater quantity of estrogen into her bloodstream, and she is receptive to the advances of the male. Only during the period of estrus can she become pregnant.

Human females differ in this respect from most other animals. A woman is receptive to sexual arousal during her whole hormonal cycle, not just when reproduction is possible. Hormones affect her fertility as they affect the fertility of lower animals, but the sex drive itself operates more or less independently of the physiological fertility cycles.

The pituitary gland in the brain controls the onset of puberty and the development of secondary sex characteristics. Sexual arousal and behavior, on the other hand, are controlled by the hypothalamus. The more highly evolved the animal, the more the cerebral cortex also plays a part in such arousal and behavior.

As the cerebral cortex becomes more and more involved, experience and learning become more and more instrumental in sexual arousal and behavior. This accounts not only for the fact that the human sex drive is not cyclical, but also for the fact that the stimuli that activate the sex drive are almost infinite—the phrase "soft lights and sweet music" immediately comes to mind. The stimulus need not be the sexual partner—it can be a visual, auditory, or tactile sensation, a picture, or a fantasy. Human sexual behavior is also affected by a wide range of variables—social experience, sexual experience, poor nutrition, emotions (particularly one's feelings about the sex partner), and age.

The picture that emerges of sexual motivation, then, is one of decreasing involvement of purely physiological factors the higher one moves up the evolutionary scale. In humans, the role of hormones is minimal compared with the importance of learning and experience, both in the stimuli that elicit the drive and the behaviors that result.

The Maternal Drive

Maternal behavior is so complex that it is difficult to attribute it to a single "maternal drive." It would be hard to say, for example, whether the mother's impulse to nurse her child springs from a motive to nourish her child, from some hormone, or from a desire to relieve the discomfort of her full breasts. In all animals, including humans, hormones influence nursing, at least to the extent that the hormone *prolactin* stimulates the mammary glands to produce milk. And if prolactin is injected into a nonpregnant female animal or human, it can bring about a variety of maternal behaviors. Yet prolactin alone cannot account entirely for maternal behavior, for when the mammary glands are removed from animals, they still try to suckle their young.

It seems likely that much of the "maternal instinct" is not instinctive at all, but learned. In one experiment, a group of monkeys was raised in isolation, with no maternal attention (Harlow & Harlow, 1966). When these monkeys matured, many were unreceptive sexually. Many of those that did give birth seemed to have no maternal interest in their babies. Out of 20 such mothers, only 5 were on the borderline of adequate maternal care, and 3 of those 5 had had at least some contact with other monkeys while growing up. Seven others were indifferent to their young, and 8 actually brutalized them. Even when the babies actively sought their attention, the un-mothered mothers would have little or nothing to do with them.

In higher animals, then, maternal behavior, and apparently the maternal drive as well, seem to require learning and experience. Moreover, it seems probable that "mother love" reflects not a single drive but a complex set of motives and emotions—responsiveness, protectiveness, tactile contact—which come together to bring about a range of behaviors that is as wide as the range of motives themselves.

STIMULUS MOTIVES

A second set of motives seems to be largely innate, but in all species these motives depend much more on external stimuli than on internal physiological states. Moreover, unlike the primary drives, their function extends beyond bare survival of the organism or species to a much less specific end—dealing with information about the environment in general. Motives such as *activity*, *curiosity*, *exploration*, *manipulation*, and *contact* are apparently innate. They push us to investigate, and often to alter, the environment. Most often, external stimuli—things in the world around us—set these motives in action, and we in turn respond with stimulus-seeking behavior.

Activity

If you get a flat tire late at night when you are driving through a small town whose sidewalks were rolled up hours ago, you go into the gas station and wait for the tire to be repaired. At first you are comfortable just sitting there, but then you get up and begin to wander around. You jangle your car keys or the coins in your pocket. You drum on a table top. You go over and read the fine print on the windshield-wiper ad. You pace about. Confined in a small space without much to do, you exhibit all the signs of boredom. When the tire is changed and you are ready to drive off again, you are likely to do so with great relief, and probably 10 miles an hour faster than you should.

The need for **activity** is apparent in all animals, but scientists cannot determine whether it is a motive in itself or a combination of other motives. Most of the experiments that have been conducted to determine whether there is a separate "activity motive" have been done with rats. A rat put into a cage so small that it cannot move around will be more active than normal when it is released (Hill, 1956). But before we draw the conclusion that activity is an innate motive, we should consider other experiments. Food deprivation also increases activity—especially running activity (measured on the cylindrical "squirrel cage"). But restless activity (pawing, climbing, moving around aimlessly) increases less. Experiments with female rats (Wang, 1923) show that the sex drive also affects activity—peak activity and peak sexual receptivity coincide.

We do not quite know where this leaves us with human beings. Age, sex, health, genetic makeup, and temperament all seem to vary the need for activity—one person may be comfortable sitting in the same position for hours, while another may begin to fidget in 5 minutes—as any professor knows.

Exploration and Curiosity

Where does that road go? What is that dark little shop? How does a television set work? What is that piece of farm equipment for? Finding answers to these questions holds no obvious advantage to you. You do not expect the road to take you anywhere you particularly need to go, or the shop to contain anything you really need. You are not about to start a TV-repair service or help out in the hay harvest. You just want to *know*. **Exploration** and **curiosity** appear to be motives activated by the new and unknown and directed toward no more specific goal than "finding out." Exploration tends to be more spatial, and curiosity may be more intellectual, but the two motives are so similar that we consider them together.

An animal will learn a behavior not only to get food or drink but also to earn the privilege of being allowed to explore its environment. The family dog will run around a new house, sniffing and checking things out, before it will settle down to eat its dinner. Exploration and curiosity thrust us forward to get to know things. They drive us to find out about new stimuli, and once these are familiar, they impel us to find new stimuli to explore. Placed in a maze that is painted black, a rat will explore it and learn its way around. The next time, given a choice between a black maze and a white one, it will choose the white one (Dember, 1965). Apparently the unfamiliarity of the unknown maze has greater appeal—the rat seems to be curious to see what the new one is like. The parent of a bored 2-year-old on a rainy day can also tell you—if not too exhausted to speak—how important novelty is.

Animals also seem to prefer complexity, presumably because more complex forms take longer to get to know and are therefore more interesting (Dember, Earl, & Paradise, 1957). We can "do more" with something complex than with something simple.

There are, of course, reservations. We have all been in situations where the unknown was distressing rather than stimulating, or when we

---

Is Work a Stimulus Motive?

A number of studies suggest that rats, pigeons, and children will sometimes perform work to gain rewards even when they can receive the same rewards without working (D'Amato, 1974).

Rats will run down an alley tripping over hundreds of food pellets to obtain a single, identical pellet in the goal box [Stolz & Lott, 1964], . . . and pigeons will peck a key, even on intermittent schedules of reinforcement, to secure exactly the same food that is freely available in a nearby cup [Neuringer, 1969, 1970]. Given the option of receiving marbles merely by waiting an equivalent amount of time for their delivery, children tend to prefer to press a lever . . . to obtain the same marbles [Singh, 1970; Singh & Query, 1971]. (D'Amato, 1974, p. 95)

Why would animals or humans work for food or other rewards when they can get the same payoff without working? Isn't there an inherent tendency to "freeload"?

Apparently, just the opposite is true: There seems to be an inherent need to work. The reason may lie in the importance of controlling the environment in order to survive. Such control is basic in all animal and human existence. The need to be in control seems to persist in animals and children even in situations where it is not immediately necessary. Thus, it may be that the work is the reinforcement, not the food. Another explanation suggested by D'Amato is that the individual's *perception* of a reward changes. "The very same wine often tastes better when drunk from a stem glass than from a paper cup" (p. 96). Thus, although they are physically the same, the free food and the worked-for food may be perceived as different.

shook our heads because something—an argument, a symphony, or a chess game—was getting too complicated for us. A young child accustomed only to her parents may withdraw from a new face and scream with terror if that face has a beard. A very unusual dress style or a revolutionary piece of art or music may evoke rejection, scorn, even anger. But here learning enters the picture again. Acquaintance with the face, dress style, or symphony may reduce its novelty from an unacceptable to an interesting level. A child who at 2 years of age is only up to "Three Blind Mice" welcomes the complexity of a popular song at age 12, and perhaps a Beethoven string quartet at age 22. As we learn—and as we continually explore and familiarize ourselves with our environment—our threshold for the new and complex is raised and our exploration and curiosity become increasingly more ambitious.

Manipulation

Why do you suppose that museums have "Do Not Touch" signs all over the place?" It's not because the museum officials are afraid some people might touch the exhibits. It's because they *know*—by hard experience—that touching is one of our more irresistible urges, and that we *all* might give in to it unless specifically asked not to. The desire to manipulate differs from curiosity and exploration in that it is directed toward a specific object that must be touched, handled, played with, and felt before we are satisfied. **Manipulation** differs from curiosity and exploration in another way, too—it is a motive that seems to be limited to primates, which have the physical structures of agile fingers and toes.

The desire to manipulate seems to be related to two things—a need to know about something at a tactile level and sometimes a need to be soothed. The Greek "worry beads"—a set of beads on a short string that are moved back and forth in the course of conversation or thought—are examples of the second sort of manipulation. Under stress, people "fiddle"—with a cigarette, a paper napkin, a fountain pen. Children are always manipulating the objects of their environment. Eyeglasses, earrings, flowers, dogs' tails—everything must be touched, played with manually. The brighter the

object, the more mixed its colors, the more irregular its shape, the more appealing it is as a potential object for manipulation. But monkeys too will take a puzzle apart for no apparent reason other than manipulation (Harlow, 1950).

Contact

People want to touch other people. The need for **contact** is much broader and more universal than the need for manipulation. Furthermore, it is not limited to touching with the fingertips—it can involve the whole body. While manipulation is active, contact can also be passive.

In a famous series of experiments (Harlow, 1958; Harlow & Zimmerman, 1959), baby monkeys were separated from their mothers at birth. In place of their real mothers, they were given two "surrogate mothers." Both were the same shape, but one was made of wire and offered no soft surfaces. The other was cuddly—layered with foam rubber and covered with terry cloth. A nursing bottle was put in the wire "mother," and both "mothers" were warmed by means of an electric light placed inside them. Thus the wire "mother" fulfilled two physiological drives for the infant monkeys: the need for food and the need for warmth. But it was to the terry-cloth "mother," which did not provide food, that the babies gravitated. When they were frightened, they would run to it, and they clung to it as they would to a real mother.

Since both mothers were warm, it seems that the need for affection, cuddling, and closeness goes deeper than a need for mere warmth.

LEARNED MOTIVES

We are not born with all our motives. We have already seen that even motives that appear to be unlearned (such as hunger, pain, and sex) are actually learned in part. As we develop, our behavior comes to be governed by new motives that are almost entirely learned. Although these new motives are learned, not innate, they can exert just as much control over our behavior as unlearned drives and motives do.

Fear

Fear is a complex motivation with a simple goal—to avoid or escape the source of the fear. If we were not afraid of certain things, we would probably not be around very long. We are brought up to be afraid of some things because they are dangerous. More often than not, we learn fear by association with pain. If a boy has once been bitten by the big dog down the street, he learns to be afraid of it and he avoids it when he sees it approaching. He may also extend this particular fear to a fear of all dogs, or of all large or strange dogs. Thus fear is important to us in dealing with the hazards in our environment.

How is fear learned? In one experiment (Miller, 1948), rats were taught to escape from a painful stimulus. They were put into a white compartment, and an electric shock was applied to the compartment's grid floor. Then they were allowed to escape to a black compartment, which was shock-free. When the rats were put back into another white compartment, also shock-free, they showed all the signs of fear, such as trembling and crouching. Although there was no actual pain the second time, the white compartment had become *associated* with pain, and therefore triggered fear in the rats. Fear can be attached to almost any stimulus. A bell ringing at the time of the shock would have made the rats afraid of bells too.

The fact that association plays a strong role in fear and that potential or even imagined harm can trigger it sets fear apart from simple pain avoidance. Once fear has been learned, it is very hard to unlearn, and it extends to things other than the feared object itself. People are said to have "irrational" fears, but in many cases these fears were learned in particular, actually dangerous situations and then extended by association to other objects or situations where the element of real danger is minimal or nonexistent. A fear of heights, for example, may have been learned from one fall or a close escape from a fall. If you are afraid of the dark, you may have once awakened in an unfamiliar dark room and been unable to find your way around. As human beings are not simple, neither are the situations that trigger fear. But behavior in fear is simple—we try to get away from whatever it is that is causing our fear.

Aggression

Human aggression includes those behaviors that are intended to inflict physical or psychological harm on others. According to Beck (1978), human behavior cannot be considered aggressive unless intent is involved. A motorist blinded by a torrential rainstorm is not displaying aggressive behavior when her car accidentally hits a pedestrian; no intent was involved. However, when poor vision is not a factor and the driver aims her car in the direction of a pedestrian with the intent to harm him, she is committing an aggressive act. If you have ever seen a toddler wham his baby sister on the head with a block, you might suppose that aggression is innate. Skimming the newspaper might give you the same impression. Some, but by no means all, psychologists go along with this view. According to those who do, like Freud and Lorenz, we are born with an **aggressive drive** and this innate motive expresses itself in destructiveness, war, and sadism.

As Lazarus (1974) points out, certain implications about human life follow from the conclusion that an aggressive drive is innate. An innate drive cannot be eliminated, so it must be directed into socially acceptable and productive activities. According to Freud, civilization as we know it is actually an elaborate channeling device for our sexual and aggressive energies. Competitiveness in the work world or controlled and limited violence in a football game can be seen as ways of redirecting innate aggression into forms that are either useful and enjoyable or, at least, of limited harm.

The innate drive concept is unpopular among many psychologists because it poses a rather negative and deterministic view of human beings. We are pictured as inherently dangerous and destructive animals whose natural instincts must be controlled or else chaos will result. Humanistic psychologists such as Fromm and Maslow see people in a more positive light and emphasize the distinctly human, cooperative tendencies in our basic nature.

The innate drive theory can also be questioned scientifically. Lazarus (1974) points out that there is no substantial research to demonstrate that people have a built-in and uncontrollable drive to attack or fight. Under the innate drive concept, aggression is constantly generating energy. If this energy is not released, the person will experience great tension and pain. Yet studies suggest that the release of such energy through aggressive behavior tends to increase, rather than decrease, the likelihood of future attack.

Another view of aggression suggests that aggression is not a motive at all, but simply a form of behavior. Aggression, according to this viewpoint, results from the nonfulfillment of other motives, which produces frustration. This frustration is then directed into aggressive behavior. According to this **frustration-aggression hypothesis**, when the stimuli associated with frustration are not present, aggressive behavior does not appear, so aggression cannot be considered a motive.

Many theorists and researchers have pointed out that laboratory studies do not support the idea that frustration inevitably leads to aggression. Bandura (1973) notes that frustration can lead to a wide variety of behaviors other than aggression. Among these are a search for help and support; achievement strivings; withdrawal and resignation; and escape into drugs or alcohol. Bandura suggests that frustration will generate aggression in those people who have previously developed aggressive attitudes and actions as a means of coping with unpleasant situations.

In any case, aggressive *behavior* is in part learned. Children raised in a competitive climate are likely to learn to fight. The boy who pushes his little sister aside to get the last swing in the playground has probably been pushed aside by someone else. In addition, aggressive behavior is sometimes learned because it is reinforced. A father who rewards his son for fighting it out with the class bully is reinforcing the child's aggression and making it more likely that he will act aggressively again. Even when no one sets out to teach children aggressive behavior, they may learn it through imitation. A mother who slaps her daughter for hitting her friend is, through her behavior, providing a model of effective aggression. Children who are severely punished for aggressive behavior are found to act aggressively toward others, even toward dolls.

Children's tendency to imitate aggressive behavior has sparked concern over the effects of televised violence on aggression. Will children whose daily television diet includes murders, beatings, knifings, and gun fights tend to act more aggressively themselves? Several studies suggest that televised violence may be a factor in the development of aggressive behavior. In tracing the viewing habits of 427 third-graders over a 10-year period, Eron and his colleagues (1972) found that "the more violent are the programs preferred by boys in the third grade, the more aggressive is their behavior both at that time and ten years later" (p. 260). Girls who participated in the study did not appear to be influenced greatly by TV violence. The sex differences in response to TV violence are striking in this experiment, as is the fact that televised violence can have such a strong and lasting effect on 8- and 9-year-old boys. In another study, a group of first-graders who viewed a 5-minute-long aggressive cartoon displayed a larger number of aggressive behaviors after the cartoon ended than their classmates who had not viewed the cartoon (Ellis & Sekyra, 1972).

In the animal kingdom, much aggressive behavior results from competition for limited resources such as food, territory, or sexual partners. Deprivation leads to competition, and the means of eliminating that competition is aggression. Bernstein and Gordon (1974) point out that aggression may also serve an important social function in animal society. While studying monkey behavior, they found that aggressive behavior is primarily motivated by efforts to maintain existing social positions in the group. A dominant male, for example, may fight a younger male who is trying to take over his position in the group. Through aggression, then, the social order is maintained. "Rather than disrupting social relationships," the researchers explain, "aggression serves to enforce regulated social interactions which maintain primate societies" (p. 308).

Social Motives

Another class of learned motives centers around our relationships with other people. Observing everyday behavior, we see that **social motives** play a very great part in our lives and that social motives are numerous and complex. Our discussion will focus on several of the most important social motives.

Achievement. Climbing Mount Everest "because it is there," sending rockets into space, making the dean's list, rising to the top of a giant corporation—these are actions whose underlying motives are probably mixed. Achievement can, of course, be sought because of other, quite different motives—curiosity, fear of failure, and so on. But in all the activities mentioned above, the desire to perform with excellence is certainly present. It is this interest in achievement for its own sake that leads psychologists to suggest a separate achievement motive. **Need for achievement**, or *nAch* as it is abbreviated, varies widely from person to person. McClelland (1958) has developed techniques to measure *nAch* experimentally. For example, one picture in the Thematic Apperception Test (see Chapter 13) shows an adolescent boy sitting at a classroom desk. An open book lies on the desk, but the boy's gaze is directed outward toward the viewer. Subjects are asked to make up stories about this picture. One person responded:

> The boy in the picture is trying to reconcile the philosophies of Descartes and Thomas Aquinas— and at his tender age of 18. He has read several books on philosophy and feels the weight of the world on his shoulders.

Another response was in sharp contrast:

> Ed is thinking of leaving home for a while in the hope that this might shock his parents into getting along.

The first response comes from someone with a very high need for achievement, the second from someone whose need for achievement is very low.

From psychological tests and personal histories, psychologists have discovered some general traits of high-*nAch* individuals. These persons function best in competitive situations and are fast learners. What drives them is not so much the desire for fame or fortune as the need to live up to a high self-imposed standard of performance. They are self-confident, take on individual responsibility willingly, and are relatively resistant to outside social pressures. They are energetic and let little get in the way of accomplishing their goals. But

they are also likely to be tense and to suffer psychosomatic illness.

How does high *nAch* relate to occupational choice? In a study of 55 college graduates who were tested for achievement levels while in college, McClelland (1965) found that 83 percent of those who had high *nAch* scores went into "entrepreneurial occupations" (p. 389). These occupations, which include sales, owning and operating a business, management consulting, and the like, are characterized by a high degree of risk and challenge, decision-making responsibility, and objective feedback on job performance. McClelland also found that 70 percent of those individuals who chose professions that were not entrepreneurial had low *nAch* scores.

Once we know that individuals are high in need for achievement, the question remains: How did they get to be that way? Two major factors have been suggested (McClelland et al., 1953). First, children must see their actions or efforts as leading to successful changes in the environment. Second, they must have the success of these actions reinforced by adult standards for excellence. Children who are exposed to such standards will soon learn how to differentiate between good and poor performance and will know that they will be praised for achievement or punished for lack of it. This may lead to a desire to do things well.

It is important to remember that our standards of achievement are often biased by our culture (Maehr, 1974). On many psychological tests, the lower-class black child shows a low achievement motivation. Yet the same black child may demonstrate an intense achievement drive on a basketball court. Similarly, disadvantaged children who exhibit language difficulties in school may be quite skillful in the use of familiar dialects within their own communities. Any serious study of the achievement needs of various Americans must avoid the dangers of *ethnocentrism*—the attitude that one's own culture is superior to all others. If white middle-class standards are the only yardstick for measuring achievement motivation, we can expect that white middle-class children will consistently appear more achievement oriented. Such studies will not help us to understand the ambitions and desires of many children who are not from the white middle class.

The Power Motive. One important type of achievement motivation is the power motive. Generally, we think of achievement in terms of specific skills—the ability to compose a sonnet, throw a football, or solve a complex physics problem. Yet some people have a strong achievement striving that aims at gaining power over others. The power motive, according to researchers, may be defined as the need to influence or control other people or groups.

Winter (1973) studied the power motives of 12 American presidents, from Theodore Roosevelt through Richard Nixon. His technique was to score the concerns, aspirations, fears, and ideas for action of each president as revealed in his inaugural speech. The highest scorers in terms of power drives were Theodore Roosevelt, Franklin Roosevelt, Harry Truman, Woodrow Wilson, John Kennedy, and Lyndon Johnson. Except for Theodore Roosevelt, all were Democrats and all six men are known as action-oriented presidents. All also scored high in need for achievement. By contrast, Republican presidents (such as Taft, Hoover, and Eisenhower) are known more for restraint and tend to score much lower in power motivation and in need for achievement. Richard Nixon scored quite high in need for achievement

but relatively low in power motivation. According to Winter, the effect of this is a tendency toward vacillation and hesitancy when faced with a power-oriented issue. Winter (1976) studied Jimmy Carter when he was still a presidential candidate and found his power motive to be about average and his need to achieve somewhat above average (about the same as Theodore Roosevelt's).

Winter suggests a number of interesting relations between the power motive and specific presidential policy decisions and actions:

Those presidents in power when the country entered wars tended to score high on power motive.

Power scores of presidents seem significantly related to the gain or loss of territory through wars, expansion, treaties, and independence struggles.

Presidents with high power scores tended to have the highest turnover in cabinet members during their administrations.

Winter does not suggest that we avoid electing presidents with high power motives. Nor does Winter feel that presidents high in power motives are always preferable, although presidents who had high power motives are rated as more effective by historians. Rather, it is more a matter of electing the right person at the right time.

Functional Autonomy

Dogs owners know that their pets will at times pick up something and shake it—just what they would do if they wanted to kill prey. But dogs do not shake things just when they are hungry. Besides, how long has it been since Rover killed rabbits for food? People, too, may keep on doing things even when the original motives for doing them seem to have disappeared (for example, misers who count their money over and over, even though they know how much is there).

R. W. Woodworth (1918a) was the first to suggest that some of the skills we learn can become motives of their own, no longer reflecting any basic motive. A woman learns to play chess because she is curious, for instance, and the skills she develops become, in effect, drives that propel her to play chess again and again.

Gordon Allport (1937) described behavior with no apparent motive beyond itself as having *functional autonomy.* Such behavior, he said, may originally have been a response to a biological need or a secondary drive, like the need for approval, but it continues to take place even though the original motivation no longer exists. Moreover, it has no present motive beyond itself. (Thus, if the chess player plays to win money, her behavior cannot be called functionally autonomous.)

Critics say that terms like functional autonomy only describe behavior but do not explain it. Others feel that different theories will work just as well to explain specific behavior. Meanwhile, the question of why a given person skydives, studies math, or tastes wine remains open.

The Motive to Avoid Success. Is there a motive to *avoid* success? Modern women who want challenging jobs are now freer to take them than ever before. However, many intelligent, skilled women fail to achieve according to their talents—especially some of those who most desire success. According to Matina Horner (1969), men develop the need to achieve, while women develop both a strong desire to achieve and a fear of success.

To tap feelings about success, Horner studied the responses of undergraduates at the University of Michigan. The men were asked to finish a story that began: "After first-term finals, John finds himself at the top of his medical school class." The women got the same story, but with "Anne" substituted for "John."

Only about 10 percent of the men gave responses revealing doubt or fear about success. But the women revealed much fear in their stories. They worried about social rejection, picturing Anne as "acne-faced," lonely, dateless—even subject to physical attack after her victory! They also expressed doubts about her femininity: "Anne feels guilty.... She will finally have a nervous breakdown and quit medical school and marry a successful young doctor." A third group of women refused to admit that Anne could have succeeded. They misread the story, writing about Anne as a "nurse" or as second in score to a male student, and so on.

Horner believes the source of this fear of success to be the way women are brought up in our society. A girl grows up hearing women who achieve outside the home called "sexless," "unfeminine," or "hard." It is not surprising that achievement—or the prospect of it—makes her feel guilty and anxious. Women would rather be liked than be successful. Unless these feelings can be resolved, Horner believes, women are unlikely to make full use of their opportunities.

Horner's work has received widespread publicity, but some of her methods and conclusions have been questioned. Tresemer (1974) stresses the small size of Horner's sample and various inconsistencies and problems in the coding of fear of success (FOS). Tresemer is also skeptical of Horner's connection between FOS imagery and nonachievement or failure in women's actual behavior. He claims that Horner's work has not established fear of success as a clear *motive* for lack of achievement in women. Tresemer poses alternate explanations for some of the same behavior that Horner sees in terms of FOS. For example, he believes that nonachievement imagery in women subjects may represent "fear of sex-role inappropriateness" rather than "fear of success."

The fear of becoming involved in behaviors that are considered inappropriate to one's sex is present in men as well as women. Whereas women may fear becoming doctors because "men are supposed to be doctors," men may fear becoming ballet dancers or nursery school teachers because these activities have traditionally been viewed as female. These individuals may not fear success as such. Rather they may fear stepping out of their sex roles and trying behaviors that in the past have been reserved for members of the opposite sex.

Whatever its cause, fear of success may be changeable. Using undergraduates from the University of Michigan once again, Hoffman (1974) repeated Horner's study several years later with some surprising results. She found that about 65 percent of the women in the study gave responses that indicated a fear of success (this was about the same percentage found in Horner's study). However, 77 percent of the men also expressed this fear, a dramatic increase from the previous study. Hoffman suggests that this turnaround may relate to men's questioning of the value of achievement—something they would not have been likely to do 6 years earlier.

Affiliation. Sometimes you want to get away from it all—to spend an evening or a weekend alone, reading, thinking, or just being by yourself. But generally, people have a **need for affiliation**, a need to be with other people. If individuals are isolated from social contact for any considerable length of time, they will become anxious. Why is it that people seek each other out? How do groups come into being, and under what circumstances do a handful of isolated individuals become a group?

For one thing, the affiliation motive is aroused when people feel threatened. Esprit de corps—the feeling that you are part of a sympathetic group—is an important sentiment to encourage among troops going into a battle. Henry V's speech to his men before the battlements of Harfleur and a football coach's pregame pep talk are both examples of an effort to make people feel they are working for a common cause or against a common enemy.

Often, affiliative behavior results from another motive entirely. For example, you may give a party to celebrate getting a job, because you want to be praised for your achievement.

It has also been suggested that fear and anxiety are closely linked to the affiliation motive. When rats, monkeys, or humans are placed in anxiety-producing situations, the presence of a member of the same species who is not anxious will reduce the fear of an anxious one. If you are sitting in a plane during a bumpy flight and are nervous, you may strike up a conversation with the calm-looking man sitting next to you, because the erratic flight of the plane does not seem to be worrying him. In a study of female college students (Schachter, 1959), the subjects were divided into two groups. The subjects in one group were told that the experiment they were participating in would involve their receiving a severe electric shock; they were labeled the high-anxiety group. The subjects in the other group were told that the sensation of shock would be merely a tickle; they were labeled the low-anxiety group. Over two-thirds of the high-anxiety group, given the choice of waiting alone or with others, chose to wait with others. Out of the low-anxiety group, only one-third chose to wait with others.

How does the motive for affiliation develop in people? It has been found (Sarnoff & Zimbardo, 1961) that firstborn or only children have stronger affiliation motives than those born later, perhaps because they were used to receiving more parental attention during the early years. Children who are brought up to be dependent, or who are raised with close family ties, show stronger affiliation motives than those coming from more loosely knit families that encouraged early independence. Many conclusions about the development of the affiliation motive are still tentative, but the evidence clearly suggests that the desire to be with others goes back to the family, the first group we were ever in.

Consistency

"I was really shocked when she said that," you might remark of someone. "It just wasn't like her." You mean, of course, that it was not like what you know of her. People have a strong desire for things to be consistent. Any disparity produces a condition known as **cognitive dissonance**. Suppose you do not believe in astrology, but you let a friend chart your horoscope, and you find it amazingly accurate. You have several alternatives—you can dismiss the whole thing as a coincidence, you can decide your friend based the horoscope on things found out about you behind your back, or you can switch over entirely and study astrology. In the first case, you have rejected the evidence entirely; in the second, you have brought in an "explanation" to reconcile the dissonance; in the third, you have changed your beliefs in the face of the evidence. Whatever you do, you have relieved the cognitive dissonance between the opinion you held and the contradictory new evidence; you have restored **consistency**.

The steps people take when faced with cognitive dissonance can depend on a number of factors. One of them is how strongly they hold their beliefs—what it "costs" them to give them up. If someone makes a good argument for cantaloupe being more nutritious than watermelon, you might change your belief accordingly because it does not matter very much to you anyway. But if you are told that your much-admired older sister has been caught cheating on an exam, you may reject the information entirely rather than change the image you hold of her. Self-image, too, is relevant—people with low self-esteem will feel a stronger need to retain their own ideas intact, while more confident people are more tolerant when faced with conflicting situations.

In terms of the pattern of motivation we have been discussing, then, we might sum up the need for consistency this way: Faced with a fact or event that is not in accord with something we believe, we experience the tension of cognitive dissonance. The tension elicits a desire for consistency, a need to restore the balance between our beliefs and the new experience. This need for consistency, in turn, activates behavior. The behavior can take several forms. We can reject or play down the dissonant fact, we can alter our beliefs, or we can bring in some new factor that reconciles the two. Whichever behavior we choose, the balance is restored and the tension is relieved.

UNCONSCIOUS MOTIVES

A new car—the BTX Super Panther II—is advertised, and a man decides he would like to own one. Why? He may tell you that his old car was running down and this one looks "pretty good" to him. But there may be other reasons, cf which he is unaware.

Theories of **unconscious motivation** vary. Freud's is probably the most extreme. According to his theory, every act—however trivial—derives from a host of unconscious motives. A Freudian might perceive the man's choice of a car as the desire to conquer a sexual object—a desire encouraged by advertisements touting it as "sleek," "purring," and "packed with power." Or Freudian theory might have cited aggression, the man's need to zoom down Main Street with as much horsepower as possible under his control.

But we do not need to interpret all acts in Freudian terms to realize that they can spring from motives we are not aware of. The man may be expressing a desire for social approval—"Be the first one on your block to own one!"—or a desire to reward himself for hard work. He could be trying to bolster a sagging self-image. He could be consoling himself for the loss of a promotion or a girlfriend.

It should be emphasized that unconscious motives are not a particular *class* of motives, as physiological, learned, and stimulus motives are. Especially in the discussion of physiological drives, we pointed out that we do not have to be aware of hunger and thirst to act in such a way as to satisfy them. An unconscious motive is any motive that we are acting to satisfy without knowing quite why we are doing so.

A HIERARCHY OF MOTIVES

You will have noticed that throughout this chapter we have been gradually working along lines leading us from very primitive motives, shared by all creatures, to motives that are more and more sophisticated, complicated, and human. Maslow (1954) proposed that all motives can be arranged in such a hierarchy, from lower to higher. The lower motives are relatively simple, and they spring from bodily states that *must* be satisfied. As the motives become higher and higher, they spring from other things—the desire to live as comfortably as possible in our environment, to deal as well as we can with other human beings, and to present ourselves to others as well as we can.

According to Maslow's theory, higher motives will appear only to the degree that the more basic ones have been satisfied. This is true on an evolutionary scale, and also on an individual one. If you are starving, you will probably not care what people think of your table manners.

Maslow believed that the most highly "evolved" motive in the hierarchy is **self-actualization**. This may be described as a desire to make the best one can out of oneself. It does not concern the respect of other human beings and their judgments of us, but rather what we ourselves want to be. People differ in how important self-actualization is in their behavior, but to some extent all of us are motivated to live according to what is necessary for our individual growth. The people who are the most self-actualizing, Maslow said, think of themselves as whole beings, not as parcels of hunger, fear, ambition, and dependency.

Although it is useful as a way of thinking about motives, Maslow's hierarchy of motives is a theory that is extremely difficult to test (Wahba & Bridwell, 1976). It has been criticized by research studies that question the evidence supporting the classification of human needs into five separate categories and the placement of these categories into a hierarchical structure. (Refer to the diagram on p. 263.)

RESOURCE CHAPTER B
Power

You can get much farther with a kind word and a gun than you can with a kind word alone.

—Al Capone

The subject of Power has been described by Bertrand Russell as "...the fundamental concept in social science..., in the same sense in which Energy is the fundamental concept in physics."[1] Although there is little controversy as to the importance of the subject, this should not be interpreted as meaning that power has been the subject of substantial research. Quite the contrary, the virtual absence of research soon becomes obvious to one reviewing the power literature. It is truly a neglected area of organizational behavior, and it may be correct to describe social scientists as having been "soft on power."[2]

Part of the problem lies in the connotation power has in a democratic society. Many believe that the overt desire for power is wrong.

In general, in American society at least...it is reprehensible to be concerned about having influence over others....In our society in our time, and perhaps in all societies at all times, the exercise of power is viewed very negatively. People are suspicious of a man who wants power, even if he does so for sincere altruistic reasons. He is often socially conditioned to be suspicious of himself. He does not want to be in a position where he

might be thought to be seeking power and influence in order to exploit others.[3]

However, this does not negate the fact that the vast majority of us do strive for power—not necessarily in order to harm others or to control others. People seek power to survive and to maximize their own interest, and this is best done by controlling the world in which we live. Absolute control, of course, can never be achieved, but the greater our power, the greater is our control over the influences that affect our lives.

Concern about power does not automatically render one a Machiavelli—that is, manipulative to the extent that one will disregard the rules of fairness and equity, ethical considerations, and allow the ends always to justify the means. The sophisticated individual recognizes that the acquisition and distribution of power is a natural process in any group. It influences what goals the group will pursue, and how the group's resources will be distributed among its members. These, in turn, play an important part in determining how effective the group will be. Failure to understand power will dramatically reduce your ability to understand organizational behavior.

A DEFINITION OF POWER

When we discuss power, we mean the ability to affect and control anything that is of value to others. If A has power over individual or group B, then A can influence certain actions of B so that the outcome is preferable to the self-interest of A.

[1] Bertrand Russell. *Power: A New Social Analysis* (London: Allen & Unwin, 1938), p. 12.
[2] Dorwin Cartwright, "Power: A Neglected Variable in Social Psychology," in *Studies in Social Power*, ed. D. Cartwright (Ann Arbor: Institute of Social Research. 1959), p. 12.

Source: Stephen P. Robbins, *Organizational Behavior* (Englewood Cliffs, N.J.: Prentice-Hall, Inc., 1979), pp. 262–79. Reprinted by permission of Prentice-Hall, Inc.

[3] David C. McClelland, "The Two Faces of Power," *Journal of International Affairs*, Vol. 24, No. 1 (1970), p. 29.

Therefore, power requires two or more people—an exerciser and a subject. Power also disregards intent. Whether A *wants* to have control over B is irrelevant. If B allows A to control certain of his or their actions, then A has power over B. Finally, power may exist but not be used. It is a capacity or potential. Just because it is not imposed does not imply that it does not exist. However, our discussion will emphasize its effectiveness when used rather than its potential capacity for influence.

A careful comparison of our description of power with our description of leadership in the previous chapter should bring the recognition that the two concepts are closely intertwined. Leaders use power as a means of attaining group goals. Leaders achieve goals, and power is a means for facilitating their achievement.

If there is a significant difference, it lies in the direction that research on the two concepts has taken. Leadership research, for the most part, emphasizes style. It seeks answers to questions like: How supportive should a leader be? How much of decision-making should be shared with subordinates? In contrast, the research on power has tended to encompass a broader area and focus on tactics for gaining compliance. It has gone beyond the individual as exerciser—power can be used by individuals or groups to control other individuals or groups. However, given the increasing interest in power and power relationships, we can expect to find a greater integration between the concepts of leadership and power in the near future.

BASES OF POWER

What are the sources or bases from which power emanates? What is it that gives an individual or group influence over others? The answer to these questions was substantially provided by French and Raven twenty years ago.[4] They proposed a classification scheme that distinguished five bases of influence: coercive, reward, expert, legitimate, and referent.

[4] John R. P. French, Jr., and Bertram Raven, "The Bases of Social Power," in *Group Dynamics: Research and Theory*, ed. Dorwin Cartwright and A. F. Zander (New York: Harper & Row, 1960), pp. 607–23.

Coercive Power

The coercive base is defined by French and Raven as depending on fear. One reacts to this power out of fear of the negative ramifications that might result if one fails to comply. It rests on the application, or the threat of application, of physical sanctions such as infliction of pain, deformity, or death; the generation of frustration through restriction of movement; or the controlling through force of basic physiological or safety needs.

In the 1930s, when John Dillinger went into a bank, held a gun to the teller's head, and asked for the money, he was incredibly successful at getting compliance with his request. His power base? Coercive. A loaded gun gives its holder power because others are fearful that they will lose something which they hold dear—their life.

> Of all the bases of power available to man, the power to hurt others is possibly most often used, most often condemned, and most difficult to control...the state relies on its military and legal resources to intimidate nations, or even its own citizens. Businesses rely upon the control of economic resources. Schools and universities rely upon their right to deny students formal education, while the church threatens individuals with loss of grace. At the personal level, individuals exercise coercive power through a reliance upon physical strength, verbal facility, or the ability to grant or withhold emotional support from others. These bases provide the individual with the means to physically harm, bully, humiliate, or deny love to others.[5]

At the organizational level, A has coercive power over B if A can dismiss, suspend, or demote B, assuming that B values his or her job. Similarly, if A can assign B work activities that B finds unpleasant or treat B in a manner that B finds embarrassing, A possesses coercive power over B.

Reward Power

The opposite of coercive power is the power to reward. People comply with the wishes of another

[5] David Kipnis, *The Powerholders* (Chicago: University of Chicago Press, 1976), pp. 77–78.

because it will result in positive benefits; therefore, one who can distribute rewards that others view as valuable will have power over them. These rewards can be anything that another may value. Again, in an organizational context, we think of money, favorable performance appraisals, interesting work assignments, friendly colleagues, and preferred work shifts or sales territories.

Coercive and reward power are actually counterparts of each other. If you can remove something of positive value from B or inflict something of negative value upon B, you have coercive power over B. If you can give B something of positive value or remove something having negative value, you have reward power over B. As we shall see later in this section, French and Raven recognize that a number of their power bases tend to exist together.

Expert Power

Expert power is that influence one wields as a result of one's expertise, special skill, or knowledge. In the mid-1960s, when Jimmy Brown of the Cleveland Browns was destroying every ground-gaining record in the National Football League, his suggestions to young rookie halfbacks must certainly have been listened to. Why? His record indicated high expertise in his field. In the same way, if basketball star Kareem Abdul-Jabbar were to give you advice on your hook shot, you would be far more likely to be influenced than if someone with no expertise or reputation were to make the same suggestion.

Valid knowledge is one of the most powerful sources of influence. For example, the accountant with twenty years' experience in the organization, who is the only one that understands the general accounting system, has power. Just such a case existed in a manufacturing firm a few years ago. It caused considerable discomfort for the controller, since he was solely dependent on this long-standing employee (let us call him A.J.) in areas pertaining to general accounting. The area supervisor was a young college graduate with little experience in how the system worked. In addition, no other employee except A.J. had performed all the general accounting functions. By reason of his

expertise, A.J. had made himself almost irreplaceable *and powerful*.

Powerful positions based solely on expert power are held by people in almost every group or organization. Physicians, in white coats and with stethoscopes around their neck, have expert power. We listen to our doctors because the five years they spent in medical school gives them credibility. Walter Cronkite's nightly comments on the state of the world probably carry greater impact than the comments of your Aunt Alice. In spite of the fact that you have known Aunt Alice all your life, love her dearly, and that you are unknown to Walter Cronkite, he has greater credibility on world affairs than your aunt. However, if you are looking for the family recipe for chocolate chip cookies, Aunt Alice's credibility may certainly outweigh Mr. Cronkite's.

In recent years, as a result of the explosion in technical knowledge that is required in order to do most jobs, expert power has become an increasingly potent influence force. As jobs become more specialized, we become increasingly dependent on "experts" to achieve group goals. As members increase their knowledge of information that is critical to the operation of the group, the more is their expertise power enhanced. If our computer system is critical to our group's work, and if I know how to repair it and no one else within 200 miles does, then the group is dependent on me. I wield expert power. If such a situation existed, you might expect the group leader or manager to have others trained in the workings of the computer or hire someone with this knowledge in order to reduce my power. As others become capable of duplicating your activities, your expertise power diminishes.

Legitimate Power

The fourth power base French and Raven identified was legitimacy, which encompasses the formal rights one receives as a result of his or her authoritative position or role in an organization. Legitimate power is closely aligned with reward and coercive powers, for individuals who have legitimacy usually also have considerable power to reward and coerce.

Legitimate power lies not in relationships but rather in position or role. For example, an army private salutes the major's gold oak leaf worn on his lapel, not the major himself. Anyone wearing a major's uniform receives a salute from a private, regardless of any private's view of the personal competence of any major. If, while driving your car, you should suddenly be closely followed by a black and white vehicle, with a flashing red light, I would expect you to pull over to the side of the road. Further, if a man in a policeman's uniform comes over to your car and asks you to get out, you probably will. Why do you obey this man? It is unlikely that you know him personally, yet you do as he requests. The reason is that his role, as identified by his costume and other official accouterments, represents a legitimate power base to you. When people with legitimacy speak—school principals, police captains, bank presidents, or city building inspectors—teachers, policemen, tellers and building contractors listen and usually obey. In the armed forces, in public agencies, in manufacturing firms, in service organizations, on athletic teams, or in social groups, there are individuals who have been given positions of authority. They hold jobs with titles like manager, administrator, director, foreman, or supervisor. The rights inherent in these positions are the basis for legitimate power.

A final point before we leave legitimate power: It tends to exist along with other power bases. Individuals who have a formal position of authority, for example, are also likely to control sources of reward, punishment, and information, which gives them reward, coercive and expert power.

Referent Power

The last category of influence that French and Raven described was referent power. Its base is identification with a person who has the resources or personal traits one believes are desirable. If A admires and identifies with B, power can be exercised by B because A wishes to please B.

Referent power develops out of admiration of another and a desire to be like that person. If you admire someone to the point of modeling your behavior and attitudes after him, he possesses referent power over you. This power base can be operative without the power holder's even recognizing it. B can potentially influence A even without attempting to do so, or without B's awareness. Referent power explains, incidentally, why celebrities are paid millions of dollars to endorse products in commercials. Marketing research shows that people like Margaux Hemingway, Joe Namath, Farrah Fawcett-Majors, and Robert Blake have power in influencing your buying behavior for products like perfumes, popcorn makers, hair conditioners, and oil additives. With a little practice, you or I could probably deliver as smooth a sales pitch as these individuals, but the buying public does not identify with you and me. On the other hand, if you have a younger brother or sister who looks up to you and wants to be like you, you may have extraordinary abilities to influence his or her attitudes or behavior. In other words, you hold referent power in your relationship.

POWER DYNAMICS

Our previous discussion focused on the need for both a power holder or exerciser and a subject or target upon which influence is exerted. The exerciser has control over a resource valued by the subject and the subject allows himself or herself to be influenced because of the exerciser's control. The valued resource can be the desire for rewards, the desire to avoid punishments, the need for information or knowledge, or the desire to be like the power holder. But we still have not discussed the dynamics of power: who wants it, how exercisers obtain compliance, or the ramifications of the various power bases on group performance and satisfaction. In the remainder of this chapter, we shall look at these issues by proposing a number of postulates that will help us to understand the dynamics of power in groups and organizations.

Who Wants Power?

Power is not equally divided among group members. Superficial observation of any group will readily show that group members have varying amounts of power. Because group members themselves differ as to knowledge, education, experience, personality traits, and physical characteristics, it would be indeed surprising to expect members to be homogeneous in their abilities to influence. Some people *are* more powerful than others. This disparity will influence the behavior and level of satisfaction of the powerful, the less powerful, and the powerless.

Different people place different values on the gain and exercise of power. The evidence suggests that the amount of power an individual exercises is dependent largely on the strength of his or her power motive.[6] Those people with a high need for power (*nPwr*) are attracted to jobs that provide latitude for defining their roles; selecting their actions; and advising, evaluating, and controlling the behavior of others. It is not our purpose to investigate why people differ in *nPwr*—for example, arguments have been made that power seeking is a neurotic behavior based on childhood deprivations.[7] Rather, we are concerned with establishing whether or not people differ.

Research indicates that there are indeed differences in *nPwr* among people and that individuals who score high on *nPwr* tend to purchase prestige objects so as to cause envy in others, seek jobs such as business managers or teachers that provide considerable opportunity to exercise influence, are more likely to run for political office, and seek to dominate others in group discussions.[8] So we can conclude that while most people strive for power, some seek it considerably more than others.

Those "in power" will resist attempts to change the distribution of power within the group. Individuals who crave power and then are successful at obtaining it are reluctant to give it up easily. They have found that having the control of power allows them to gratify their desires more readily. It provides the opportunity for the powerful to allot for themselves more of those things that provide satisfaction.[9]

As a result, those in power will attempt to maintain the status quo. For example, one researcher uses the label "intimidation rituals" to describe the devices that the power holders in an organization's authority structure use to resist changes they do not sanction.[10] Intimidation begins by attempting to nullify the would-be reformer's impact by claiming that the accusations or suggestions for change are the result of misunderstandings or misconceptions. If nullification fails, those in power will isolate the reformer. By limiting the reformer's communication links, restricting her freedom of movement, or restricting her resource supply, those in power hope to lessen the impact of the crusader and reduce her ability to mobilize support for her changes. Should isolation fail, the efforts by the power holders become more overt. They will attempt to reduce the influence of the reformer through defamation, hoping to reduce her following by publicly questioning the reformer's motives or her competence. Finally, if the three previous approaches fail to reduce the reformer's impact, those in power will resort to their "ace in the hole"—they will expel her. In a business organization, this is illustrated by the power holders (management) firing the employee who challenges management decisions or who becomes respected by her peers and develops strong abilities to influence other workers. Such activities or abilities represent a potential threat to those decision makers in power, and terminating the dissident is the final alternative if it appears that she may be successful in changing the power structure.

Those "out of power" and seeking to be "in," will first try to increase their power individually, but if ineffective, will then resort to forming a coalition.* The natural way to gain influence is to become a powerholder. Therefore, those who want power will attempt to build a personal power base. But in many instances, this may be difficult, risky, costly, or impossible. In such cases, efforts will be made to form a coalition of two or more "outs" who by joining together can each better them-

[6] D. G. Winter, *The Power Motive* (New York: Free Press, 1973).

[7] Alfred Adler, *Understanding Human Nature* (New York: Fawcett World Library, 1959).

[8] Kipnis, *Powerholders.*

[9] *Ibid.*, pp. 171–72.

[10] R. O'Day, "Intimidation Rituals: Reactions to Reform," *Journal of Applied Behavioral Science*, Vol. 10 (1974), pp. 373–86.

selves at the expense of those outside the coalition.

In the late 1960s, college students found that by joining together to form a "student power group," they could achieve ends that had been impossible individually. Historically, employees in organizations who were unsuccessful in bargaining on their own behalf with management resorted to labor unions to bargain for them. In recent years, even some managers have joined unions after finding it difficult to individually exert power to attain higher wages and greater job security.

Dependency and Uncertainty

The greater A's dependency on B, the greater power B has over A. When you possess anything that others require but that you alone control, you make them dependent upon you and, therefore, you gain power over them.[11] Dependency, then, is inversely proportional to the alternative sources of supply. If something is plentiful, possession of it will not increase your power. If everyone is intelligent, intelligence gives no special advantage. Similarly, among the super-rich, money is no longer power. But as the old saying goes, "in the land of the blind, the one-eyed man is king!" If you can create a monopoly by controlling information, prestige, or anything that others crave, they become dependent on you. Conversely, the more that you can expand your options, the less power you place in the hands of others. This explains, for example, why most organizations develop multiple suppliers rather than giving their business to only one. It also explains why so many of us aspire for financial independence. Financial independence reduces the power that others can have over us.

A recent example of the role dependency plays in a work group or an organization is the case of Mike Milken, the 30-year-old head of the corporate bond department at a major New York City brokerage firm.[12] A native Californian, Milken grew disenchanted with New York and decided to

return to southern California and a warmer climate. But Milken made so much for his employer that they were not about to let him go. The solution: Rather than lose his trading skills to some competitor with West Coast connections, the company agreed to move its entire bond department. Milken and the staff of 20 people working for him were, in the spring of 1978, all being moved to Los Angeles. The cost of setting up this office, moving employees and their families, and absorbing housing subsidies all being part of the price Mike Milken's employer was willing to pay to keep his skills.

A concept referred to as the "elasticity of power" can help to illustrate the interrelationship between power and dependency. In economics, considerable attention is focused on the elasticity of demand, which is defined as the relative responsiveness of quantity demanded to change in price. This concept can be modified to explain the strength of power.

Elasticity of power is defined as the relative responsiveness of power to change in available alternatives. One's ability to influence others is viewed as being dependent on how these others perceive their alternatives.

As shown in Figure 12–2, assume we have two individuals. Mr. A's power elasticity curve is relatively inelastic. This would describe, for example, an employee who believed that he had a large number of employment opportunities outside his current organization. Fear of being fired would have only a moderate impact on Mr. A, for he perceives that he has a number of other alternatives. Mr. A's boss finds that threatening A with termination has only a minimal impact on influencing A's behavior. A reduction in alternatives (from X to X − 1) only increases the power of A's boss slightly (A' to A"). However, Mr. B's curve is relatively elastic. He sees few other job opportunities. His age, education, present salary, or lack of contacts may severely limit his ability to find a job somewhere else. As a result, Mr. B is dependent on his present organization and boss. If B loses his job (Y to Y − 1), he may face prolonged unemployment, and it shows itself in the increased power of B's boss. As long as B perceives his options as limited and B's boss holds the power to terminate his employment, B's boss will hold

[11] R. E. Emerson, "Power-Dependence Relations," *American Sociological Review*, Vol. 27 (1962), pp. 31–41.
[12] Sharon Johnson, "Mohammed and the Mountain," *New York Times*, January 29, 1978, p. F5.

FIGURE 12–2 Elasticity of Power

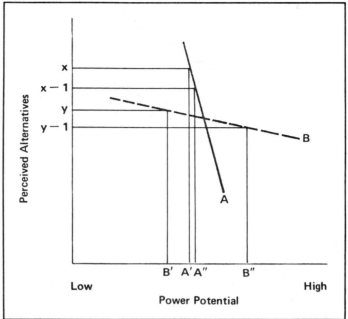

considerable power over him. In such a situation, it is obviously important for B to get his boss to *believe* that his options are considerably greater than they really are. If this is not achieved, B places his fate almost entirely in the hands of his boss and makes him captive to almost any demands the boss devises.

Higher education provides an excellent example of how this elasticity concept operates. In universities where there are strong pressures for faculty to publish, we can say that a department head's power over a faculty member is inversely related to that member's publication record. The more recognition the faculty member receives through publication, the more mobile he or she is. That is, since other universities want faculty who are highly published and visible, there is an increased demand for his or her services. Although the concept of tenure can act to alter this relationship by restricting the department head's alternatives, those faculty members with little or no publications have the least mobility and are subject to the greatest influence from their superiors.

To the extent that a low-ranking member has

important expert knowledge not available to high-ranking members, the low-ranking member is likely to have power over the high-ranking members. This statement is the natural result when we combine our previous statement regarding dependency with what we have previously discussed in the section on expert power. It explicitly states that one does not have to hold a legitimate hierarchical role in a group or organization in order to have power. Individuals who are low-ranking in the hierarchy can develop a strong and potent power base by acquiring expert knowledge or information that high-ranking participants are dependent upon. This may be achieved by destroying the procedure manuals that describe how a job is done, refusing to train people in your job or even to show others exactly what you do, creating specialized language and terminology that inhibits others from understanding your job, or operating in secrecy so the activity will appear more complex and difficult than it really is.

A person difficult to replace has greater power than has an easily replaceable person. This statement also evolves out of the role dependency plays in power positions. The more unique your skills, the greater advantage you have in influencing others in ways that are personally satisfying. This applies to occupational categories as well as to unique individual talents:

> In the late 1950s, when there were relatively few engineers to service an expanding American economy, engineers had great prestige and power. They could force employers to provide them with large salaries and benefits, by threatening to withhold their services. By the 1970s, however, many persons had become engineers and consequently the bargaining power of engineers with employers was practically nil.[13]

The same thing happened among elementary and secondary school teachers. In the 1940s and 1950s, there was a significant shortage. Today, literally hundreds of thousands of individuals with teaching credentials look in vain for teaching jobs. School administrators no longer fear that competent teaching replacements cannot be found. In contrast, if you had a degree in accounting in the 1970s, you found yourself in a powerful position in negotiating with your employer or prospective employers. In the late 1970s, at least, accountants were more difficult to replace than elementary or secondary teachers.

The ability to decrease group uncertainty increases an individual's potential power. Just as dependency is an effective approach for developing power, the evidence suggests that individuals who can reduce the uncertainties that their group or organization faces possess a valuable resource that can create power.

Organizations seek to avoid uncertainty.[14] Those individuals who can absorb the organization's uncertainty will have influence in the organization. In a French factory, one researcher noticed that maintenance engineers exerted considerable power in spite of their generally low rank in the hierarchy.[15] Why? The researcher found that the only major remaining uncertainty confronting the

organization was the breakdown of machinery— and only the maintenance engineers could control this uncertainty.

Another researcher studied departmental power in a group of industrial organizations and found that the marketing department was consistently rated as the most powerful.[16] He concluded that the most critical uncertainty facing these firms was selling their products. This might suggest that during a labor strike, the organization's negotiating representatives have increased power or that engineers, as a group, would be more powerful at IBM than at Procter & Gamble. These inferences appear to be generally valid. Labor negotiators *do* become more powerful within the personnel area and the organization as a whole during periods of labor strife. An organization such as IBM, which is heavily technologically oriented, is highly dependent on its engineers in order to maintain its product superiority. And, at IBM, engineers are clearly the most powerful group. At Procter & Gamble, marketing is the name of the game, and marketers are the most powerful occupational group.

Compliance

Individuals perceive reward and coercive powers as weak reasons for complying with a superior's requests. Of the five power bases, reward and coercion are the least preferred. Individuals perceive these bases as having the weakest potential for enacting compliance. Studies of college teachers[17] and salesmen[18] both demonstrated the same conclusion: Reward and coercive power bases are the lowest in the preference scale. This may be explained by the fact that expert and referent bases refer to something inherent in the individual rather

---

[13] Kipnis, *Powerholders*, p. 159.
[14] Richard M. Cyert and James G. March, *A Behavioral Theory of the Firm* (Englewood Cliffs, N.J.: Prentice-Hall, 1963).
[15] Michel Crozier, *The Bureaucratic Phenomenon* (Chicago: University of Chicago Press, 1964).

[16] Charles Perrow, "Departmental Power and Perspective in Industrial Firms," in *Power in Organizations*, ed. M. N. Zald (Nashville, Tenn.: Vanderbilt University Press, 1970).
[17] Jerald G. Bachman, "Faculty Satisfaction and the Dean's Influence: An Organizational Study of Twelve Liberal Arts Colleges," *Journal of Applied Psychology*, Vol. 52 (1968), pp. 55–61.
[18] Jerald G. Bachman, C. G. Smith, and J. A. Slesinger, "Control, Performance and Satisfaction: An Analysis of Structural and Individual Effort," *Journal of Personality and Social Psychology*, Vol. 4 (1966), pp. 127–36.

than in the position held. It is more palatable to be influenced by someone who uses knowledge or respect than his ability to reward or punish. The probable reason that legitimacy is more acceptable than either reward or coercive bases is the role that authority plays in our society. The home, school, and church have historically reinforced the authority of parents, teachers, and religious doctrine, respectively. With rare exception, we recognize and accept the legitimacy of those in authority. We may not be in agreement with their decisions, but we will almost always abide by them.

Coercion causes a decrease in attraction for the power center and higher resistance. Few people enjoy functioning under the fear of punishment. As a result, there tends to be resistance to coercive efforts and to the individual doing the coercing. As one might realize intuitively, users of reward power are liked better than those depending on coercive power.[19]

Compliance with the demands of coercive power increases with the strength of the potential punishment. Though individuals may not prefer coercion, it would be naive to assume that it is ineffective. But coercion's ability to exact compliance tends to increase with the strength of the potential punishment.[20] Again, this should not be surprising. As was mentioned earlier, in our discussion of John Dillinger, a loaded gun does tend to bring about compliance, generally a lot more readily than loud talk or threats. This may explain why, during a holdup, the perpetrator may fire his gun: just to demonstrate that he or she "means business."

When resistance to influence is attributed to lack of motivation rather than lack of ability, a power holder is most reliant on coercion. When noncompliance is attributed to motivational causes ("I refuse") rather than to a lack of ability ("I can't"), the power holder's expectations of successful influence are lowest, and reliance upon coercion becomes the greatest.[21] If there is a lack of motivation, there is a tendency toward using the

stick rather than the carrot. For example, among first-line supervisors, it was found that 63 percent who attributed their workers' unsatisfactory performance to a lack of motivation, poor attitudes, or discipline used coercive means in attempts to alter this behavior. Among supervisors who attributed unsatisfactory performance to the workers' lack of ability, only 26 percent used coercion.[22] In summarizing the research on this point, one author concluded: "It appears to be a safe generalization that more workers are fired for poor attitudes and lack of discipline than for a lack of ability."[23]

Expertness on one task increases the ability of an individual to exert influence on a second task. There appears to be a halo effect operating with expert power. If an individual holds expertise in one activity, it increases the probability of his being able to exert influence in another activity.[24] Your accounting instructor may have a Ph.D. in accounting, hold a C.P.A. certificate, and be highly learned in his field. But if the topic in class diverts to premarital sexual relations, and he voices a position, is it given less, equal, or greater weight than the opinions of other members in the class? Probably greater, as a result of his accounting expertise. His knowledge on the subject of premarital sexual relations may be the least of anyone in the class, but we tend to allow expertise to expand into areas beyond its original focal point.

Expert power is reduced when its exercise is attempted outside the perceived limits. When others perceive expert power to be used beyond those limits or areas for which it was originally accepted, the base becomes less effective. Dr. Benjamin Spock, for example, a well-known pediatrist, lost a great deal of credibility in the 1960s when he proclaimed to be knowledgeable in foreign affairs. The public's first response was to accept his views on foreign affairs as they had his opinions on raising children. But, very quickly, it

[19] John Schopler, "Social Power," in *Advances in Experimental Social Psychology*, Vol. 2, ed. Leonard Berkowitz (New York: Academic Press, 1965), pp. 177–218.
[20] *Ibid.*

[21] B. Goodstadt and L. Hjelle, "Power to the Powerless," *Journal of Personality and Social Psychology*, Vol. 27 (1973), pp. 190–96.
[22] D. Kipnis and J. Cosentino, "Use of Leadership Styles in Industry," *Journal of Applied Psychology*, Vol 53 (1969), pp. 460–66.
[23] Kipnis, *Powerholders*.
[24] Schopler, "Social Power."

became apparent that Dr. Spock was outside his range of competence, thus reducing his overall power of influence.

Effectiveness

Expert power is the base most strongly and consistently related with effective performance. In a study of five organizations, expertise appeared to be the best of the five power bases for getting others to perform as desired.[25] We can conclude, therefore, that competence appears to offer very wide appeal.

Referent power tends to be positively related with group effectiveness. The evidence on referent power is not as strong as that on expertise. It appears to be of more intermediate importance in explaining compliance, though in most cases it is positively related with group effectiveness.[26]

Legitimate power does not appear to be related to performance differences. In spite of legitimacy being the most widely given reason for complying with a superior's wishes, it does not seem to lead to higher performance, though the findings are far from conclusive. Among blue-collar workers, one researcher found significantly positive relations between legitimate power and four of six production measures. However, it was not related with average earnings or performance against schedule.[27] Another study could find no relationship between the use of legitimate power and high efficiency ratings.[28] Legitimacy is effective for exacting compliance, but there is little evidence to suggest that it leads to higher levels of performance. This may be explained by the fact that legitimate power tends to be fairly constant, especially within a given organization.

The use of reward and coercive power has a significant inverse relationship to performance. Given the negative view that individuals have toward reward and coercion as reasons for complying with a superior's requests, the above statement appears logical.[29] Research finds the use of coercive power to be negatively related to group effectiveness.[30]

Legitimate, expert, and referent power bases generally produce both public and private compliance, while reward and coercive bases produce only public compliance. Our previous findings on the relationship between various power bases and performance effectiveness may be explainable by differentiating between public and private compliance.[31]

All the power bases can produce public compliance; that is, individuals will comply as long as their behavior is monitored. But without private compliance—the internal acceptance of the influence—the power holder must continually monitor the behavior of the subject. Private compliance indicates that the subject has undergone a relatively permanent change in his or her behavior that will continue independently of the power holder's influence. This could explain why reward and coercive power bases tend to be ineffective—they are publicly accepted, but if the power holder fails to continually monitor his or her subject(s), compliance declines.

Situational Factors

To this point we have sought to identify general statements that can help us to better understand power. But the concept is obviously complex, and we can increase our predictive ability by trying to isolate situations where certain power bases are more effective than others.

The greater the professional orientation of group members, the greater relative strength referent power has in influencing them. Profes-

[25] Jerald G. Bachman, D. G. Bowers and P. M. Marcus, "Bases of Supervisory Power: A Comparative Study in Five Organizational Settings," in *Control in Organizations*, ed. Arnold S. Tannenbaum (New York: McGraw-Hill, 1968), p. 236.
[26] *Ibid.*
[27] K. Student, "Supervisory Influence and Work-Group Performance," *Journal of Applied Psychology*, Vol. 52 (1968), pp. 188–94.
[28] John Ivancevich, "An Analysis of Control, Bases of Control, and Satisfaction in an Organizational Setting," *Academy of Management Journal,* December 1970, pp. 427–36.

[29] Bachman, "Faculty Satisfaction"; and Bachman, Smith, and Slesinger, "Control, Performance and Satisfaction."
[30] Bachman, Bowers, and Marcus, "Bases of Supervisory Power."
[31] D. Warren, "Power, Visibility, and Conformity in Formal Organizations," *American Sociological Review*, Vol. 33 (1968), pp. 951–70.

sionalism has been found to be negatively related to performance with all bases with the exception of referent power.[32] This may be due to more status consciousness among professionals and concern with modeling their behavior after their more successful contemporaries.

Professionals relate to their larger professional body rather than to the specific group or organization in which they work. The professional might say, "I am a teamster," or "I am a nurse," whereas the individual with a local orientation might say, "I work for Consolidated Trucking," or "I am employed by the Miami General Hospital." The professional tends to be more independent and autonomous from the group or organization, and this tendency impacts on the effectiveness of power bases.[33]

The less effort and interest high-ranking participants are willing to allocate to a task, the more likely are lower-ranking participants to obtain power relevant to this task. Motivation of members is an influence in power distribution. Certain tasks within a group must be performed, but the power holder, who may be expected to complete these activities, may be uninterested or ambivalent toward the tasks. The opportunity, therefore, exists for low-ranking members to assume influence. This statement explains how a secretary frequently acquires a powerful position in a department. Because of pressing time constraints, the boss will often allow her secretary to schedule her appointments. The secretary, then, possesses the power to determine who the boss sees and when she will see them. The result is that a lower participant obtains power over the boss' schedule. When a void exists, lower-level participants can increase their power by filling it.

Satisfaction

Expert power is strongly and consistently related with satisfaction. The evidence overwhelmingly indicates that expert power is most satisfying to subjects of the power.[34] Knowledge-based power

obtains both public and private compliance, and avoids the problem of making subjects comply merely because the power holder has the "right" to request compliance. Additionally, our value system is built on the idea of merit and competence, and expert power appears to most closely align with these values. If individuals find expert power to be most compatible with American values, it should logically give the greatest satisfaction.

Interestingly, one study of salesmen found legitimacy to be the most satisfying, with expertise second.[35] Again, societal values can be used to explain the results: Legitimacy of position is an established and therefore satisfying part of our culture. The use of legitimate "rights," however, may be less satisfying to professionals than to nonprofessionals.

The use of coercive power is inversely related to individual satisfaction. Coercion not only creates resistance, it is generally disliked by individuals. The previously mentioned studies of college teachers and salesmen found coercion the least-preferred power base.[36] A study of insurance company employees also drew the same conclusion.[37]

Power Corollary

For every use of power, there is a corollary use of power. We can conclude our review of the dynamics of power by recognizing that all forms of power are not alike. Some are accepted more readily than others and there are many instances when the costs of applying influence exceed the derived benefits from such action. The benefits of power are quite obvious, but we should consider the costs of using power.

It may be nice to have power, but the use of resources is always costly. Power is effective when held in balance. As soon as power is *used*, it gets out of balance and the person *against whom* the power is used automatically resorts to some activities designed to correct the power imbalance.[38]

[32] Ibid.

[33] Alan Filley and A. Grimes, "The Bases of Power in Decision Processes," *Proceedings of the Academy of Management*, December 1967, pp. 133–60.

[34] See footnotes 29 and 30.

[35] Bachman, Smith, and Slesinger, "Control, Performance and Satisfaction."

[36] See footnote 29.

[37] Ivancevich, "Analysis of Control."

[38] David J. Lawless, *Effective Management* (Englewood Cliffs, N.J.: Prentice-Hall, 1972), p. 243.

In physics, we know that for every action there is a reaction. We should also know that for every use of power there is a corollary use of power. Therefore, we understand why French and Raven suggest seeking legitimacy in the exercise of power.[39] It reduces a subject's options in counteracting the power holder's influence. Coercion would then be used only as a last resort.

In a power relationship, one party obtains another's compliance, while in a situation involving force, one's objectives must be achieved, if at all, in the face of the other's noncompliance. Thus, if A's demand for B's money or his life prompts B to surrender his wallet, A has exercised power—he has won B's compliance by threat of even more severe deprivations. But if A must kill B to get the money, A has to resort to force—he must actually invoke the threatened sanction—and thereby perhaps expose himself to more severe deprivations too.[40]

Effective power holders seek to use their power with a minimum of counterpower attacks and "bluff calls." Whenever one uses the "do this or..." approach, there is a risk that one's bluff will be called. In such cases, one must be prepared to follow through with the "or" action, which may prove dysfunctional to the group's overall effectiveness.

IMPLICATIONS FOR PERFORMANCE AND SATISFACTION

Five power bases have been discussed—expert, coercive, reward, legitimate, and referent. They have proven to have different effects on individual satisfaction and on peformance.

In addition to isolating five bases of power, we have considered the role that dependency and uncertainty play in power dynamics. Those individuals who can make others dependent upon them—either actually or perceived—will increase their power over these others. Because groups avoid uncertainty, individuals who appear to possess the ability to reduce uncertainty will also gain power. This explains why group members withhold information or keep their activities shrouded in secrecy. This approach can make one's activities appear more complex and important than they may well be. The *perception* that one's activities are critical to the group's effectiveness and reduce external threats to the group is more important than whether the activities *actually* perform these functions.

We found that power *does* influence performance and individual satisfaction. Different power bases produce different effects on performance and satisfaction.

Expert power demonstrates the most consistent relationship with high performance; referent power is the next strongest, especially among professionally oriented individuals. While legitimate power does not appear to be related to performance, reward and coercive bases generally tend to be negatively related. Further, coercion's effectiveness varies proportionately with the strength of the potential punishment, and tends to be resorted to when the power holder perceives that the subject lacks motivation.

Expert power also scored high on satisfaction. Legitimacy scored well among nonprofessionals. And, again as with performance, reward and coercive power bases tend to be negatively related to satisfaction.

From the above, we can conclude that with expertise and coercion, there is close alignment between what people like and how they perform. Expert power is a positive force and coercion is negative. Referent and reward powers appear to be more effective with professionals than with nonprofessionals.

Point

McClelland: An Advocate of Power

David C. McClelland, the fifty-eight-year-old professor of psychology at Harvard University, could be described as the maverick of the behavioral

[39] French and Raven, "Bases of Social Power," p. 165.
[40] Peter Bachrach and Morton A. Baratz, *Power and Poverty* (New York: Oxford University Press, 1970), p. 27.

Source: An Interview with David McClelland. Adapted and excerpted by special permission from the July 1975 issue of *International Management*. Copyright © McGraw-Hill International Publication Company Limited. All rights reserved.

scientists. His research findings on what motivates entrepreneurs and managers seem to run counter to the beliefs of an entire generation of behavioral science pioneers. His views contrast sharply with such internationally acclaimed experts as Douglas McGregor, Abraham Maslow, Rensis Likert, and Chris Argyris, who have spearheaded a trend away from autocratic management toward greater participation and more democratic organizational systems.

Relaxing in the Boston office of McBer and Company, the consulting firm he founded in 1963, McClelland, sporting a white goatee beard and dressed in a green corduroy suit, dismisses the work of these management theorists with a casual air. He simply believes that their conclusions are based on insufficient evidence. He claims that a second generation of behavioral scientists, following in the spirit of his own beliefs, will eventually come up with well-researched data to show today's widely held views on motivation are wrong.

McClelland has identified three main motivational characteristics—the need for power, for achievement, and for affiliation.

During an interview in Boston, deputy editor David Oates asked McClelland how these characteristics relate to management:

One of the things my latest research shows is that the best managers are high in the need for power and low in the need for affiliation. They're not interested in people. They are interested in discipline. The evidence is very clear cut. The subordinates of such managers have high morale, whatever McGregor says.

Isn't this power element in the most successful managers surprising when there is so much talk these days about a relaxation of authority and greater emphasis on participation?

I think the basic problem with society today is a tremendous disillusionment with power. The revolt everywhere is basically the revolt of the oppressed against the exercise of authority and power. I see two faces of power. The face which social science has presented has been the Nazi face, the face of Theory X, which says that power is bad; we must do away with it. But there is another face of power. This is the one to be found in the successful manager.

The successful manager has four discernible power-oriented characteristics. Firstly, he believes

in an authority system, that the institution is more important than the individuals in it. Secondly, he likes to work and he likes the discipline of work, which leads to orderly management. Thirdly, he is altruistic in that he will sacrifice his own self-interest for the welfare of the company and does this in some obvious way that everybody can see. And fourthly, he believes in justice above everything else, that people must have even-handed treatment.

Are you saying firms that adopt a more democratic approach to management never succeed?

I can think of one particular electronics company that hired some eminent business school types to come and analyze them and who went away and wrote books about it being entirely possible to manage a company without authority. But 94 percent of that company's business comes from government contracts. You can do damn near anything when people are just dumping money on you, and if you have a cost overrun the government just picks up the bill.

Would you say then that too much participation can be harmful to an organization?

I can answer that from personal experience. We founded this firm twelve years ago under very democratic management. Even the secretaries sat in on the board meetings. We had endless staff meetings which drove me up the wall. The first thing we did was run ourselves into a debt of $800,000. It took us eight years to get out of debt.

Another example is the young people in the counterculture movement in this country who produce these radical-type newspapers. They are very intelligent, well-educated, liberal people and the papers were quite successful in terms of a good circulation. But every single one of them became broken up internally because people got into the most awful fights with each other. None of them were prepared to put the interests of the organization above their own personal, self-expressive interests.

When you get those people in an organization in sufficient numbers they destroy it.

Chris Argyris has this big thing about how awful it is that he studied 200 American companies and found them all authority conscious. He is dead set against that. I said: "Chris, did it ever occur to you that the reason you didn't get a chance to study the organizations which are democratic is because they didn't stay in business long enough?"

In addition to identifying three motivational characteristics McClelland has devised a method to measure how strongly they exist in individual businessmen. Participants at his training courses are given pictures about which they are invited to write short descriptions. For example, several business managers might be asked to describe a picture of two executives standing together in a factory. One manager might depict the scene as a factory manager telling a supervisor to make more effort to meet production targets. This description indicates a strong need for power. Another manager might describe the same scene as depicting two executives of equal rank discussing their prospects in a forthcoming golf competition, indicating an affiliative motive pattern.

McClelland's consulting firm also trains managers how to recognize their prevailing motivational attitudes and to adapt these where necessary to the motivational requirements of the job they are doing.

How do you make people want a change?

They learn a lot of very specific behavioral things in the seminar, such as the fact that an affiliative person makes more telephone calls, spends more time on the telephone, likes to drop in on people for a chat, and, worst of all from the management point of view, he likes to take individuals needs into account too much. We find an affiliative manager is always making exceptions in terms of personal needs. For example, he gives somebody a raise because they really need the money. He forgets that there are maybe six other people who feel they have been unjustly treated as a result.

A prominent example of this is President Ford, who is a very affiliative manager if ever there was. We know that because we coded his inaugural address—affiliative images versus achievement and power. When he said, in pardoning Nixon, "The man has suffered enough," that was a typical affiliative response, and the response of everybody else was also typical: "Well, maybe *he* has suffered enough but what about all these other guys he ordered around and who are now made to suffer more by going to jail?"

Counterpoint

Maccoby: The New Manager: A Game-Player Rather than Power-Seeker

This is a study based on interviews with 250 managers from twelve major companies in different parts of the country. When we scored all the interviews in terms of dynamic character traits, different types began to emerge as distinct from one another in terms of the individual member's overall orientation to work, values, and self-identity. We eventually came to name four main psychological types in the corporate technostructure: the craftsman, the jungle fighter, the company man, and the gamesman. These are "ideal types" in the sense that few people fit the type exactly and most are a mixture of types. But in practically every case, we were able to agree on which type best described a person, and the individual and his colleagues almost always agreed with our typing. Here are brief introductions to each type.

1. *The craftsman.* The craftsman holds the traditional values of the productive-hoarding character—the work ethic, respect for people, concern for quality and thrift. When he talks about his work, his interest is in the *process* of making something; he enjoys building. He sees others, co-workers as well as superiors, in terms of whether they help or hinder him in doing a craftsman-like job.

2. *The jungle fighter.* The jungle fighter's goal is power. He experiences life and work as a jungle (not a game), where it is eat or be eaten, and the winners destroy the losers. A major part of his

Adapted and edited from Michael Maccoby, *The Gamesman* (New York: Simon & Schuster, 1976), pp. 15, 46-49, 188-89. Copyright © 1976 by Michael Maccoby. Reprinted by permission of Simon & Schuster, a division of Gulf & Western Corp.

psychic resources is budgeted for his internal department of defense. Jungle fighters tend to see their peers in terms of accomplices or enemies and their subordinates as objects to be utilized. There are two subtypes of jungle fighters, lions and foxes. The lions are the conquerors who when successful may build an empire; the foxes make their nests in the corporate hierarchy and move ahead by stealth and politicking.

3. *The company man.* In the company man, we recognize the well-known organization man, or the functionary whose sense of identity is based on being part of the powerful, protective company. His strongest traits are his concern with the human side of the company, his interest in the feelings of the people around him, and his commitment to maintain the organization's integrity. At his weakest, he is fearful and submissive, concerned with security even more than with success.

4. *The gamesman.* The gamesman is the new man, and, really, the leading character in this study. His main interest is in challenge, competitive activity where he can prove himself a winner. Impatient with others who are slower and more cautious, he likes to take risks and to motivate others to push themselves beyond their normal pace. He responds to work and life as a game. The contest hypes him up and he communicates his enthusiasm, thus energizing others. He enjoys new ideas, new techniques, fresh approaches, and shortcuts. His talk and his thinking are terse, dynamic, sometimes playful and come in quick flashes. His main goal in life is to be a winner, and talking about himself invariably leads to discussion of his tactics and strategy in the corporate contest.

The new corporate top executive combines many gamesman traits with aspects of the company man. He is a team player whose center is the corporation. He feels himself responsible for the functioning of a system, and in his mind, his career goals have merged with those of the corporation. Thus he thinks in terms of what is good for the company, hardly separating that from what is good for himself. He tends to be a worrier, constantly on the lookout for something that might go wrong. He is self-protective and sees people in terms of their use for the larger organization. He even uses himself in this way, fine-tuning his sensitivity. He has succeeded in submerging his ego and gaining strength from this exercise in self-control.

How hardhearted are corporate managers? This is a complicated question. Many of the most hardhearted people in corporate roles are ambitious but neurotic failures, petty bureaucrats (hopeless company men) who have been so humiliated and discouraged by life and by their parents and bosses that they have chosen to use the little power they have to make others squirm. Only a very few of the individuals we interviewed expressed such destructive tendencies.

In contrast, some of the high-level power seekers were more complex people, combining ruthlessness to outsiders with benevolent justice for their own people. Thus, the head of a major company, a lionlike jungle fighter, likened corporate growth to the conquest of Genghis Khan, and spoke coldly about the survival of the fittest, writing off the people of whole continents as "fauna" that no longer could compete with the new managerial breed for scarce resources. Yet the same man kept an open door at work so that any employee could seek "the king's justice," and he worried that his business school-trained vice-president was unfeeling. In contrast to this industrial baron, the average gamesman would be both less imperial and less concerned about his employees.

While some corporate jungle fighters are exceptionally hardhearted and sadistic, on the whole, the modern corporate executive is much less so and is more concerned about being liked than the empire builder of the past. The modern corporation has been built in such a way as to minimize the need for people with a hardened heart. Still, the logic of corporations is to optimize profit and power, and the corporate managers must serve it. Most become comfortable servants of the company. Unlike the kings and conquerors of old or the modern robber barons, they do not boast of their glory or power. Many executives of elite corporations have never fired anyone, and if they are forced to, they feel terrible about it. Beneath the protective shell, they are rather softhearted.

RESOURCE CHAPTER C
The Behavioral Sciences in Management

The field of management has had a longstanding concern with the impact of individuals and groups on the effectiveness of organizations. It has been over 50 years since the beginning of the now-classic Hawthorne studies. These experiments are an excellent illustration of how scientific endeavor often leads to findings completely unexpected by the investigators at the outset.

What began in 1924 as an investigation of the impact of alternative lighting methods on employee productivity ended up ten years later providing the field of management with the knowledge that a number of psychological and sociological factors influenced productivity at

Source: Joseph L. Massie, *Essentials of Management*, 3rd Edition (Englewood Cliffs, N.J.: Prentice-Hall, Inc., 1979), pp. 135–53. Reprinted by permission of Prentice-Hall, Inc.

least as much as such characteristics as physical conditions, work methods, technology, and organizational structures.

In the ensuing time period a great deal of effort has been expended by behavioral scientists in a variety of fields, building upon the Hawthorne findings and expanding our understanding of the impact of human behavior upon the effectiveness of organizations. The purpose of this chapter is to summarize these findings and to evaluate them in terms of how useful they are to the practicing manager interested in increasing his or her effectiveness. In other words, this chapter will limit itself to the question: What does the practicing manager need to know about the impact of individuals and groups upon organizational functioning and effectiveness?

BEHAVIORAL DISCIPLINES RELEVANT IN MANAGEMENT

Since the conclusion of the Hawthorne studies in the 1930s, investigators in a number of closely related scientific disciplines have explored the nature and dynamics of individuals and groups within work organizations. Of primary interest to us are the contributions made by the fields of psychology and sociology. The fields of history, economics, political science, and anthropology have also contributed (although in a secondary fashion) to this understanding.

Psychology, itself, is divided into a number of sub-disciplines, many of which have led to significant findings about the nature of individuals in organizations. *Motivational* psychologists, for example, have concentrated their efforts on identifying the kinds of needs or motives that influence work behavior. In addition, they and other psychologists interested in the phenomenon of *learning* have examined the processes by which behavior occurs and is changed over time. Still other psychologists engaged in the field of *personality* have attempted to predict and understand the influences of moods, interests, needs, tendencies, intelligence, aptitudes, capacities, and values on work behavior. Those psychologists who have applied basic knowledge in the sub-disciplines of *motivation*, *learning*, and *personality* to an understanding of work behavior in organizations have identified themselves as **industrial psychologists** and, in fact, constitute a formal division within the American Psychological Association, the professional body of practicing psychologists in the U.S.

Overlapping somewhat with the interests of industrial psychologists are the concerns of **industrial sociologists**, who have applied basic knowledge in the field of sociology to an understanding of the behavior of individuals in formal and informal groups. The difference between industrial psychology and sociology is a matter of degree rather than any fundamental qualitative distinction. We might say that the primary focus of the psychologist is on the employee as an individual. In contrast, the sociologist focuses on that individual employee's interactions with others, formally and informally. Industrial sociologists have tended to define their field in a combination of three position statements:

1. Sociology is the study of *interactions* between people. Interactions can involve power, influence, status, authority, affiliation, support, or common interests and objectives.

2. Sociology is the study of *group behavior*. Two or more people, whether joined formally or informally, have a joint impact on organization.

3. Sociology is the study of *social systems* or *organizations*. These may be formal (e.g., having a written charter) or informal (e.g., a clique of co-workers). Such organizations have a variety of characteristics that influence the behavior of individual employees. These include values, norms, communication channels, and roles.

THREE ILLUSTRATIONS OF APPLIED BEHAVIORAL RESEARCH

A complete examination of industrial psychology and sociology's contributions since the Hawthorne studies is well beyond the scope of this chapter. Instead, three cases of behavioral research will illustrate the kinds of efforts made between the 1930s and the present.

Human Relations—A Case of Applied Sociology

The recognition of the importance of individual and group dimensions of behavior led to a series of investigations carried out by William F. Whyte and his associates during the 1940s and 1950s that have collectively become known as the **human relations** school of thought.

Analyzing individual responses to a number of management policies, including incentive payment programs, Whyte and his co-workers were impressed by the formal work group's influence on individual behavior. In fact, they concluded that informal work-group norms are more important than formal organizational rules in influencing individual decisions about level of work performance.

Investigators in the human relations tradition, including Whyte, Leonard Sayles, George Strauss, Orvis Collins, Melville Dalton, and Douglas McGregor, concluded that two sets of factors are critical as determinants of employee work behavior:

1. *Individual Motives*: The human relations school reacted sharply to the earlier premise that employees have an inherent dislike of work and must be closely supervised and directed. In addition, they rejected the earlier belief that money is the only basis for motivating work behavior. McGregor characterized these assumptions as Theory X. In contrast, he proposed a set of premises, labeled Theory Y, that best summarize the human relations school beliefs concerning the individual. McGregor believed that physical and mental effort is as natural to an individual employee as play or rest. Furthermore, if allowed, an employee will exercise self-direction and self-control in his or

her work behavior. Indeed, the opportunity to take on responsibility, exercise discretion, and direct one's own actions in the completion of meaningful tasks is far more powerful as a motivator than threats, coercion, or money rewards.

2. *Informal Groups*: The human relations school concluded that the informal group is the greatest single source of influence on an employee's behavior. Informal work groups establish very important rules or norms regarding appropriate and inappropriate behavior. In addition, according to this reasoning, informal groups can dispense or withhold very attractive rewards in order to assure compliance with such norms. These rewards include: (a) the satisfaction of *affiliation* needs, (b) a sense of *identity* with a recognized and respected group, (c) a confirmation of *self-esteem*, (d) a means for *testing reality*, and (e) a means for *assistance* in accomplishing work tasks.

Recognizing the importance of individual motives and informal work groups, the human relations school of thought rapidly developed into the human relations *movement*, a strongly expressed set of managerial prescriptions for designing and directing work organizations. This set of prescriptions focused principally on three areas of managerial activity: (1) encouraging employees to *participate* in decisions regarding their work and the operations of the organization, (2) implementing job *enlargement* or *enrichment*, i.e., redesigning jobs to allow for a broader degree of discretion and breadth of activities, and (3) improving the flow of *communications* between managers and subordinates as well as all employees.

The early work of the human relations school is an excellent example of industrial sociology, especially in their research of small group dynamics. Unfortunately, the field slipped prematurely away from description and understanding to prescription. Subsequent analysis critical of the human relations school has cited a number of important weaknesses in such prescriptions:

1. They tend to oversimplify the complexity of human behavior and group dynamics. They do not take account of the varying situations under which work is carried out.

2. Their assumptions about the nature of human motives are as simple and sterile as those they sought to replace. Money, for example, remains an important work-related incentive for employees.

3. They lack an underlying model of sufficient richness to allow testing major human relations propositions or extending knowledge gained in one administrative setting to another.

Although its impact was felt through the 1960s, the human relations school is more an item of historical interest than a modern, contributing body of theory and knowledge about work behavior. It did, however, make an important and lasting contribution in (a) demonstrating that employees are motivated by a variety of needs, not just monetary needs, (b) discovering the importance of informal work groups in organizations, and (c) recognizing the importance of communication channels in influencing employee behavior and performance.

Work Motivation—A Case of Applied Psychology

The sociological approach of the human relations school over the past 40 years has been paralleled by the efforts of industrial psychologists to understand the nature and operation of motives in influencing work behavior and performance. Industrial psychologists' efforts originated in an attempt to identify the specific needs that motivate work behavior; in effect, they concentrated on the *content* of work motivation. More recently, they have begun to address themselves to *process* questions, that is, issues regarding the dynamics or mechanics by which motives influence work behavior and performance.

Industrial psychologists, then, initially undertook the task of identifying those work-related motives that influence work behavior. Several hundred attempts have been made to identify and classify the multitude of work-related motives. Out of these, three or four have emerged to influence managerial thought and practice. The first of these is the work of Abraham Maslow, who introduced the notion of a **Need Hierarchy**. Maslow's principal argument is that employee needs emerge in a hierarchical fashion; lower-order needs are experienced first and must be satisfied by the work environment before higher-order needs are perceived. The implication is that rewards of higher-order needs will have no incentive effect upon employee motivation until lower-order needs are satisfied (Maslow labeled this phenomenon the concept of **prepotency of needs**).

Maslow's hierarchy is illustrated in Figure 11–1. From lowest to highest, the needs are defined as:

Physiological needs: These include hunger, sex, thirst;

Safety needs: These represent the need to be free of bodily threat;

Social needs: These represent the need to love and be loved. They include affection, friendship, and affiliation;

Esteem needs: These include an employee's need for self-respect and respect from others;

Self-actualization: This need has never adequately been defined either by Maslow or subsequent theorists. In an existential sense, the term refers to becoming all that one chooses and is capable of becoming.

Most industrial psychologists agree that Maslow identified several classes of needs that are important sources of work motivation. The theory has been faulted, however, over the prepotency issue. Very few management theorists believe anymore that a strict ordering exists in the sequence in which needs are felt (except, possibly, for physiological and safety needs). Perhaps the most important managerial implication emerging from Maslow's work is that most employees experience a variety of needs motivating them to come to work and perform at a given level of effort. It is important for a manager to consider each employee's unique profile of felt needs when explaining his or her response to the organization.

A second famous statement of employee needs was made by Frederick Herzberg and his associates. Herzberg is credited with a **two-factor** model of motives that (like Maslow's) was adequate in describing the content of work motives but failed to describe adequately their impact on work behavior and performance. Herzberg and his associates analyzed the content of interviews carried out with approximately 200 employees about their jobs. Respondents were asked to think of times when they felt particularly good and particularly bad about their jobs, and to describe the conditions leading to these feelings in as much detail as possible.

An analysis of these interviews led Herzberg to propose that the conditions leading to positive feelings about the job were fundamentally different from those leading to negative feelings. The former were called satisfiers and the latter were

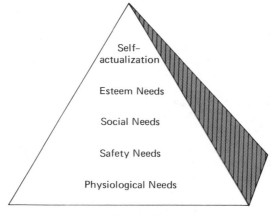

Figure 11-1
Maslow's Need Hierarchy

labeled dissatisfiers. He inferred from these findings that needs were discontinuous as far as their impact on motivation and performance is concerned. Positive work motivation (factors leading to enhanced performance) would only be influenced by **satisfiers** (e.g., the satisfaction of achievement needs, recognition, advancement, the work itself, personal growth). Later theorists agreeing with Herzberg considered these factors intrinsic because they exist primarily within the context of the work being carried out.

Dissatisfiers, according to Herzberg, could only lead to dissatisfaction with the job, and therefore could not positively motivate job performance. Dissatisfiers include such factors as company policy and administration, technical supervision, interpersonal relations with supervisors and peers, salary, job security, work conditions, and status. Later theorists referred to these elements as **extrinsic factors**, because they exist outside the context of the immediate work being performed on the job.

As was the case with Maslow, Herzberg's ideas gave us an interesting and a useful framework for considering a variety of needs and rewards that are important to employee motivation. His model, however, has failed as an accurate statement of the process by which these needs influence behavior and performance. Few serious students of management today accept the notion of a discontinuity between satisfiers and dissatisfiers. These constitute two opposite ends of the same continuum, and both have measurable impacts on employee motivation and performance.

In recent years the field of psychology has given us three models of motivation that focus on the process (as opposed to the content) of motivation. When combined, these have provided a rich and fruitful approach to understanding employee effort, behavior, and performance. These are: (1) the **behaviorist-reinforcement model**, (2) **expectancy theory**, and (3) **equity theory**.[1]

The behaviorist-reinforcement model is a product of over 70 years of scientific investigation,

beginning with the work of John Watson at the turn of the twentieth century, continuing with the work of Clark Hull during the 1930s, 1940s, and 1950s, and developing further in the more recent work of B. F. Skinner in the 1960s and 1970s.

Three concepts are fundamental to the behaviorist model diagrammed in Figure 11–2:

1. *Drive* is an internal state of need. It can be started by a variety of conditions, including the needs described above in the content models of motivation. Under conditions of drive, an individual is aroused—his or her behavior is energized. Needs then arouse the drive that motivates behavior. Needs, furthermore, fall into two classes: (a) primary and (b) secondary. Primary needs (like hunger and thirst) are unlearned. Secondary needs (like money, power) are learned; they must be acquired through experience.

2. *Habit* is a learned connection between a condition or event in the employee's environment and a response (behavior) to that event. Behaviorist psychologists label the event S and the response R. The habit itself is denoted as "S-R," indicating a stimulus-response connection. The habit (S-R connection) determines the *choice* and *direction* of employee behavior. If an employee, for example, has learned that he can reduce the need for money by working at a given level of performance, the next time he has been aroused by a need for money he can be expected to work at the same level of performance.

The notions of drive and habit combine in multiplicative fashion to result in observed behavior. The *product* of drive times habit (S-R) leads to the selection of a specific behavior or response in a *given* set of stimulus conditions. Note that the S-R model deals explicitly with the issues of strength and direction of employee effort and performance. Without the presence of drive, performance would not be energized. Without the presence of habit (S-R), behavior and performance would be random, unorganized, and not directed toward specific actions.

3. *Reinforcement* is an event (stimulus) that follows a response or action. A reinforcer or reward has two impacts on the employee: (1) Reinforcement reduces drive; that is, the

[1] Much of the discussion is drawn from W. Haynes, J. Massie, and M. Wallace, *Management: Analysis, Concepts, and Cases,* 3rd ed. (Englewood Cliffs: Prentice-Hall, 1975), Chapter 5.

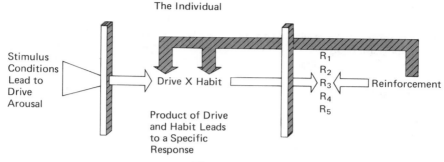

The Individual

Stimulus
Conditions
Lead to
Drive
Arousal

Drive X Habit

Product of Drive
and Habit Leads
to a Specific
Response

R₁
R₂
R₃
R₄
R₅

Reinforcement

Figure 11-2
An Outline of Hull's Model

employee's need is satisfied. Most psychologists add, therefore, that the experience of reinforcement is pleasurable and attractive to the individual. (2) Reinforcement strengthens habit (S-R) connections. Through the process of reinforcement, therefore, new habits are learned.

Understanding of the behaviorist model is central to an explanation of a great deal of employee behavior and employee learning. The experience of a need or set of needs leads to the arousal of drive. Such arousal energizes behavior—makes the employee capable of performance. Habits (both learned and unlearned) serve to direct behavior and make it predictable under the same need conditions. Finally, reinforcement is a powerful force that (a) reduces a felt need and (b) leads to both learning new behaviors and retaining other behaviors under similar circumstances.

B. F. Skinner has made a valuable contribution to our understanding of reinforcement as a powerful managerial tool for controlling and shaping patterns of employee behavior. Two generalizations about reinforcement emerge from his work. First, the timing or *scheduling* of reinforcement is at least as important as the absolute level of reinforcement. He has demonstrated, for example, that intermittent reinforcement (rewarding the desired behavior only part of the time) is more effective than constant reinforcement (rewarding the desired behavior each time that it occurs). Second, Skinner has demonstrated a vital distinction between the notion of *reinforcement* on one hand, and that of *punishment* on the other:

Reinforcement can be positive or negative. Positive reinforcement is the presentation of an attractive stimulus following the desired behavior. Negative reinforcement is the *removal* of an aversive or unpleasant stimulus following the desired response.

Punishment, on the other hand, consists of *removing* a pleasant event following an undesired behavior or *presenting* an aversive or unpleasant stimulus following an undesired response.

Note the important differences between reinforcement and punishment. According to strict Skinnerian logic, behavior can only be positively influenced and learned under conditions of reinforcement (positive or negative). The reason for this is that reinforcement focuses upon the desired behavior, and therefore gives the employee a great deal of information. Punishment, in contrast, can only serve to disrupt an undesired behavior. It carries no informational content about the desired behavior. Under conditions of punishment, the employee only knows that whatever he or she is doing is wrong.

The behaviorist-reinforcement model has two major qualities associated with it. First, it has been developed and thoroughly tested in a rigorous scientific fashion. Generalizations made from it to applied settings are on firm theoretical and empirical ground. Second, much of the content of the model lends itself directly to one of the most cogent and pressing concerns of managers: how does one influence the behavior and performance of others? This model is only now influencing the applied field of management. We should expect to see a great deal more influence and application of the model in future years.

The major weakness of the behaviorist-reinforcement model is that it tends to be mechanistic in its conception of the human mind and thought processes. Indeed, strict Skinnerian thinking downplays the necessity even to be very explicit about what goes on in the mind of a person in the process of motivation. According to such thinking, the scientist need only predict tangible behavior (observable actions) from tangible events (stimuli) in order to understand motivation. In a sense, therefore, the individual is quite passive in the behaviorist model. In contrast to the behaviorist-reinforcement models, cognitive models focus directly on the individual employee as an active and conscious agent in his or her work environment. A basic premise of the cognitive models we are about to examine is that the individual is a conscious decision maker. Indeed, these models propose that an employee's decision is a result of (1) the outcomes he or she believes will result from the response, and (2) the value or importance of such outcomes to the person.

Although early cognitive models of behavior are credited to the work of such psychologists as Kurt Lewin and E. C. Tolman during the 1930s and 1940s, the work of Victor Vroom has had the most pronounced effect upon management's thinking about employee motivation in recent years. In 1964, he published what has become a standard reference statement about the process of employee motivation. His model has become known as **Expectancy Theory** and represents the translation of a normative statistical decision model (often found in economics) into the language of psychology.

Expectancy theory focuses directly on the process of human decision making and emphasizes the cognitive processes by which alternatives are evaluated in terms of valued outcomes and likelihoods that such outcomes will occur if a given alternative is chosen. Accordingly, Vroom argues that an employee's motivation is the effort or force driving a person to a specific act. In the case of employment the act will most likely be some level of job performance. The motivation or force behind a specific level of work performance will

be a function of two perceptions on the part of the employee:

1. the probability or perceived likelihood that certain outcomes will result from the person's effort; and,
2. the value or utility of such outcomes to the employee.

Figure 11-3 outlines the way an expectancy theorist explains employee behavior. Before expending a given level of effort, a worker will likely ask, "If I make a strong effort on this job, will a superior level of performance be achieved? And, if I do achieve such an outstanding level of performance, what kinds of rewards (or negative outcomes) will occur?"

The answer to this line of questioning is what Vroom characterizes as an **expectancy**, that is, the personal probability estimate that a given level of effort will result in a given outcome (superior performance). The expectancy alone, however, is not all the employee needs to know before acting. The person also needs to know how valuable that outcome or performance level is to him or her. Vroom calls this value a **valence** and argues that the valence associated with a first-level outcome (like performance) is in turn determined by the personal probability that the performance will lead to a series of **second-level outcomes** together with the valences associated with those outcomes (e.g., income, social approval, job security, promotion, and accomplishment).

The employee described in Figure 11–3, for example, may believe that performance at a high level (first-level outcome) will result in being paid a higher wage (second-level outcome). The degree to which the worker believes that high performance will lead to higher pay is also a subjective guess or probability, which Vroom calls an **instrumentality** perception. In addition, high pay has some value or valence associated with it. The combination of the valence of secondary outcomes and the instrumentality that first-level outcomes (such as high performance level) will result in a secondary outcome (e.g., higher pay) determines the valence associated with first-level outcomes. Finally, the force, effort, or motivation to achieve first-level outcomes is determined by the valence

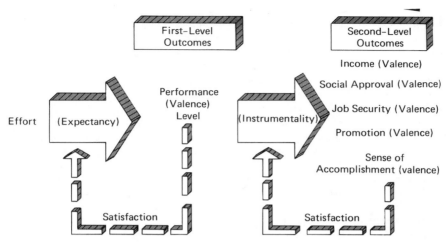

Figure 11-3
An Outline of Expectancy Theory

of the first-level outcome combined with the expectancy that a given level of effort will actually result in the desired first-level outcome.

A final note on expectancy theory relates to the notion of **job satisfaction** or **morale**, a topic that has long been discussed by students of management. Job satisfaction is characterized most frequently by behavioral scientists as an attitudinal reaction to the job. It represents a reflection on the employee's part about how happy or unhappy he or she is with various aspects of the job, including the work itself, supervision, pay, and other, peripheral matters. Psychologists call such a reaction an **affective reaction** or attitude. The concept of satisfaction fits in very nicely in expectancy theory. Accordingly, employees consciously evaluate the results of their behavior. If the outcomes experienced confirm the expectancies and instrumentalities originally experienced, satisfaction will result. If not, dissatisfaction will result. Note the close similarity between the behaviorists' notion of reinforcement and that of satisfaction. Both are rewarding, both tend to reinforce learning. Indeed, satisfaction plays an extremely important role as feedback (indicated by the dotted line in Figure 11–3), which causes the individual to readjust efforts and behavior in response to changing work conditions.

In addition to the behaviorist and expectancy models, a third area of theory development has influenced management thought about employee motivation during the late 1960s and 1970s. This model has been named **Equity Theory** and brings together two quite different lines of theoretical development: the notion of Distributive Justice and the concept of Cognitive Dissonance. The name most often cited for developing the equity model is J. Stacy Adams. According to equity theory, each employee constantly engages in a form of social comparison. In this process employees attempt to evaluate each other's returns from the work experience relative to the contribution each has made. This kind of comparison can be represented as follows:

$$\frac{\text{Person's Outcomes}}{\text{Person's Inputs}} \quad \text{vs.} \quad \frac{\text{Others' Outcomes}}{\text{Others' Inputs}}$$

If these two ratios are equal (that is, returns are proportionate to inputs), then **distributive justice** is said to exist. The achievement of distributive justice (or equity) is said to be a powerful and overriding motive for employees. If these two ratios diverge in either direction, a state of cognitive dissonance is said to develop. Social psychologists use the term **cognitive dissonance** to describe a situation in which a person experiences something that he or she neither expects nor desires to experience. The experience of dissonance is a motivating event, very similar to the behaviorist's notion of drive. Its experience is unpleasant, and the individual will behave in ways expected to reduce dissonance. In fact, the reduction of dissonance following some action on the employee's part serves the same purpose as reward or reinforcement. It is experienced as pleasurable, and it will reinforce whatever behavior preceded it. Hence, dissonance reduction influences the direction of behavior—it serves to shape behavior.

All three process theories we have considered so far—the behaviorist-reinforcement model, expectancy theory, and equity theory—are complementary to each other; they fit nicely together to provide a rounded view of employee motivation. This comparison is illustrated in Figure 11-4. Basically, questions of employee motivation boil down to three major issues:

What arouses or energizes behavior?

What directs behavior?

What outcomes that occur as a result of behavior tend to feed back and influence subsequent behavior?

Figure 11-4 illustrates the complementary ways in which the three theories address these three questions. With respect to arousal, the behaviorist model proposes drive, while the expectancy model describes valence and equity theory discusses cognitive dissonance.

Similarly, direction of behavior is explained by habit in the behaviorist model and by expectancy and instrumentality in expectancy theory. This is the only motivational question not directly addressed in equity theory. Finally reinforcement, satisfaction, and equity all play similar roles in addressing the question of outcomes that feed back and influence subsequent behavior.

The great contribution of the process theories of motivation has been in increasing our understanding of the processes or mechanisms by which employee behavior occurs. Both the behaviorist and expectancy models suggest specific mechanisms by which individual responses to the work environment are aroused and directed. When combined with the content theories which suggest specific kinds of needs or motives operating among employees, the process theories show a great deal of promise as sources of information to guide practicing managers in directing the activities of employees.

Leadership—A Case Combining Applied Sociology and Psychology

A third important line of research and theoretical development over the last 30 years combines the work of applied sociologists and psychologists:

Aspect of
Motivation

	Arousal	Direction	Outcome
Behavioral Model	Drive	Habit	Reinforcement
Expectancy Model	Valence	Expectancy and Instrumentality	Satisfaction
Equity Model	Dissonance	—	Equity or Distributive Justice

Figure 11-4
Integrating the Behaviorist, Expectancy, and Equity Models

the study of leadership. Leadership has long been considered one of the most important factors influencing organizational performance and achievement of goals.

Although a variety of definitions of leadership have been proposed over the years, we can say that leadership is the practice of influence. Thus, **leadership** is a process through which the performance of others is influenced by a person occupying a leadership role. Leadership is thus an important part of study in management, though it is by no means synonymous with management.

The primary emphasis of early research on leadership was psychological in nature and focused on the *traits* or personality characteristics typically found among successful leaders. Such researchers began a long task of "laundry-listing" all conceivable personal characteristics of so-called "great" leaders. Such compilations included the following kinds of characteristics:

Age	Extroversion
Maturity	Verbal skills
Intelligence	Prestige
Physical bearing	Attractiveness
Height	Charisma
Education	Popularity
Decisiveness	Aggressiveness

The problem with these early efforts was that they left too many questions about leadership unanswered. For example, is there any optimal combination of traits that is most critical in determining one's success as a leader? In what ways do such characteristics influence one's ability to lead? Are these characteristics that one can learn, or must one be born with them? Although such qualities might have fit popular stereotypes characterizing popular leaders or great personalities, their citation did little to expand our knowledge about the *process* of leadership.

It was not until a sociological view of the problem was combined with the psychological approach that headway was made in understanding leadership. Characteristic of these efforts was work carried out by researchers at Ohio State University in the 1950s. They recognized that leadership involves an interpersonal *relationship* between a leader and subordinates. Furthermore, the most critical element in this relationship is the

behavior of the leader toward the subordinates.

This realization led them to focus their research efforts on the set of behaviors or actions that constituted leader behavior. Their basic approach was to isolate and measure the dimensions underlying leader behavior that could be used to define leadership; it was an empirical approach. A questionnaire was designed, with over 100 specific kinds of acts or behaviors a manager might engage in while supervising the work of others. The leader's subordinates were asked to use the questionnaire to describe the leader's behavior. The following is an illustration of the kinds of questions contained in the instrument that has come to be known as the **Leader Behavior Description Questionnaire** (LBDQ).

The subordinate indicates the degree to which each of the following statements describes the actions of the supervisor:

Refuses to give in when people disagree with him
Is easy to understand
Refuses to explain his actions
Encourages overtime work
Tries out his new ideas
Assigns people under him to specific tasks

Subsequent analysis of several thousand subordinates' responses to such questions consistently yielded two dimensions or factors that underlie subordinates' descriptions of their leaders: **Initiating Structure** and **Consideration.** In other words, the actions a leader takes regarding subordinates tend to cluster in one of these two major kinds of leader activities. Consideration is the extent to which the leader's behavior toward subordinates is characterized by mutual trust, mutual respect, support for subordinates' ideas, a climate of rapport, and two-way communication. A low score on consideration reflects an impersonal way of dealing with subordinates.

Initiating Structure, on the other hand, is the extent to which a leader defines and structures his role and those of subordinates. A high score reflects a leader who is likely to play a very active role in directing, planning, and scheduling the group's activities. Initiating Structure and Consideration have come to refer to kinds of leadership behavior that constitute a leader's style, the way the person influences subordinates.

As so often happens with attractive models, the work of the Ohio State researchers was prematurely applied by others as a set of **normative prescriptions** for leaders to follow, rather than being used as a model to be tested further in order to enhance our understanding of leadership. Many entrepreneurs traveled the country assessing supervisors on their measures of initiating structure and consideration. For some reason, they presumed that the ideal leader is one who is high on both leadership dimensions.

For a fee, they would then provide two kinds of services: (1) diagnose a particular leader's style, using this two-dimension framework, and (2) propose changes (usually involving expensive training programs) in leadership style that should lead to improved leader effectiveness.

In all this entrepreneurial flurry two major questions went unanswered: (1) How do we know when a leader is effective? and (2) What factors determine whether or not a given style of leadership behavior will be effective? Reliable answers to the first question remain the subject of continuing research. The problem is that the goals of a leader are many, and each constitutes a valid dimension of leader effectiveness. At the very least, we can say that the following are elements of leader effectiveness: (a) individual effectiveness of subordinates in accomplishing their tasks, (b) the morale or satisfaction of subordinates, (c) the productivity or efficiency of groups of subordinates in accomplishing their tasks, (d) the quality of products or services generated by subordinate groups.

Fortunately, research on what constitutes the most effective leadership style has become the topic of serious research efforts during the 1970s. Two such efforts deserve our particular attention: (1) the work of Fred Fiedler and (2) the path-goal theory of leadership. Building upon the results of the Ohio State studies, Fiedler reasoned, as was mentioned in Chapter 8, that there was probably no single best leader style to fit all work situations. His research has identified three major situational factors that determine the appropriateness of a given style of leadership:

1. *Leader-member relations*: the quality of the leader's relations with subordinates, the confidence they have in the leader, and their loyalty.

It is generally measured by asking the leader to rate the atmosphere of the group on a number of dimensions.

2. *Task structure*: the degree to which the work tasks are routinized. This is generally measured by asking observers to rate the degree of routine observed in carrying out assigned tasks.

3. *Position power*: the amount of formal authority vested in the leader's formal position, including the degree of control over rewards and the degree to which upper management supports the leader in the use of authority.

Fiedler collapsed the original Ohio State dimensions into a single dimension of leader style with employee-oriented behaviors (high consideration) at one extreme and task-oriented behaviors (high initiating structure) at the other extreme. His research (as well as that of subsequent investigators) has found that the most successful style of leader behavior depends upon the situation defined by the three conditions just listed. These contingencies are summarized in Table 11-1. A task-oriented style, for example, appears to be most effective where leader member relations are good and the task is structured. A task-oriented style is best, furthermore, when leader-member relations are good, the task is unstructured, and the leader's position power is strong. Under similar conditions, however, if the leader's position power is weak, an employee-oriented style is more effective. An examination of Table 11-1 will reveal the varying situational conditions under which two entirely different styles of leader behavior can be equally effective.

The major importance of Fiedler's work lies in the discovery that the situation surrounding the leadership role has a critical bearing upon the success of any given leadership style. Subsequent management students have credited Fiedler with introducing a **contingency** or **situational** approach to the study of leadership.

A second theory of leader effectiveness also concentrates on contingencies as they influence the effectiveness of various leader behavior styles. According to the work of House and his colleagues, leaders can choose the degree to which they engage in four kinds of leader behaviors:

1. *Instrumental Behavior*: very similar to Initiating Structure, consisting of planning, organiz-

Table 11-1
Summary of Research Findings Regarding Fiedler's Theory

Situational factor			
Leader-member relations	*Task structure*	*Position power*	*Most effective leadership style*
Good	Structured	Strong	Task-oriented
Good	Structured	Weak	Task-oriented
Good	Unstructured	Strong	Task-oriented
Good	Unstructured	Weak	Employer-oriented
Moderately poor	Unstructured	Strong	Employee-oriented
Moderately poor	Structured	Weak	Employee-oriented
Moderately poor	Structured	Strong	Employee-oriented
Moderately poor	Unstructured	Weak	Task-oriented

ing, controlling, and coordinating subordinates closely in their tasks;

2. *Supportive Behavior*: very similar to Consideration, consisting of displaying concern for the interests, needs, and well-being of subordinates;

3. *Participative Behavior*: characterized by sharing information and an emphasis on consultation with subordinates;

4. *Achievement-Oriented Behavior*: setting challenging goals, expecting subordinates to perform at the highest level, and continually seeking improvement in performance.

This model has been labeled a **Path-Goal Theory** of leadership effectiveness, because it proposes that a leader's choice of these behaviors should be premised upon a goal of increasing personal payoffs to subordinates for work-goal attainment, and making the path to these payoffs as free of obstacles as possible. The path-goal model, furthermore, is a contingency model, in that it posits that the appropriate mix of such leader behaviors depends on two major sets of factors: (a) the individuals being supervised, and (b) the characteristics of the work environment.

Individual characteristics influencing the impact of leader behaviors include: (1) Ability—the greater the employee's perceived level of ability to accomplish a task, the less the individual will accept direction or instrumental behavior on the part of the leader. (2) Locus of control—this is the degree to which employees believe they have control over what happens to them. Those who

believe that they have a great deal of control over what happens to them are said to react more favorably to a participative leader, and others would prefer a more directive leader. (3) Needs and motives—the particular set of needs that are felt strongly by an employee will affect the impact of a particular set of leader behaviors on that person's performance. People with a high need for autonomy will probably react negatively to instrumental kinds of leader behavior.

A number of organizational characteristics, in addition to subordinates', are also proposed by path-goal theory as influences on the effectiveness of leader behavior. Specifically, three broad groups of work environment properties have been studied: (1) subordinates' tasks—the degree of structure involved in work operations; (2) the work group—informal work group norms and cohesiveness; and (3) organizational factors—stress levels in the work situation, situations involving high uncertainty, and the degree to which rules, procedures, and policies govern an employee's work.

A full explication of contingency leadership theories is beyond the scope of this chapter. It is important, however, to note that present research on the topic of leadership is just now beginning to yield an understanding of the complexities of leadership phenomena. The practice of leadership involves elements of the leader's own personality and behavior, complex relationships between the leader and subordinates, informal group characteristics, and a variety of characteristics of the formal environment within which work activities are carried out. Any formula, then, that proposes to make one an effective leader by adopting a single ideal leader style is hopelessly wrong, and anyone purporting to sell such a formula is no more of a help than were the snake oil salesmen of 70 or more years ago.

ORGANIZATIONAL BEHAVIOR: A SUMMARY CONCEPT

We have examined three illustrations of theoretical development and research in the behavioral sciences that are important and representative of the work this field has contributed to the field of management. Furthermore, we have said that the fields of industrial psychology and industrial sociology have contributed heavily to this tradition.

Actually the 1970s has seen a blending and integration of such efforts into a recognizable field that is now called **organizational behavior (OB)**.

Organizational behavior is a field that is primarily concerned with an understanding and prediction of *performance* at the organizational, group, and individual level. To accomplish this, the field focuses on a study of three broad areas: (1) formal organizations and their processes, (2) informal groups and their dynamics, and (3) individual behavior (including the topics of motivation, perception, learning, and personality). Finally, the field of organizational behavior can be identified by its emphasis on the employment of scientific method in conducting investigations and accumulating knowledge. The term *scientific method* implies that a heavy reliance is placed on logically consistent models in developing questions for research and that all such models are submitted to the test of data; that is, all propositions about individual and organizational behavior are subjected to carefully controlled empirical studies. Only after a model or proposition has passed the test of data is it considered confirmed and treated as knowledge.

Index